The Estate and Household Accounts of
William Worsley,
Dean of St Paul's Cathedral, 1479–1497

Edited by
Hannes Kleineke and Stephanie R. Hovland

RICHARD III AND YORKIST HISTORY TRUST

LONDON RECORD SOCIETY
PUBLICATIONS
VOLUME XL

THE ESTATE AND HOUSEHOLD ACCOUNTS OF WILLIAM WORSLEY DEAN OF ST PAUL'S CATHEDRAL 1479–1497

Edited by

HANNES KLEINEKE

and

STEPHANIE R. HOVLAND

RICHARD III AND YORKIST HISTORY TRUST

LONDON RECORD SOCIETY

in association with

SHAUN TYAS

DONINGTON

2004

.

Typeset and designed from the disc of the authors by
Shaun Tyas

Published by
SHAUN TYAS
(an imprint of 'Paul Watkins')
1 High Street
Donington
Lincolnshire
PE11 4TA

on behalf of
Richard III and Yorkist History Trust
and the
London Record Society

ISBN 1 900289 70 9
(Richard III and Yorkist History Trust)
ISBN 0 900 95240 7
(London Record Society)

Printed and bound by Woolnoughs of Irthlingborough

CONTENTS

Acknowledgments   vii

List of Abbreviations   viii

Part 1: Introduction: William Worsley, Dean of St. Paul's (1479–99), His Estates and Household   1

I.   William Worsley – Life and Career   3

     The Deanery of St. Paul's   8

     The Warbeck Conspiracy and Worsley's Final Years   12

II.   The Accounts I: The Economy of the Dean's Estates and Worsley's Income   17

III. The Accounts II: The Dean's Household   31

     Provisioning of the Household   34

     Servants' Allowances   35

IV. The Accounts III: The Manuscripts   37

     Note on Images   39

Part 2: Calendar of the Estate and Household Accounts of Dean William Worsley, 1479–1498   41

Editorial Method   41

1.   Receiver's Account 1479–1480   43

     Receipts from Rents and Farms   43

     Expenditure   44

2.   Receiver's Account 11 July 1480–18 July 1481   47

     Receipts from Rents and Farms   47

     Expenditure   50

3.   A Full Translation of the Receiver's Account, 11 July 1481– 13 July 1482   57

     Receipts from Rents and Farms   57

     Expenditure   60

4.   Receiver's Account 18 July 1482–18 July 1483   67

     Receipts from Rents and Farms   67

     Expenditure   69

5.   Receiver's Account 1484–1485   73

     Receipts from Rents and Farms   73

	Expenditure	75
6.	Receiver's Account 20 July 1487–20 July 1488	79
	Receipts from Rents and Farms	79
	Expenditure	81
7.	Receiver's Account 20 July 1488–7 August 1489	85
	Receipts from Rents and Farms	85
	Expenditure	87
8.	Receiver's Account 1489–1490	91
	Receipts From Rents And Farms	91
	Expenditure	93
9.	Receiver's Account 10 July 1495–21 July 1496	97
	Receipts from Rents and Farms	97
	Expenditure	99
10.	View of Account for the Estates and Household, 1496–1497	105
	Receipts from Rents and Farms	105
	Expenditure	106
11.	Accounts of Ministers on Certain Estates of William Worsley 1493–1494	108
12.	Accounts of Ministers on Certain Estates of William Worsley 1495–1498	113
13.	Account of the Rent Collector of the Deanery of London for Some of Worsley's Lands in the City of London and in Norton Folgate, Middlesex 1483–1484.	124
Appendix 1: The Chapter of St. Paul's at Worsley's Election		127
Appendix 2: Biographical Details of Individuals Mentioned in the Accounts.		129
Glossary		
Glossary of Unusual English Words		179
Feast Days and Term Dates used in the Accounts		181
Bibliography		182
I. Original Sources		182
1. Manuscripts		182
2. Printed		183
II. Secondary Material		186
III. Unpublished Theses		189
Index		191

ACKNOWLEDGMENTS

In preparing this edition, we have incurred many debts that we acknowledge with gratitude. Tony Pollard guided the book through its draft stages towards publication with kindness, perception and, above all, patience. He and Christopher Woolgar both read the entire manuscript and made a number of valuable suggestions. Caroline Barron kindly read and commented on an early draft of the introduction and biographical appendix. Clive Burgess, David Grummitt and Mark Forrest commented on individual chapters of the introduction. Linda Clark, Sean Cunningham, Matthew Davies, Jessica Freeman, Elizabeth New and Eleanor Quinton all contributed information on various aspects of the introduction and biographical appendix. A paper based on the introduction was read to the seminar on Medieval and Tudor London at the Institute of Historical Research in Trinity Term 2000, and we are grateful to the members of the seminar for their comments and criticisms.

Thanks are also due to the librarians and archivists of the Public Record Office and the British Library, whose collections we have drawn upon extensively in preparing the introduction and appendices.

The majority of the MSS edited in this volume are the property of and are published by permission of the Dean and Chapter of St. Paul's Cathedral, and we are grateful to the Cathedral's librarian, Jo Wisdom, for his assistance. MS 25,166/6A was formerly owned by the Church Commissioners of the Church of England. All MSS are now deposited in the Guildhall Library, Corporation of London, by whose kind permission they are published here. We are particularly grateful to the Keeper of Manuscripts, Stephen Freeth, and his staff for their assistance.

We are further indebted to the Richard III and Yorkist History Trust whose funding has made this publication possible.

Finally, we are grateful to our friends and families who have long suffered the presence of this 'turbulent priest' in our lives.

London, the Conversion of St. Paul, 2002

Stephanie R. Hovland   Hannes Kleineke
Royal Holloway   History of Parliament Trust
University of London   London

LIST OF ABBREVIATIONS

BI	Borthwick Institute, York
BIHR	*Bulletin of the Institute of Historical Research*
CAD	*A Descriptive Catalogue of Ancient Deeds* (6 vols., London, 1890–1915)
CCR	*Calendar of the Close Rolls* (61 vols., London, 1892–1963)
CFR	*Calendar of the Fine Rolls* (22 vols., London, 1911–62)
CIPM Hen. VII	*Calendar of Inquisitions post Mortem, Henry VII* (3 vols., London, 1898–1955)
CP	Complete Peerage
CPL	*Calendar of Entries in the Papal Registers Relating to Great Britain and Ireland: Papal Letters* (14 vols., London, 1893–1960)
CPR	*Calendar of the Patent Rolls* (53 vols., London, 1891–1916)
DNB	*Dictionary of National Biography*
Fasti	*Fasti Ecclesiae Anglicanae*, ed. J. M. Horn and B. Jones (12 vols., London, 1962–67)
GL	Guildhall Library, London
L&P Hen. VIII	*Letters and Papers, Foreign and Domestic, of the Reign of Henry VIII* (22 vols. in 38, London, 1862–1932)
PRO	Public Record Office
RP	*Rotuli Parliamentorum* (7 vols., London, 1832)
Reg. Stat.	*Registrum Statutorum et Consuetudinum Ecclesiae Cathedralis Sancti Pauli Londiniensis*, ed. W. Sparrow Simpson (London, 1873)
VCH	Victoria County History

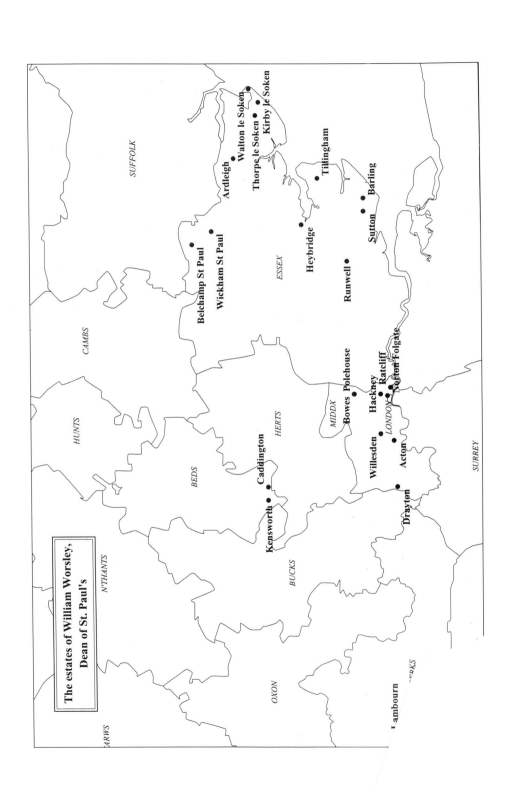

The estates of William Worsley, Dean of St. Paul's

SUFFOLK

Walton le Soken
Kirby le Soken
Thorpe le Soken
Ardleigh

Tillingham
Barling

Heybridge
Sutton

Belchamp St Paul
Wickham St Paul

ESSEX

Runwell

CAMBS

HUNTS

HERTS

MIDDX

Bowes Polehouse
Hackney
Ratcliff
Norton Folgate
LONDON

Caddington

BEDS

Willesden
Acton

Kensworth

Drayton

SURREY

N'THANTS

BUCKS

OXON

Lambourn

ARWS

RKS

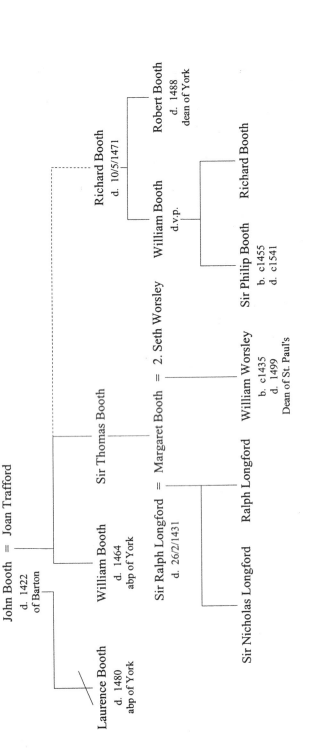

2. The Worsleys and Booths

3. Head of a kneeling cleric from a mural formerly in Brooke House, Hackney
(by permission of the London Metropolitan Archives).

4. Figure of a kneeling cleric from a wall painting formerly at Brooke House, Hackney (by permission of the London Metropolitan Archives).

5. Fragment of the wall painting formerly at Brooke House, Hackney and now at the Museum of London, showing the figure of a late medieval cleric kneeling before St Peter (by permission of the London Metropolitan Archives).

6. William Worsley's petition for a pardon following the Warbeck conspiracy, signed by Henry VII (PRO, C82/135) (by permission of The National Archives [PRO]).

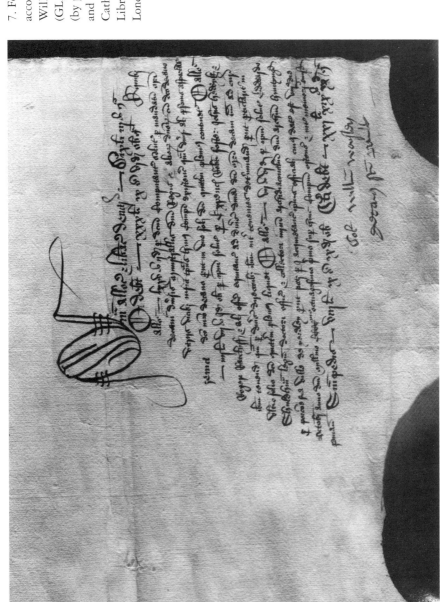

7. Foot of the Receiver's account for 1481–2, bearing William Worsley's signature (GL, MS 25, 166/3) (by permission of the Dean and Chapter of St. Paul's Cathedral and Guildhall Library, Corporation of London).

8. Drawing of Dean Worsley's tomb brass in pre-fire St Paul's, from
Sir William Dugdale's *History of St. Paul's Cathedral* (1658; 1818 edn).

PART 1: INTRODUCTION

WILLIAM WORSLEY, DEAN OF ST. PAUL'S (1479-99), HIS ESTATES AND HOUSEHOLD

'Also I will þat [...] myn executors be not troubled nor vexed be the Chirch of Poules for such maners and londes as I have hadde in ferme of the seid Chirch and also [...] myn executors be not interupted of the said fermes bot soo as thei may enioie the same acordyng to a leese made to me be the Chapiter and also challeyns no thyng for reparacons of the seid fermes, for so moch as I knowe well þat the said maners be in ferre bettyr condicion then I receyved them ...'[1] Thus boasted William Worsley, Dean of St. Paul's cathedral, London, in 1499 when he came to draw up his will.

Like their lay peers, the greater clergy of later medieval England throughout their lives faced the twin challenges of managing often sizeable landed estates and maintaining from the revenues produced by these estates household establishments in keeping with their social status. An often complex administration was one of the prerequisites of meeting these challenges, and a bevy of officials was required to draw up financial accounts of their activities at varying points in the year. Ultimately, a chief financial officer would draw together all the different threads of his lord's economic affairs and compile his own annual account for inspection by his master. In varying degrees of detail, such accounts provide an impression of the lord's finances, the administrative structures of his establishment, and sometimes his activities and movements over a period of time.[2]

Yet, although sizeable numbers of these documents survive to the present day, some sections of society are better served than others, and the secular clergy are just one group who have only limited amounts of such material to illuminate their lives. In particular, there are few instances of runs of accounts, rather than just isolated chance survivals. From the end of the fourteenth century the accounts of the household of Robert Braybroke, Bishop of London, are extant, and a century later we are fortunate to have a series of the accounts of the receiver of William Worsley, Dean of London's

---

[1] Register of Wills of Dean and Chapter of York, vol. ii, fol. 22d, printed in *Testamenta Eboracensia*, iv (Durham *et al.*, Surtees Soc. 53, 1869), p. 157.

[2] Some of the difficulties involved in using medieval receivers' accounts are discussed by C. Dyer, *Standards of Living in the Later Middle Ages* (Cambridge, 1989), pp. 34-35.

1

cathedral church from 1479 to 1499.[3]

In the accounts he prepared for his master, Worsley's receiver – for much of his life one Roger Radcliff – itemised the sums of money he had received from farmers and ministers throughout the Dean's estates, as well as routine items of expenditure. Extraordinary items of annual expenditure were often listed in great detail, offering fascinating insights into some aspects of Dean Worsley's daily life. Thus, the receiver recorded the acquisition of new liveries and other items for important events in the life of the household, such as the visit of a great magnate, or national events such as royal funerals. The Dean's travels around his estates and benefices in the south-east left their traces, as did the flurry of activity caused by an expedition further afield. More mundanely, the accounts noted the routine maintenance of buildings and illustrate the exploitation of the estates in an age after the manorial demesnes had ceased to be cultivated directly.

In many respects, William Worsley's way of life may have been characteristic of the lives of many of the greater clergy of the late fifteenth century. Only occasionally do the accounts offer us tantalising glimpses of the man himself: they record the clothing he wore, and tell of an ointment purchased for the ageing man's back. Yet, Worsley was a man who allowed himself to be drawn into at least one of the great political crises of his age, and the accounts reflect some of the consequences that befell him, if not his motivation. It may thus be worthwhile, by way of introduction to this collection, to take a closer look at William Worsley's career, his income and finances, and the life they served to support.

---

[3] *Household Accounts From Medieval England*, ed. C. M. Woolgar (2 pts., Oxford 1992–93), ii. 721; *9th Report of the Royal Commission on Historical Manuscripts* (3 pts., London, 1883), pt. i, pp. 42b–43a. For examples of later fifteenth-century accounts cf. Woolgar, ii. 693, 695, 703, 704, 709, 712. A cash, corn and stock account of Richard Bell, bishop of Carlisle, for 1485–86 is edited *ibid*. 557–63; for a diet account of John Hales, bishop of Coventry and Lichfield, for part of the year 1461 see *ibid*. 451–86. A diet account of the household of William Smith, archdeacon of Winchester and later bishop of Coventry and Lichfield, for the quarter year from December 1491 to March 1492 survives at Westminster Abbey: WAM 5474, 31795. Braybroke's accounts are edited by L. H. Butler, 'Robert Braybrooke, bishop of London (1381–1404) and his kinsmen' (University of Oxford, D.Phil. thesis, 1951), pp. 457–77. For the household accounts of some late thirteenth and early fourteenth-century bishops see *A Roll of the Household Expenses of Richard de Swinfield, Bishop of Hereford, during part of the years 1289 and 1290*, ed. John Webb (2 vols., London, Cam. Soc. O. S. 59–60, 1854–55), and 'Household Roll of Bishop Ralph of Shrewsbury', ed. J. A. Robinson in *Collectanea* (Som. Rec. Soc. xxxix, 1924), 72–165.

I. *William Worsley – Life and Career*

William Worsley was born around 1435 into a gentry family from Booths, in the Lancashire parish of Eccles.[4] His parents' marriage was a late product of a close friendship, formed half a century earlier, between his great-grandfather, Robert Worsley, and one of his neighbours, the Lancashire landholder John Booth of Barton.[5] The two families continued their close association in subsequent decades, and eventually cemented their alliance by the marriage of Robert Worsley's grandson, Seth, to John Booth's granddaughter, Margaret, widow of the wealthy Sir Ralph Langford. Seth's and Margaret's union resulted in a number of children, including William, the later Dean of St. Paul's.[6]

Seth and Margaret Worsley's offspring formed part of an extensive family, many of whose younger scions were provided for in the Church. In this vocation, two siblings of Margaret's father, Thomas Booth, rose to particular prominence. William and Laurence Booth both held important offices under the Crown while pursuing their ecclesiastical careers and were ultimately preferred to the archbishopric of York.[7] Their advancement in the Church allowed them to provide patronage for many of their younger kinsmen. Robert Booth, a younger son of Richard Booth of Bergham, Suffolk, became Dean of York in 1477, a year after Laurence Booth had been translated to the archbishopric.[8] Three other kinsmen, Thomas (d. 1501),

---

[4]   The date of Worsley's birth is estimated from his entry into Winchester College in 1442. William Worsley's career has been the subject of a number of short studies, most notably A. F. Pollard's account in the Dictionary of National Biography, soon to be superseded by Michael Bennett's biography in the *Oxford DNB*. Other brief notes can be found in C. N. L. Brooke, 'The Deans of St. Paul's, *c.* 1090–1499', *BIHR*, xxix (1965), 231–44, p. 244.

[5]   *The History of Parliament, The Commons 1386–1421*, ed. J. S. Roskell, L. Clark and C. Rawcliffe (4 vols., Stroud, 1992), iv. 902–3.

[6]   *Testamenta Eboracensia*, iv. 155 and *A Biographical Register of the University of Cambridge to 1500*, ed. A. B. Emden (Cambridge, 1963), p. 651 call Dean Worsley's father Robert, but the description of a Ralph Langford as his brother in the 1497–98 account provides conclusive evidence of the Dean's parentage (cf. below, p. 122). A biography of Sir Ralph Langford will appear in *The History of Parliament, The Commons 1422–1504*, ed. L. S. Clark (forthcoming).

[7]   E. Axon, 'The Family of Bothe (Booth) and the Church in the 15th and 16th Centuries', *Transactions of the Lancashire and Cheshire Antiquarian Society*, 53 (1938), 32–82; A. Compton Reeves, 'William Booth, Bishop of Coventry and Lichfield (1447–52)', *Midland History*, iii (1975–76), 11–29; *idem*, 'William Booth, Bishop of Coventry and Lichfield, Archbishop of York', in *Lancastrian Englishmen* (Washington D.C., 1981), 265–362; *idem*, 'Lawrence Booth: Bishop of Durham (1457–76), Archbishop of York (1476–80)', in *Estrangement, Enterprise and Education in Fifteenth Century England*, ed. S. D. Michalove and A. Compton Reeves (Stroud, 1998), 63–88.

[8]   *Testamenta Eboracensia*, iv. 31–32; PRO, C1/86/20; *Fasti*, vi. 8, 28, 91. Like his son, Richard Booth maintained close links with Laurence Booth: PRO,

John (d. 1496), and his brother Ralph Booth (d. 1497) were respectively made prebendaries of Ampleforth and Rikhill and Archdeacon of York at Archbishop Booth's cathedral, and the latter's nephew, Charles, later also entered the Church.[9] Along with the younger Booths, their Worsley relatives benefited from William and Laurence's successful careers. The later Dean's father, Seth Worsley, maintained close links with both Archbishops Booth throughout his career. A younger kinsman, Benjamin Worsley, became a trusted servant of William Booth in later life, was remembered in the Archbishop's will, and appointed keeper of his manor of Scrooby.[10] William Worsley's brother Thomas (d. 1501), was sent to study at Cambridge, where Laurence Booth was chancellor of the university. In June 1452 he became a canon of Lichfield and prebendary of Tachbrook in succession to his brother William, and he continued to hold this benefice until his death. In December 1471, after receiving his B.Cn.L., he was in addition granted the rectory of Waltham in Lincolnshire. Eventually, he received preferment to the prebend of St. Mary's Altar at Beverley, Yorkshire.[11] An illegitimate kinsman, John Worsley, was ordained acolyte in 1446. He went on to study at Oxford, where he gained his LL.B. by December 1455. During the same year he was preferred to the rectory of Bolton le Moors in Lancashire. In subsequent years, Archbishop William Booth continued to dispense patronage to him: in December 1458 he was collated canon and prebendary of the chapel of St. Mary and the Holy Angels at York, and in 1461 he became vicar of Felkirk. That same year the Archbishop also appointed him his commissary general. Two further benefices followed: in November 1465 John became canon of the royal free chapel of Wolverhampton, Staffordshire, and prebendary of Kynwaston *alias* Stonhall, and eventually rector of Bilton in Warwickshire, before dying at the end of the 1470s.[12] A fourth relative, Richard Worsley (d. 1491), became chaplain of Laurence Booth's chantry at Southwell.[13]

Likewise, William Worsley's career was from an early date shaped by the influence of his maternal great-uncles. By 1442, he had begun his education at Winchester College. While still under age, he received extensive preferment,

KB27/790, rot. att. 1; KB27/791, rot. 21.

9   *Fasti*, vi. 19, 29, 76; PRO, PROB11/10, fol. 259v (PCC 33 Vox). On the younger Booths see also A. Compton Reeves, 'Bishop John Booth of Exeter, 1465-78', in *Traditions and Transformations in Late Medieval England*, ed. D. Biggs, S. D. Michalove and A. C. Reeves (Leiden *et al.*, 2002), 125-44.

10   *CCR*, 1429-35, pp. 232, 243; *Testamenta Eboracensia*, iv. 156; PRO, KB27/790, att. rot. 1; KB27/791, rot. 21; CP25(1)/294/75/5.

11   Emden, *Cambridge*, p. 651; *Fasti*, x. 59.

12   *A Biographical register of the University of Oxford to AD 1500*, ed. A. B. Emden, (3 vols., Oxford 1957-59), iii. 2089.

13   *Visitations and Memorials of Southwell Minster*, ed. A. F. Leach (London, Camden Soc. n.s. 48, 1891), p. 108.

for which he later had to seek papal licence.[14] In March 1449, he was collated to his first benefice, the prebend of Tachbrook at Lichfield cathedral.[15] He vacated this three years later, in June 1452, in favour of his brother Thomas,[16] and, in March 1453, instead became a canon of the collegiate church of Southwell, Nottinghamshire, and prebendary of Norwell Overall. He was to retain this benefice until his death.[17] Southwell Minster was a favourite church of the Booths, and both William and Laurence eventually chose to be buried there.[18] By the time of this preferment, Worsley had entered the university of Oxford where he read civil law, but preferments continued to flow: in July 1457 Archbishop William Booth secured the prebend of South Cave at his own cathedral church for his protégé.[19] Meanwhile, the Archbishop's younger brother, Laurence, had studied law at Cambridge. Elected master of his college, Pembroke Hall, in 1450, Laurence rose to become chancellor of the university in about 1458. There is little doubt that Worsley's decision to leave Oxford and move to Cambridge owed a great deal to Booth's influence. In December 1459, William was consequently granted a grace for a degree at that university, and by 1460 had been admitted to the degree of LL.B. there.[20] In the same year, he was also successively ordained deacon and priest within a period of six months. In the years immediately following, Worsley remained at Cambridge, but in March 1462 he was dispensed from further study for the degree of B.Cn.L. He nevertheless appears to have continued his education, perhaps even outside England, for by 1468 he also held a doctorate in the law, although it is not known where he obtained this degree.[21]

Although Worsley was already a significant pluralist at this date, his standing and wealth were further increased by the Booths' continued patronage. Before Archbishop William Booth died in 1464, he made provision for his great-nephew who appears to have been his particular favourite. In his will, he settled his holdings in Hackney and Tottenham on Worsley, thus providing him with a personal landed income in addition to any revenues he might draw by virtue of his benefices.[22] More of the latter were still to follow: Worsley was instituted to the rectory of Eakring in Nottinghamshire on 19 May 1467, and by 16 July 1468 was also prebendary of Willesden at St. Paul's cathedral, London, where Laurence Booth had briefly been dean in 1456–57.[23]

---

14 *CPL*, xii. 311–12.
15 Lichfield Joint Record Office, Reg. B/A/1/10, fol. 8v; *Fasti*, x. 59.
16 *Fasti*, x. 59; Register of Wills of Dean and Chapter of York, ii, fol. 23r; Lichfield Joint Record Office, Reg. B/A/1/10, fol. 13v.
17 BI, Register xxiii, Thomas Rotherham, fol. 110v.
18 *DNB*, ii. 850.
19 *Fasti*, vi. 43; BI, Register xx, William Booth, fols. 42–42v.
20 *Grace Book A*, ed. S. M. Leathes (Cambridge, 1897), pp. 21, 25.
21 University Library Cambridge, EDR G/1/5, fol. 208; Emden, *Cambridge*, p. 651; Emden, *Oxford*, vol. iii, p. 2089; *Grace Book A*, pp. 32, 39; *CPL*, xii. 311.
22 *CCR*, 1476–85, no. 39.

It was, however, at Southwell, his first prebend, that Worsley mainly exercised his residency during these early years. The church there had no dean and its chapter was presided over by the senior residentiary.[24] As many of the residentiaries were absent for large parts of the year, a heavy administrative burden fell on those remaining. Throughout the 1470s it was rare for even three of the canons to attend chapter, and Worsley, who stood out as a frequent attender, often transacted business alone.[25] In 1472, the chapter appointed him its special commissioner to settle disputes among the chantry chaplains at the minster, and in the following years he regularly conducted the triennial visitations of the church.[26]

While the administrative experience that William was thus able to gain would stand him in good stead in his later career, his duties at Southwell nevertheless also saw some unpleasant and time-consuming incidents. One of these arose from corrective action taken by Worsley against one of the vicars choral at Southwell, Thomas Gurnell, in 1470. At the time, Gurnell already had a record of unruly behaviour. He had been cited in November 1469 to appear before the canons to answer charges of having taken possession of the goods of John Terold, a deceased former residentiary, despite their formal sequestration by the chapter. He had shown himself contumacious and refused to acknowledge the chapter's jurisdiction and as a result had been excommunicated. He had nevertheless continued to farm his prebend of Normanton and, although on one occasion in August 1470 he had agreed on his knees to pay for its procuration, he had ignored the chapter's order to surrender the living. Now it was stipulated that not only had he openly engaged in trade, but he had insulted the canons, both in chapter and publicly, and had threatened them with physical injury. As a result, he was once more suspended from his benefice and ejected from the choir. On 13 September 1470, after hearing the evidence of the other vicars choral, who unanimously described Gurnell as headstrong and of bad morals, a panel of three canons headed by Worsley formally excommunicated him a second time. As a result of his continued refusal to surrender his benefice, Gurnell was bound by an obligation for a hundred marks to submit to the chapter's decision. However, he brought a suit against Worsley in the court of Chancery, accusing the later Dean of having caused him to be arrested and imprisoned at London out of sheer malice and ill will. It was only under such duress, he claimed, that he had bound himself to surrender his vicarage. He said that even though he had complied with this condition, Worsley had nevertheless brought a suit at common law to force him to pay the hundred marks. Worsley, by contrast, denied these accusations and claimed that

23   BI, Register xxiii, Thomas Rotherham, fol. 178D; *Fasti*, v. 71.
24   A. H. Thompson, *The English Clergy and their Organization in the Later Middle Ages* (Oxford, 1947), p. 79.
25   *Visitations of Southwell*, pp. 7–8, 13, 14, 16, 17, 18–19, 26–27, 29, 161, 168.
26   *Visitations of Southwell*, pp. 12, 20–26, 32, 42–43.

Gurnell had forfeited his obligation because he had broken its terms by inducing Henry, Lord Grey of Codnor, to interfere in the matter on his behalf.[27]

Such issues as these no doubt absorbed much of Worsley's time at Southwell. Yet he may have found time to attend to his other benefices during the occasional spells when the residentiaries granted themselves leave of absence for weeks, and often months, on account of epidemics of the plague at Southwell. Even so, it is not surprising that one of the complaints raised during the 1481 visitation was that the canons were usually in residence for only eight months in the year.[28]

Although Worsley was clearly pre-eminent among the canons of Southwell and dominated the conduct of their business in the 1470s, he had not reached the apex of his career. In 1476 his patron Laurence Booth was translated from the bishopric of Durham to his brother William's former see at York. In September of that year he appointed his protégé, Worsley, archdeacon of Nottingham.[29] Further preferment was clearly intended, for the following February Worsley secured papal dispensation to hold three incompatible benefices.[30] There is no indication to what extent he found time to attend to his pastoral duties, but he did find time to exercise his legal knowledge on the affairs of various members of the middling and more important clergy, and it is not improbable that the expertise he revealed at Southwell also placed him at the forefront of administrative business elsewhere.[31]

An opportunity for advancement finally presented itself in the autumn of 1478 as a result of the death of the dean of St. Paul's cathedral, London, Thomas Winterbourne. The election of a new dean was invariably a complicated administrative exercise, as a number of the cathedral's prebends were held by absentees who had to be given time to appoint proxies to exercise their votes. Unfortunately, the record of Worsley's election as dean in Bishop Kemp's register is incomplete, with a whole quire missing since medieval times, as is apparent from a marginal entry.[32] Thus, thirteen of the thirty-one canons who might have exercised their vote are unaccounted for. Only eight prebendaries are known to have been present, either because their presence is recorded, or because their presence may be conjectured from their appointment as another canon's proxy. John Sutton, prebendary of Rugmere, presided over the election and Richard Martyn, prebendary of Hoxton and archdeacon of London, publicly announced the election result. Richard

---

27   PRO, C1/1502/12–13; C253/44/9; *CCR*, 1468–76, no. 765; *Visitations of Southwell*, pp. 1–11. For Grey see *CP*, vi. 130–32.

28   *Visitations of Southwell*, pp. 10, 11, 40, 43.

29   *Fasti*, vi. 24; BI, Register xxii, Laurence Booth, fol. 241.

30   *CPL*, xiii, pt. ii. 540.

31   *CCR*, 1468–76, nos. 1330, 1359.

32   GL, MS 9531/7, pt. ii, fol. 9v. See appendix 1.

Lichfield, prebendary of Newington and archdeacon of Middlesex, acted as a procurator shortly afterwards and may therefore be thought also to have been present at the election.[33] Five other canons, Thomas Chaundeler, Thomas Jane, Richard Luke, William Worsley and William Wylde attended as proxies for between one and six other canons. Seven canons, Edmund Audley, Ralph Byrd, Thomas Hall, Robert Morton, Robert Pevesey, William Pykenham, and James Stanley had nominated proxies, while three men (John Bourgchier, John Davyson and William Kempe) were missing unexcused. The prebend of Tottenham was vacant by the death of Dean Winterbourne.[34]

Under these circumstances it was perhaps not surprising that William Worsley, who controlled five proxy votes, as well as his own, was promptly chosen as the new dean.[35] His election was confirmed by the bishop on 4 March, and he took up residence in London. Although he continued to take an interest in the affairs of Southwell minster, his attendance there grew increasingly irregular. He was absent from chapter at Southwell in February and when he next occurs in the chapter acts there, it was for a meeting at which the canons granted themselves leave of absence for the whole summer on account of the plague.[36]

The Deanery of St. Paul's

The cathedral chapter of St. Paul's had been headed by a dean since at least the eleventh century, one of the earliest instances of the office at an English cathedral. In the early years of its existence, the dean's authority was somewhat overshadowed by that of the archdeacons, but from the early twelfth century the dean emerged clearly as leader of the chapter and his role as such was reflected in its documents.[37] By the mid-fifteenth century the office's responsibilities were well-defined and enshrined in the cathedral statutes, a collection of which was compiled by Dean Lisieux in the 1450s. The dean's first responsibilities were of a pastoral nature. His particular ministry was directed at the cathedral clergy: he judged their morals, heard their confessions and administered the last rites. Beyond these internal duties within the cathedral community, there were more important pastoral tasks to be undertaken. In the bishop's absence, the dean would take his place as head of the church. He might then assume the more solemn duties during the

---

[33] GL, MS 9531/7, pt. ii, fol. 13v.

[34] GL, MS 9531/7, pt. ii, fols. 9v–12v; *Fasti*, v. 63.

[35] GL, MS 9531/7, pt. ii, fols. 9–15; C. N. L. Brooke, 'The Earliest Times', in *A History of St Paul's Cathedral and the Men Associated with it*, ed. W. R. Matthews and W. M. Atkins (London, 1957), pp. 54–55.

[36] *Fasti*, v. 6; *Visitations of Southwell*, pp. 40–41.

[37] K. Edwards, *The English Secular Cathedral in the Middle Ages* (Manchester, 1967), p. 140; C. N. L. Brooke, 'The Composition of the Chapter of St. Paul's, 1086–1163', *Cambridge Historical Journal*, x (1950–52), 111–32, pp. 118–19; *idem*, 'The Deans of St. Paul's', p. 233.

offices, such as giving the benediction, or the celebration of divine service on greater feast days. He was also expected to preach public sermons on other feast days.[38] Further duties were defined by the different cults in existence within the cathedral church: within the Jesus chapel in the crypt of St. Paul's, the dean had an honorary stall as rector of the fraternity of the Holy Name.[39]

Alongside its pastoral duties, the office of dean brought with it extensive responsibilities of a secular nature, both within the cathedral close and without. In the first instance, there was the business transacted by the cathedral chapter. The statutes of St. Paul's stipulated that only residentiary canons who had held their prebends for more than a year could attend chapter, but as Worsley had been prebendary of Willesden for more than ten years when he became dean, he was able to take his place at the chapter's head immediately.[40] The dean had a responsibility not only to attend chapter but to summon it and, either in person or by deputy, to expound the business to be transacted. Yet, the extent to which the dean could act independently from the chapter remained limited, and many important decisions could only be taken by the full chapter, where the dean's vote was equal to that of any other canon.[41] Similarly, the statutes of St. Paul's placed severe limits on the dean's jurisdiction over the major canons and the sanctions available to him for their correction. By contrast, he had extensive powers and responsibilities concerning the administration of the chapter's common lands, an area in which some of Worsley's twelfth- and thirteenth-century predecessors made their marks.[42] These powers included the right of triennial visitations of the chapter's churches and manors, accompanied by a residentiary canon elected by the chapter. This power, however, did not extend to the estates held by the dean himself, which in their turn were visited triennially by two canons appointed by the chapter.[43]

Further afield, by the fifteenth century the dean of St. Paul's also customarily played a part in matters of state. Several fifteenth-century deans served as members of the King's council, while some others rose even further: Thomas Lisieux and Laurence Booth had served as Keepers of the Privy Seal while Roger Radcliff and Thomas Winterbourne had both been members of Henry VI's council.[44] Worsley never rose to such high office, but nevertheless

---

[38] Edwards, p. 143; *Reg. Stat.*, p. xxiii.

[39] *Reg. Stat.*, pp. 437, 440.

[40] *Reg. Stat.*, pp. 129–30.

[41] Edwards, pp. 144–45.

[42] *Reg. Stat.*, p. 163; Edwards, p. 147; *The Domesday of St. Paul's*, ed. W. H. Hale (London, Camden Soc. o.s. 69, 1858); *Radulphi de Diceto Opera Historica*, ed. W. Stubbs (2 vols., London, R.S., 1876), i, pp. lvi–lxi.

[43] *Visitations of Churches belonging to St. Paul's Cathedral in 1297 and 1458*, ed. W. Sparrow Simpson (London, Camden Soc., n.s. 55, 1895); *Reg. Stat.*, pp. xxiv, 96, 247; W. Dugdale, *The History of St. Pauls Cathedral in London from its Foundation untill these Times* (London, 1658), pp. 310–35.

played his part in the governance of the realm. He was appointed to royal commissions under both Edward IV and Richard III,[45] and regularly summoned to convocation, the assembly of the clergy of the province of Canterbury, into whose remit fell decisions such as grants of taxation to the King or the Pope (cf. pp. 21–22, below). In the fifteenth century convocation invariably met in the chapter house of St. Paul's and ten assemblies were convened during Worsley's time as dean. His activities in several of them are documented, and that which gathered at the cathedral on 21 March 1481 may serve as an example. On this occasion convocation was asked to consider a series of issues and financial demands. Worsley took a prominent role from the outset. On 26 March he and John Bourgchier, the archdeacon of Canterbury, presented the archdeacon of Suffolk, Master William Pykenham, as speaker (*prelocutor*) of convocation.[46] Although grants to the King and archbishop were quickly agreed, the issue of a papal subsidy proved more controversial and was referred to a committee of convocation that was first summoned to meet on 5 June. Worsley was one of three deans of cathedrals included in this body.[47] As the committee continued to meet at St. Paul's, Worsley was regularly present. By contrast, many of its other members frequently defaulted, and the committee was prorogued several times before being dissolved without result in mid-November 1482, as sickness and death had taken too much of a toll among the original membership.[48] On several occasions thereafter, when convocation was in session it fell to the dean of St. Paul's to present the chosen *prelocutor* to the assembled prelates.[49]

Otherwise, only limited information is available on Worsley's activities as dean. His lack of involvement within St. Paul's contrasts sharply with the enthusiasm and reforming zeal of some of his predecessors and successors, such as Thomas Lisieux, who left his mark on the statutes and administration of the cathedral, or John Colet, who refounded St. Paul's school. At the same time, he failed to play as central a part in royal government as had Lisieux or Laurence Booth. It is, however, interesting, and perhaps even suggestive, that the surviving evidence appears to place stronger emphasis on his secular and political activities than on his conduct of his pastoral duties, or even on his conduct of the office of dean.[50] Indeed, this may be indicative of Worsley's approach to his responsibilities.

[44] R. Virgoe, 'The Composition of the King's Council, 1437–61', *BIHR*, xliii (1970), 134–60, p. 159; J. R. Lander, 'Council, Administration and Councillors, 1461–1485', *BIHR*, xxxii (1959), 138–80, p. 172.

[45] *CPR*, 1476–85, pp. 215, 466.

[46] *Registrum Thome Bourgchier*, ed. F. R. H. Du Boulay (Oxford, 1957), p. 133.

[47] The others were the Deans of Wells and Chichester (*Registrum Bourgchier*, p. 147).

[48] *Registrum Bourgchier*, pp. 148ff.

[49] *The Register of John Morton, Archbishop of Canterbury, 1486–1500*, ed. C. Harper-Bill (2 vols. [Canterbury and York Soc. 75, 78], Leeds, Woodbridge, 1987–91), no. 102, where Worsley is erroneously called Thomas.

Although formally more distant from the government than his predecessors, Worsley nevertheless found himself in close proximity to the King and court in other ways. The hospitality of the dean and chapter was famous,[51] and great lords with blood ties to the King such as Edward IV's stepson, the Marquess of Dorset, were entertained in the Dean's house.[52] Yet, Worsley also maintained close links with the King himself. In the months following his election, in the course of the year 1479, Anglo-Scottish relations – generally amiable since the treaty of October 1474 – had deteriorated rapidly. The Scottish government became increasingly tolerant of its subjects' breaches of the truce and raids on English territory. In early 1480 King Edward sent Alexander Legh to Scotland to demand not only reparations for the Scottish violations of the truce, but to threaten open war and demand the surrender of Berwick. In the first half of the same year Edward also began preparations for open warfare in the north, should it become necessary to back his demands up with force. When the Earl of Angus crossed the border and burnt Bamborough in the summer of 1480, the retinues of the Duke of Gloucester, warden of the West March since 1470, and the Earl of Northumberland rapidly retaliated. James III of Scotland now sent Ross herald to Westminster in an attempt to negotiate and sought to blame the English borderers for the breach of the truce, but his overtures were dismissed by Edward, who in November 1480 decided to lead an expedition to Scotland in person. Although preparations for this campaign progressed rapidly, Edward himself delayed in the south-east until September 1481. He only reached Nottingham at the end of October and remained there for three weeks before returning to London, leaving his commanders to besiege Berwick.[53]

Worsley appears to have been caught up in the general excitement of the preparations for the expedition to the north in the final months of 1480. His intention was obviously to accompany the King himself and, moreover, the provisions listed in the accounts indicate that he was to take a personal retinue of seven men.[54] The Dean had to be fully equipped for the expedition and, for

---

[50] The authors are grateful to Dr. Elizabeth New for her comments on this point.

[51] J. H. Lupton, *A Life of John Colet, D.D., Dean of St. Paul's and Founder of St. Paul's School* (London, 1909), pp. 148–49; *The Collected Works of Erasmus, vol. 8: The Correspondence of Erasmus*, ed. R. A. B. Mynors and P. G. Bietenholz (Toronto etc., 1988), p. 235.

[52] Document 3, below.

[53] C. Ross, *Edward IV* (London, 1974), pp. 278–83. The chronology of these events is problematic. Ross dates Legh's mission to early 1480, Ranald Nicholson, *The Edinburgh History of Scotland*, ii: Scotland: the Later Middle Ages (Edinburgh, 1974), p. 491, to the early months of 1481.

[54] It was not unknown for deans of St. Paul's to travel to the Scottish Marches on the King's business. In the Spring of 1375 Dean John de Appelby went there for a meeting with the deputies of the King of Scotland: PRO, E101/317/8.

his protection his retinue was armed with bows and arrows. For the company's transport, a wagon and a cart with six horses as well as six additional horses were acquired. The potential hardships of setting up camp in the field could not be avoided, but a degree of comfort and ostentation were nevertheless intended, and tents and pavilions were provided for the party's accommodation. Worsley seems to have set out before the King: in June 1481 he drew £80 in gold from his receiver for his journey to Southwell and the following month he was conducting a visitation there.[55]

The Warbeck Conspiracy and Worsley's Final Years

It is impossible to tell whether the death of Edward IV and the turbulence of Richard III's accession had any impact on Worsley's relationship with the court. There is no suggestion that he was either particularly close or particularly hostile to Richard, with whom he may be thought to have become acquainted either at court or in the course of the expedition of 1481. If anything, the transition appears to have been a smooth one, for he did not think it necessary to sue for a personal pardon from the new King for his protection.[56] It may have been as a consequence of this apparent indifference that the accession of Henry VII brought Worsley neither difficulties nor immediate benefit, even though two of his kinsmen, Edward and Seth Worsley, had been in exile with the pretender.[57] Unlike many others associated with Richard III, the Dean again saw no need to sue for a pardon from the new King.[58] For the first time since his installation as Dean, however, he was granted a further benefice: in February 1493 he was made Archdeacon of Taunton and prebendary of Milverton in Wells, resigning the Nottinghamshire rectory of Eakring in return. It was a significant preferment, and boded well for Worsley's further career: three of his five predecessors since the early 1440s had been elevated to bishoprics from the benefice.[59]

---

[55] *Visitations of Southwell*, pp. 42–3; document 2, below.

[56] PRO, C67/51, 52.

[57] *CPR*, 1485–94, p. 32; *Testamenta Eboracensia*, iv. 155 suggests that Seth may have been the Dean's brother. Within weeks of Bosworth Edward was rewarded for his service by a grant of the farm of the lordship of Ballingham in Calais: D. Grummitt, '"For the Surety of the Town and Marches": Early Tudor Policy towards Calais 1485–1509', *Nottingham Medieval Studies*, xliv (2000), 184–203, p. 186.

[58] The pardon Worsley was granted in December 1485 related to his service as one of the feoffees of Richard Culpeper and included all his co-feoffees: PRO, C67/53, m. 4.

[59] Adam Moleyns, archdeacon 1441–45, became bp. of Chichester, Robert Stillington, archdeacon 1450–65, became bp. of Bath and Wells, Oliver King, archdeacon 1490–92, became bp. of Exeter. Only Andrew Holes, archdeacon 1446–50, was merely moved to the archdeaconry of Wells, while Richard Langport died as archdeacon in 1490. Likewise, Worsley's immediate successor in the archdeaconry, Robert Sherborne, became bp. of St. David's in 1505 when he

Nevertheless, it is possible that he had hoped for more significant preferment on that occasion, perhaps even for immediate elevation to a bishopric on this occasion, and that it was dissatisfaction that caused him to become involved in the extensive conspiracy against Henry Tudor that came to light in late 1494. Certainly, like the Archdeaconry of Taunton, the Deanery of St. Paul's had been a stepping stone leading to further preferment for several of Worsley's predecessors, including his great-uncle, Laurence Booth.

The apparent aim of the conspirators of 1494 was to replace Henry with the Flemish pretender Perkin Warbeck, posing as Richard, duke of York, Edward IV's younger son. Henry VII's spies infiltrated the ranks of the conspirators at an early stage and the principal men involved were arrested at the beginning of 1495. Apart from Worsley, three other clergymen were arrested: William Richford (d. 1501), prior provincial of the English Dominicans, Thomas Powys, the Dominican prior of Langley, and William Sutton (d. 1503), the distinguished preacher and parson of St. Stephen Walbrook in London.[60] The leading laymen involved were John Radcliff, Lord FitzWalter, Sir Simon Mountfort, Sir Thomas Thwaites, William Daubeney, Robert Ratcliffe and Richard Lacy.[61] Mountfort, Robert Ratcliffe and William Daubeney were executed as leaders of the plot, while the rest, including the priests were spared.[62]

The background to Worsley's involvement in the plot and its extent remain obscure. It has been argued that the link between the main conspirators was their common connection with Edward IV and senior members of his family surviving into Henry Tudor's reign, a theory prevalent by the sixteenth century which survived into James I's reign.[63] A similar

---

surrendered the benefice: *Fasti*, viii. 16–17; *The Registers of Robert Stillington, Bishop of Bath and Wells, 1466–1491, and Richard Fox, Bishop of Bath and Wells, 1492–94*, ed. H. C. Maxwell-Lyte (Som. Rec. Soc., lii, 1937), p. 179; *The Register of Richard Fox while Bishop of Bath and Wells, A.D. MCCCCXCII–MCCCCXCIV*, ed. E. C. Batten (n.l., 1889), p. 28.

[60] For Sutton see Emden, *Oxford*, iii. 1826–27, for Richford, *ibid.*, p. 1575, for Powys, Emden, *Cambridge*, p. 459.

[61] For biographical details of the conspirators cf. *CP*, v. 486–87; *The History of Parliament: Biographies of the Members of the Commons House 1439–1509*, ed. J. C. Wedgwood (London, 1936), p. 706 (FitzWalter), Wedgwood, p. 603 (Mountfort), *ibid.*, p. 855 (Thwaites), and also see Grummitt, "Surety of Town and Marches", p. 191.

[62] *Memorials of King Henry VII: Historia Regis Henrici Septimi a Bernardo Andrea Tholosate Conscripta*, ed. James Gairdner (London, R.S. 10, 1858), p. 69; *The Anglica Historia of Polydore Vergil A.D. 1485–1537*, ed. D. Hay (London, Camden Soc. lxxiv, 1950), p. 72; Ian Arthurson, *The Perkin Warbeck Conspiracy* (Stroud, 1994), pp. 84–86. For Sutton's bond for future good behaviour see PRO, C54/376, m. 19d. The authors are indebted for this reference to Dr. Sean Cunningham, who is preparing an edition of the document.

[63] Arthurson, pp. 87–88; *The History of King Richard the Third (1619) by Sir George*

explanation appears possible in Worsley's case. The Dean had connections with the court, and members of the royal family were guests at his table. Worsley's kinsman and patron, Laurence Booth, Archbishop of York, had served as King Edward's chancellor and been elevated by him to the archbishopric.[64] Although the Marquess of Dorset, a guest in Worsley's household in 1481, played a part in trying the rebels of 1495, he was nevertheless viewed with suspicion by the King and in 1496 had to find substantial sureties for his good behaviour.[65] Perhaps even more suggestive is Worsley's close connexion with Sir Thomas Montgomery, whom he retained at an annual fee of £4, and who had been one of King Edward's executors. Although Montgomery was never charged with involvement in the plot, he may have escaped merely by his death in January 1495, before the conspirators' arrest.[66]

Worsley also had links among the other men arrested: in 1491 William Sutton and the Dean's kinsman, the mercer Edmund Worsley, jointly acquired the Essex manor of Uphavering and other lands in the county from Anne, widow of Sir Thomas Urswick.[67] Furthermore, one of the men who stood surety for Sutton's good behaviour in 1496 in the aftermath of the conspiracy was Richard Lee, who had earlier served alongside the Dean as a feoffee of Richard Culpeper, first husband of Worsley's kinswoman Isabella. Through his mercer relatives, who by the later fifteenth century were established at Calais as well as in London, the Dean was well placed to sustain contacts with conspirators further afield. Members of the London Mercers' Company and their mercantile contacts across the Channel played a central role in communications between the plotters, and the close connexion between William Worsley and his merchant kinsmen is illustrated by his appointment of Edmund Worsley to a central position in his household after the death of the steward Roger Radcliff in late 1496.[68]

Whatever the reason, Worsley was attainted and placed in the Tower. Yet, in keeping with his status, his imprisonment was not an uncomfortable one. He took his servants along, and Simon Digby, the deputy lieutenant of the Tower, received 16s. 8d. for them each week from Worsley's receiver.[69] Similarly, the Dean's diet remained a varied one. Various kinds of meat and fish were bought and sent to the Tower for Worsley's table.[70] Nevertheless, the Dean soon opened negotiations for a reconciliation with the King. It was not long before his efforts bore fruit: he was released from the Tower after

---

    Buck, ed. A. N. Kincaid (Gloucester, 1979), p. 161.

[64] See appendix 2.

[65] Arthurson, pp. 86, 138; *CCR*, 1485–1500, no. 972.

[66] See the entry for Montgomery in appendix 2.

[67] *CAD*, ii. C.2366, vi. C.6991.

[68] Arthurson, p. 90. See the entry for Edmund Worsley in appendix 2.

[69] *Statutes of the Realm* (11 vols., 1810–28), ii. 619; document 9, below.

[70] Document 9, below.

only sixteen weeks,[71] his attainder was reversed in parliament, and on 6 June 1495 Henry granted him a general pardon.[72] However, the pardon cost Worsley dearly. In the first instance, he had to find eight mainpernors who each pledged £200 for his loyalty. He drew most of these from among his own household, and they included the faithful Roger Radcliff, three kinsmen, Edmund Worsley, Philip Booth and Thomas Orston, who had long administered Worsley's Southwell prebend, as well as the chaplain William Roke.[73] Immediately following the grant of his pardon, Worsley had to grant an annual rent of £200 from his ecclesiastical estates, payable for the rest of his life, to Lord Daubeney, Sir Reginald Bray, Sir Thomas Lovell, Andrew Dymmok, James Hobart and Richard Empson, to the King's use. For added security, he had to renew this commitment twice in the following years, and the Dean's receivers' accounts record the payment of the sum in subsequent years.[74] There also appears to have been another agreement made some days later on 28 June. The terms of this separate bond are obscure, but under it Worsley paid another £35 *p.a.* to King Henry.[75] Furthermore, the Dean had to surrender his archdeaconry of Taunton, which was regranted before the end of 1496.[76]

The King's close advisors were personally rewarded for their part in securing Worsley's pardon:[77] the Dean had little personal estate, but what he had – the lands in Tottenham and Hackney that he had inherited from Archbishop Booth – he was forced to make over to Sir Reginald Bray and the London goldsmiths John Shaa and Bartholomew Rede, joint masters of the mint, in March 1496.[78] While Worsley remained resident at Hackney, from this date on he had to pay £8 6s. 8d. in rent to Bray every half year.[79] In

---

[71] The receiver's account allows for payment to Digby for this period of time: document 9, below.

[72] PRO, C65/128, m. 17; *CPR*, 1494–1509, p. 23; *RP*, vi. 489; *Statutes of the Realm*, ii. 619; C82/135. The authors are indebted to Dr. David Grummitt for this latter reference.

[73] *CCR*, 1485–1500, no. 863; PRO, E101/414/16, fol. 127.

[74] *CCR*, 1485–1500, nos. 795, 910, 965; documents 9, 10, below. In November 1498 Thomas Lucas replaced Dymmok among the beneficiaries.

[75] Documents 9, 10, below.

[76] *The Registers of Oliver King, Bishop of Bath and Wells 1496–1503, and Hadrian de Castello, Bishop of Bath and Wells 1503–1518*, ed. H. Maxwell-Lyte (Som. Rec. Soc. liv, 1939), no. 9, p. 2; *Fasti*, viii. 17.

[77] The role of Henry VII's inner circle, including Daubeney, Bray, and Lovell, in controlling access to the King is discussed by M. M. Condon, 'Ruling Elites in the Reign of Henry VII', in *Patronage, Pedigree and Power*, ed. C. Ross (Gloucester, 1979), 109–42. Specifically for Bray see M. M. Condon, 'From Caitiff and Villain to Pater Patriae: Reynold Bray and the Profits of Office', in *Profit, Piety and the Professions in Later Medieval England*, ed. M. A. Hicks (Gloucester, 1990), 137–68.

[78] *CCR*, 1485–1500, no. 910.

[79] Documents 9, 10, below.

addition, Bray was granted an annual fee of £10, as was Sir Thomas Lovell, while Simon Digby, the deputy lieutenant of the Tower, annually received half that sum.[80]

If the financial constraints resulting from the need to make substantial payments for renewed royal favour were not enough, Worsley's final years were to be further overshadowed by the death of his trusted receiver, Roger Radcliff, in December 1496. Two of the Dean's kinsmen who had stood surety for him in 1496, Edmund Worsley and Philip Booth, now took control of his finances, probably to keep their own interest secure. As a result, William's relations with Booth and Worsley were cool, and before long led to litigation in the court of Chancery.[81]

To compound his troubles, Worsley's health now also began to fail. His stay in the Tower – however comfortable – may have adversely affected his constitution, for in 1496-97 the steward accounted for an ointment for his master's back. In this sense there may have been an element of truth in the claim of the author of the Great Chronicle of London that he had died as a consequence of his actions in 1494, although probably not of shame, as the chronicler asserted.[82] Feeling death approaching, Worsley made his will on 12 February 1499. He asked to be buried on one side of the choir of St. Paul's in London. He made fairly sumptuous provision for his funeral, providing for black liveries for his servants, as well as black gowns for a number of poor people. On the day of his funeral the sum of £3 6s. 8d. was to be distributed among the poor. For three years after his death a chantry priest was to sing for his soul in the chapel of St. Laurence in St. Paul's and for the same period of time his obit was to be kept in St. Paul's, with 20s. being distributed among poor people on each occasion. Having thus provided for his soul's salvation, Worsley's next thought was for his servants. He asked that his household be kept intact for their benefit for a month and that each of them should be paid their full wages for the quarter he died in. In addition, each of them was to receive a suitable reward. Further bequests went to the choristers and minor canons of St. Paul's.[83] Thomas Worsley, the Dean's brother, refused the execution of William's will, so it was entrusted to the lawyer William Ayloff,[84] and to the Dean's household retainers Thomas Shaa and John

[80] Document 9, below. For Lovell cf. appendix 2, below.

[81] PRO, C1/453/2-3.

[82] The Great Chronicle of London, ed. A. H. Thomas and I. D. Thornley (London, 1938), p. 257.

[83] Testamenta Eboracensia, iv. 155-57.

[84] William Ayloff of Breteyns in Hornchurch, Essex, was a lawyer trained at Lincoln's Inn with landholdings in Essex and Suffolk. He died in the late summer of 1517, leaving two legitimate sons and a daughter, as well as two bastards. In his will he bequeathed most of his books of law to his elder son William, but left a yearbook of Edward III's reign and a book of assize proceedings to the library of Lincoln's Inn: PRO, PROB11/19, fols. 1-4 (PCC 1 Ayloffe); M. K. McIntosh, A

Saperton.[85] The exact date of the Dean's death remains obscure, but he was dead by 7 September 1499, when Bishop Savage collated his successor to the prebend of Willesden.[86] As he had requested, Worsley was buried in the cathedral, close to the chapel of St. Laurence. Apart from the inscription on his tomb brass, a further epitaph was engraved on a pillar close to the tomb, perhaps on the initiative of Ayloff, who in his own will of 1517 made provision for masses for Worsley's soul.[87]

II. *The Accounts* I: *The Economy of the Dean's Estates and Worsley's Income*
As William Worsley's chief financial official, the receiver – for most of the Dean's life Roger Radcliff – had overall control both of his master's income and of his expenditure. This did not, however, mean that all of Worsley's income passed through Radcliff's hands: entries in several of the receiver's accounts show that some of the Dean's ministers and farmers would regularly make payments either to Worsley himself or to household officials other than the receiver. On these occasions, only the revenue paid to Radcliff appears in the accounts, making it difficult to draw conclusions as to the total revenue annually at the Dean's disposal. Equally, it is impossible to calculate accurately Worsley's full potential income, as the receiver was only concerned with the sums in actuality paid to him. Some approximation to such sums is possible by drawing on two surviving sets of accounts of individual ministers and farmers, which provide a valuable impression of what was due to the Dean from his estates and the proportion of them actually collected.[88]

Worsley's estates fell into four categories. In the first instance, there were the lands he held by virtue of his deanery. The deanery estates incorporated a number of properties, mainly in the city of London, which had been assembled over the course of time. Characteristic of the process of assembly was the house bequeathed to the deanery by Dean Ralph Diceto in the twelfth century, on condition that future deans should annually pay 10s. towards the keeping of his anniversary.[89] Further holdings of the deanery were situated in Ivy Lane and Knightrider Street, and included the Middlesex manor of Norton Folgate (in Shoreditch).[90] Other cathedral estates of St.

Community Transformed, The Manor and Liberty of Havering 1500–1620 (Cambridge, 1991), pp. 52, 84, 272, 274, 374, 424, 440; N. Pevsner, *Buildings of England, Essex* (2nd ed., Harmondsworth, 1965), p. 245; *VCH Essex*, vii. 33, 48.

[85] The manuscript of Worsley's will is damaged and missing the appointment of executors. However, it is likely that the men to whom the administration of his goods was committed when the will was proven on 8 Nov. 1499 were also the Dean's choice of executors. For Shaa and Saperton see appendix 2.

[86] GL, MS 9531/8, fol. 33.

[87] PRO, PROB11/19, fols. 1–4 (PCC 1 Ayloffe); John Weever, *Ancient Funeral Monuments* (London, 1767) pp. 158–59.

[88] Documents 11, 12, below.

[89] *Radulfi de Diceto Opera*, ed. Stubbs, vol. i, p. lxxiii.

Paul's were by the fifteenth century customarily assigned to support the dean alongside the traditional parcels of the deanery. These included the rectory of Cheping Lambourn (Berks.), lands at Acton and the mill of Ratcliff (in Stepney). In addition, there were the lands pertaining to Worsley's other benefices. These included the prebends of Willesden at St. Paul's cathedral (1468–99), South Cave at York Minster (1457–99), Milverton at Wells cathedral (1493–96), and Norwell Overall in the parish of Nowell at Southwell Minster, Notts. (1453–99).

Worsley further augmented his holdings with a number of manors which he took to farm from the cathedral chapter. These extended across three counties and included the manors of Caddington and Kensworth in Bedfordshire, Bowes and Polehouse in Edmonton, Drayton and the rectory of Willesden in Middlesex, and Belchamp St. Paul, Wickham St. Paul, Walton-le-Soken, Thorpe-le-Soken, Kirby-le-Soken, Heybridge, Tillingham, Sutton, Barling and Runwell in Essex.[91] Not all of these manors were in the Dean's hands throughout his period at St. Paul's: the receiver's accounts suggest that Worsley only took Tillingham to farm in about 1486, and his lease had expired or been terminated by 1494, when Sir John Shaa was leasing it directly from dean and chapter. Similarly, the manor of Sutton was leased to Master Walter Odeby, the prebendary of Harleston, from 1489 and Drayton to Edmund Audley, bishop of Hereford, by 1495. Finally, Worsley personally owned a number of properties in Tottenham and Hackney which his patron William Booth had bequeathed to him, and which were transferred to him by Booth's feoffees by May 1476.[92]

The bulk of Worsley's income from his estates came from the annual farms of his demesne lands. As on other estates, the direct cultivation of the dean's demesnes had by the later fifteenth century long been abandoned in favour of their leasing for annual payments.[93] The majority of Worsley's

[90]   Document 13, below.
[91]   For these manors and their acquisition by the Dean and chapter cf. *Visitations of St. Paul's*, pp. xv–xxiii; *VCH Middlesex*, v. 151; vii. 213–14. Walton-le-Soken is today called Walton-on-the-Naze.
[92]   *CCR*, 1476–85, no. 39. Cf. p. 5, above.
[93]   For the chronology of demesne leasing on other ecclesiastical estates see P. J. Taylor, 'The Estates of the Bishopric of London from the Seventh Century to the early Sixteenth Century', (2 vols., unpubl. Univ. of London Ph.D. thesis, 1976), ii. 294–96; F. R. H. Du Boulay, 'Who Were Farming the English Demesnes at the End of the Middle Ages?', *Economic History Review*, 2nd Ser. xvii (1964–65), 443–55, p. 445; B. Harvey, 'The Leasing of the Abbot of Westminster's Demesnes in the Later Middle Ages', *ibid.* xxii (1969), 17–27, p. 19; *eadem*, *Westminster Abbey and its Estates in the Middle Ages* (Oxford, 1977), pp. 148–51; C. Dyer, *Lords and Peasants in a Changing Society: The Estates of the Bishopric of Worcester 680–1540* (Cambridge, 1980), p. 209. By 1450 the bulk of the estates held by M. John Bernyngham, a prebendary of St. Paul's, including Worsley's later manors of Drayton, Norton and Ardleigh, were in the hands of farmers, and the same was

manors were leased *en bloc* to a single farmer or a pair of joint farmers.[94]
Where there are examples of apparent piecemeal leases of parcels within a
manor, these were usually parcels originally separate from the demesne, such
as 'Kent's tenement' in Thorpe, which appears to have evolved from the
former rectory lands,[95] or 'Cootes' in Wadende in the manor of Ardleigh, the
origins of which are more obscure. Where Worsley's holdings included the
demesnes of both a manor and a rectory, the farms of the two units were
formally kept separate, even if they were let to the same tenant. Often, corn
mills were let separate from the manors as well. This was the case at Drayton,
where throughout Worsley's tenure the mill was farmed on a lease of its own,
and at Heybridge, where one of the mills was kept distinct, except for the
years 1488–96, when Geoffrey Dallyng, farmer of the demesne, was able to
secure its lease. Individual demesnes were let as complete units, including a
variety of buildings, on rare occasions a mill, and on at least one manor a herd
of livestock: in 1496–97 the bailiff of the soke accounted for the replenishing
of a flock of sheep at Thorpe, which the recently dismissed farmer had
allowed to diminish.[96]

In the absence of any original lease indentures from Worsley's estates,
and with only a few such documents from the chapter estates, it is difficult to
gain an impression of the length and terms of the leases taken by the farmers.
In 1450 several of the manors then held by Master John Bernyngham,
including Worsley's later manors of Drayton and Ardleigh, had been farmed
out on an annual basis,[97] but in the second half of the century, leases may
generally have become longer.[98] So, in 1500–01 it was stipulated that Thomas

---

probably true of other Dean and chapter properties: PRO, SC6/1108/19. For
    Bernyngham cf. below, n. 97.

[94] Wholesale leasing was also dominant on the estates of the bishops of London and
    Worcester: Taylor, 'Estates', p. 307; Dyer, *Lords and Peasants*, p. 209.

[95] This appears to be the implication of the farms paid: John Kent, who from 1479
    to 1483 held Thorpe rectory at an annual farm of £4, in 1484–85 held 'Kent's
    tenement' which continued to be let for the same amount until 1497. John Percy,
    farmer of 'Thorpe Hall' in 1487–88, was said from 1488–89 to be farmer of the
    manor and rectory at a farm unchanged since the early 1480s. Cf. documents 1–4,
    6–8, below.

[96] Document 12, below. By contrast, the tenants of the bishopric of Worcester
    received no livestock (Dyer, *Lords and Peasants*, p. 210), and on the estates of the
    bishop of London the practice of letting livestock with the demesne continued
    only on a few select manors, probably at the farmers' insistence (Taylor, 'Estates',
    pp. 312, 314), whereas on the estates of Westminster Abbey the practice varied
    between manors (Harvey, *Westminster Abbey*, pp. 153–54).

[97] It is possible that this practice resulted from Bernyngham's need to let his
    demesnes for terms shorter than those for which he himself held his manors from
    the cathedral chapter: PRO, SC6/1108/19. For Bernyngham cf. *Fasti*, v. 26, 46, 53
    and above, n. 93

[98] Dyer, *Lords and Peasants*, pp. 210–11.

Garrard's lease of the rectory of Chepyng Lambourn, which he held to farm by 1495, had not yet expired,[99] while in 1508 Dean Colet granted the manor of Runwell to William Ayloff for a term of twenty years, with a promise of renewal for a similar term on expiry.[100] As on neighbouring ecclesiastical estates, the length of leases of smaller parcels of the estate varied widely.[101] Thus, the succession of tenants of Heybridge mill indicates short leases ranging from annual farms to at most eight years,[102] whereas 'Cootes' tenement at Wadende was held by William Frost for at least fifteen years between 1482 and 1497. Frost may have held on similar terms to the London tailor John Bygland, who took various houses and tenements in the city from Worsley year by year during pleasure.[103] By contrast, in the 1460s Robert Nundy leased a London brewhouse from the chapter for a term of twenty-five years.[104] Elsewhere on the chapter estates unusually long farms are documented: in 1457 Richard Lee leased a house in the London parish of St. Stephen Walbrook from Dean Laurence Booth and the chapter of St. Paul's for a term of ninety-five years, and in 1460 Roger Frende took to farm several parcels of land in Acton and Willesden from Dean Say and the chapter for a term of ninety-nine years, but these terms may have been atypical, as Lee committed himself to repairing a decayed and ruinous holding.[105]

Although some leases specifically required the farmer to keep his holding in repair, this was not uniformly the rule. Indeed, several farmers complained that after they had invested substantial sums in the repair of their holdings, the chapter authorities had sought to relet the improved properties at increased rents.[106] It was not uncommon for late fifteenth-century ecclesiastical lords to continue to take an active interest in the maintenance of their leased properties. The archbishop of Canterbury allowed his farmers up to 20% of their annual rents, and the bishop of London usually retained at least some, sometimes all, of the liability for repairs.[107] Similarly, Worsley's farmers in the 1490s could be allowed between 10% and 20% of their annual farm for necessary repairs.[108] In the soke in Essex the costs of repairs were not

---

[99]   PRO, C1/240/7.
[100] PRO, C1/534/6.
[101] Taylor, 'Estates', p. 323.
[102] John Candish until 1481, Robert Pere 1481–82, John Pere, by 1484–1488, Geoffrey Dallyng 1488–96, Robert Bette from 1496.
[103] PRO, C1/258/85.
[104] PRO, C1/61/553.
[105] GL, MS 25342; PRO, C106/149.
[106] PRO, C1/61/553, 258/85.
[107] Du Boulay, 'Demesne Farming', p. 446; Taylor, 'Estates', p. 308. By contrast, the abbot of Westminster's farmers were generally required to repair any defects at their own expense, even if the abbot provided the necessary timber: Harvey, 'Demesne Leasing', p. 24.
[108] Substantially higher expenses such as were incurred at Runwell in 1496–97, where the farmer was allowed 59% of his farm for repairs, were the exception: document

allowed to individual farmers, but were paid and accounted for by the lord's bailiff. Particularly extensive was the maintenance required by the Dean's mills: for that of Ratcliff (Mdx.) some 4,000 tiles were purchased in one year. A new millstone was provided in 1489, and the same year improvements were made to the ditches supplying the mill with water. This was a costly affair: whereas repairs to the mill regularly accounted for between £3 and £8, the millstone alone cost £5, and the improvements to the ditches came to more than £28.[109]

Other aspects of the leases of Worsley's farmers, besides the Dean's policy regarding repairs on the estates, were common on south-eastern estates in the fifteenth century. So, in addition to their cash farm, some farmers were required to make an annual livery in kind. Thus, Roger Frende's lease at Acton required him to deliver four bushels of wheat flour and four bushels of oatmeal to the Dean's mansion house in London, although these might be commuted at a rate fixed in the lease indenture, thus preventing the provision of sub-standard produce.[110] Similarly, a number of Worsley's farmers benefited from grants of gowns on taking up their farms, and in some instances on an annual basis thereafter, a practice also followed on the archbishop of Canterbury's demesnes. On Worsley's lands, this is documented at Acton, Ardleigh, Willesden, Belchamp St. Paul and Wickham St. Paul in 1495-96.[111]

More unusual was the Dean's practice of exonerating some of his farmers from payments of tax to King and Pope. Whereas Worsley's benefices were taxed in accordance with the grants made by convocation (cf. below, p. 30), his temporal holdings were, like those of secular lords, subject to the taxation granted by Parliament. As a rule, these payments would be made locally by Worsley's farmers and could then be allowed to them in their annual accounts. Consequently, however, this taxation left few traces in the accounts of the Dean's receiver general. Only one of Roger Radcliff's accounts, that of 1488-89, records a payment of 13s. 4d. as a fifteenth for the manors of Bowes and Polehouse in Edmonton.[112] A similar payment is also recorded there in the farmer's account of 1496-97 for a tenth, with an additional payment of 6s. 8d. for the part of the farmer's lands at Tottenham, and further payments for an earlier instalment. In the same year there is also a record of a payment of 2s. 4d. for the first 'aid' to the King by the farmer of 'Kent's tenement' at

12, below.

[109] Document 8, below. On mills and their repair more generally see R. Holt, *The Mills of Medieval England* (Oxford, 1988), esp. pp. 99–101.

[110] GL, MS 25342. The livery is documented in the 1480–81 receiver's account, albeit by then commuted (cf. below, p. 49).

[111] Document 9, below. A similar practice was followed by the archbishop of Canterbury on some of his demesnes: Du Boulay, 'Demesne Farming', p. 445.

[112] Document 7, below; M. Jurkowski, C. L. Smith, D. Crook, *Lay Taxes in England and Wales 1188–1688* (Kew, 1998), p. 122.

Thorpe-le-Soken in Essex.[113]

The King's taxation aside, several of the accounts also record payments of 'Peter's Pence', also called 'Romeshott'.[114] 'Peter's Pence' was a levy dating back to Anglo-Saxon times and reinstituted by William the Conqueror after a brief lapse during the late Anglo-Saxon period. Originally it was levied at 1d. for every hearth, but by the later middle ages England paid a fixed annual sum of 299 marks (£199 6s. 8d.). While in some dioceses the collection was supervised by the bishop, in the diocese of London this responsibility rested with the archdeacons of Middlesex, Essex and Colchester, each of whose districts annually returned the sum of £5 10s.[115] The collection of the levy on the ground fell to local parish priests or manorial lords. Thus, the dues from the manors of Bowes and Polehouse were annually paid to the lord of manor of Edmonton, who acted for the archdeacon of Middlesex. As in the case of the King's taxes, the Peter's Pence from Bowes and Polehouse were often either paid directly by the receiver or allowed in the farmer's account.[116]

These concessions to the farmers of Bowes and Polehouse were exceptional on Worsley's estates. Although the Dean's concessions to his tenants elsewhere also seem extensive, they did not differ significantly from the terms on offer from other ecclesiastical landowners in the south-east. The accounts do not indicate holdings standing vacant for any length of time or in any number, and it appears unlikely that the concessions resulted from difficulties in finding farmers. Rather, it is probable that in the competitive landmarket of south-eastern England where large amounts of ecclesiastical demesne lands were available to potential farmers, the dean of St. Paul's simply had to match the terms on offer elsewhere. Bowes and Polehouse may have been the exception. Even in years where allowances for taxes and repairs are not expressly documented, the farmers' payments often fell short of the annual farm of £26 13s. 4d., and yet the farmers were not replaced. Even in 1496–97, when elsewhere farmers were being replaced with a view to maximising revenue, John Fox remained in place, paying just £16 13s. 4d., of which only £5 4s. 6d. was delivered in cash.

---

[113] Document 12, below.

[114] Documents 7, 8, 9, 12, below. For the background and early development of this levy see O. Jensen, 'The "Denarius Sancti Petri" in England', *Transactions of the Royal Historical Society*, n.s. xv (1901), 171–247, based on his doctoral thesis 'Der englische Peterspfennig und die Lehensteuer aus England und Irland an den Papststuhl im Mittelalter' (Doctoral thesis, Heidelberg, 1903); William E. Lunt, *Papal Revenues in the Middle Ages* (2 vols., New York, 1934), i. 65–71; *idem*, *Financial Relations of the Papacy with England 1327–1534* (Cambridge, Mass., 1962), pp. 1–54.

[115] Jensen, 'Denarius Sancti Petri', pp. 186–88, 206; Lunt, *Papal Revenues*, i. 65–69, ii. 69.

[116] J. J. Scarisbrick, 'Clerical Taxation in England, 1485 to 1547', *Journal of Ecclesiastical History*, xi (1960), 41–54, p. 42; documents 7–9, 12, below.

The farmer of Bowes and Polehouse was not alone in sometimes failing to pay his farm in full. Elsewhere, substantial arrears were also on occasion allowed to mount up in individual farmers' accounts. As Radcliff's accounts were concerned with the sums of money he had received, rather than those that remained outstanding, we can only glimpse such debts in the middle years of the 1490s, for which individual farmers' accounts survive.[117] Several of the Dean's farmers seem to have been dismissed because of their persistent shortfalls and replaced by men who were prepared to do better. At Runwell, farmer John Bek owed almost two thirds of his annual farm of £36 10s. in the summer of 1493 and further increased his debt to £26 in the following year. This may account for his dismissal by the summer of 1496, when he was replaced by William Aleyn, who promptly ended his first year with a surplus. At Thorpe, John Percy owed more than double the annual farm of £18 by the summer of 1493 and twelve months later his arrears had further risen to £53. As Percy's management of his holding had also been unsatisfactory in other respects – he had allowed the manor's livestock to deteriorate and diminish – his rent arrears were deemed intolerable and he was removed in the following year. When Robert Palmer took up the farm in the summer of 1496, he started with a clean slate, but he also ran up arrears of £9 in his first year, even though he promised to pay £3 6s. 8d. thereof at Martinmas (11 November). At Walton the farmer's arrears remained static from 1493 to 1497 at exactly half the annual farm of £38 6s. 8d. Even though this meant that farmer John Toose was effectively paying his full annual farm, in the summer of 1496 he was replaced by John Horward, who at the end of his first year promised to pay 100s. of the arrears by the following Martinmas. Other farmers were more fortunate during the documented period. As at the main manor of Walton, exactly half the annual farm was outstanding at the rectory of Bancroft in the summer of 1493, yet by the following summer farmer William Carter owed more than two thirds of his farm (£10 16s. 8d.). Nevertheless, he remained and in the summer of 1497 promised to pay £3 6s. 8d. of his arrears at Martinmas. John Harnes, farmer of 'Kent's tenement' in Thorpe, owed half his annual farm of £4 by the summer of 1493 and, even though he paid his full annual farm, these arrears remained outstanding until at least 1497, when he promised to pay in full at Martinmas. Elsewhere, arrears fluctuated. In the summer of 1493 Geoffrey Dallyng, farmer of Heybridge manor and mills, owed the substantial sum of £28 (more than half the annual farm of £43). He reduced this debt to £16 1s. 4d. by the following summer, but two years later he once more owed £36 18s. 6d., which over the course of the following year increased further to £37 2s. 10d. At Caddington John Bray owed £16 18s. 6d. (almost half his farm) in the summer of 1493. He reduced these arrears to just

---

[117] Documents 11, 12, below. On the subject of arrears more generally see R. R. Davies, 'Baronial Accounts, Incomes and Arrears in the Later Middle Ages', Ec.H.R., 2nd ser., xxi (1968), 211–29.

£6 4s. 2d. over the course of that year, but in the summer of 1496 he was once more £18 behind, paying all outstanding monies in full by the summer of 1497. Even good farmers who could normally be relied on to pay their farm in full could occasionally fall into arrears, perhaps through unforeseen circumstances. Richard Wynche, who in the early 1490s had replaced another persistent debtor, Edmund Counteys, as farmer of Kensworth ended the years 1492-93, 1493-94 and 1496-97 quit, but in 1495-96 he fell behind by the sum of £3.[118]

The differences between individual manors both in the regularity with which farmers incurred arrears and in their scale, suggest that the debts were not simply the result of a wider economic downturn, but depended on local circumstances. It seems likely that in many instances Worsley's administration of his estates had simply failed to keep control of his farmers' mounting arrears, perhaps in part as a result of the ageing Roger Radcliff's failing capacities. Perhaps under the pressure of payments to the Crown following the Warbeck conspiracy, the administration of the Dean's finances after Roger Radcliff's death was tightened and the mounting arrears of many farmers were tackled.[119] Several persistent debtors were replaced by new farmers and, although the Dean's new receivers (his kinsmen and mainpernors Edmund Worsley and Philip Booth) recognised that a farmer could not reasonably be expected to pay the full sum owing all at once, they lost no time in making sure that the debtors agreed a date for the payment of at least a partial sum.

The men who took the Dean's lands to farm came from a variety of backgrounds. Several were senior clerics, such as Thomas Jane, the archdeacon of Essex, and Richard Nykke, both later bishops of Norwich (who held houses in the city of London from the Dean), Edmund Audley, bishop of Hereford (who was tenant of Drayton in 1495) and Robert Stillington, bishop of Bath and Wells (who held a tenement in Sutton). Others were lesser clergy. Into this category fell men like John Lokear, vicar of Belchamp St. Paul, a naturalised Scotsman, and William Hill, a minor canon of St. Paul's cathedral. A number of tenants were London merchants who were investing profits made in trade into estates in the south-east. These included the goldsmiths Sir Edmund and Sir John Shaa who successively took Worsley's lands at Tillingham to farm. Other farmers were members of the gentry, either more substantial men like William Say of Brokesbourne, or gentlemen like Edward Westby, farmer at Bowes and Polehouse. Whereas these men may be thought to have sublet the lands they leased from the Dean, at the lower end of the social scale a majority of the farmers were peasants who cultivated the lands themselves, men like John Fox, farmer at Bowes and Polehouse, a

---

[118] In the two years of his tenure for which separate figures for Caddington and Kensworth survive, Counteys paid less than a third of his farm: documents 7, 8, below.

[119] A similar tightening up of the administration is documented on the bishop of Worcester's estates after 1450: Dyer, *Lords and Peasants*, p. 171.

husbandman, John Lindsey at Heybridge, and the rather more substantial yeomen Roger Frende, farmer at Acton, and Edmund Prentesse, farmer at Drayton.

In several instances, leases remained in the same families for more than one generation. At Bancroft rectory, by 1493 John Carter had been succeeded by William Carter. At Acton, Roger Frende's lands were taken up first by his widow, Joan, and later by their son Robert. 'Kent's tenement' at Thorpe passed from John Saver to William Saver junior in 1488, and in the same year Sir Edmund Shaa was succeeded by his nephew Sir John Shaa as farmer of Tillingham, where Sir Edmund's son Hugh had also held land from the Dean.[120] The mills of Ratcliff and Heybridge were respectively held by successive generations of the Hewet and Pere families, while Norton Folgate was held in succession first by William and Edmund Hill, and later by John Stephens, whose widow Joan took up the farm on his death.

As on other estates, considerations for household and estate servants could play a part in the choice of tenants and farmers. Thus, John Fox, joint farmer of Bowes and Polehouse by 1481, was possibly the same man, a probable household servant, who went to Scotland with the Dean that year. Thomas Bogas, bailiff of the soke of St. Paul, took the rectory of Kirby to farm in about 1488 and William Hill, rent collector of the Dean and Chapter by 1480 held Norton Folgate to farm.[121]

A small part of the demesne remained in the Dean's hand. These lands were chiefly woodland, including a wood at Willesden, 'le Parke' at Ardleigh and 'Deane Wodde' at Acton, and farmers and local officials occasionally accounted for sales of timber. The income derived from the sale of such demesne produce was usually added to the accounts at the time of the audit, as it did not form part of Worsley's regular income. More important as a source of income were the manorial courts, which remained in the Dean's hand and were held annually by his steward. Apart from the tenants' amercements, large sums were collected annually in entry fines and heriots.[122] Whereas these latter payments seem to have been leviable, it appears that, as elsewhere, amercements were often ignored: in 1496–97 the bailiff of the soke had to be allowed 1s. 5d. of amercements remaining unpaid from the previous year.[123] As a result, the revenues returned by the courts fluctuated, depending chiefly on the incidence of such fines. Thus, in the years when the returns of the courts in the soke in Essex were recorded separately, they varied from £4 13s. 4d. in 1482–83 (just 3.16% of Worsley's total revenues from the soke) to £16

---

[120] For Hugh Shaa: *CIPM Hen. VII*, iii. 677.

[121] For biographical details of all these individuals see below, app. 2.

[122] E.g. in 1480–81 John Nayller paid an entry fine of £16 15s. 4d. for his holdings in the soke in Essex: document 2, below. For estreat and court rolls of the Dean's manors see GL, MSS 25281/1, 25311 (Heybridge), 25287 (Norton Foliot), 25301/1 (Ardleigh).

[123] Dyer, *Lords and Peasants*, pp. 267–68; document 12, below.

15s. 4d. in 1480–81 (their highest share of the total revenue being 12.87% in 1487–88).

More reliable than the fines and amercements of the conventionary tenants, both free and unfree, were their fixed rents. Although of lesser importance than the farms of the demesnes as a proportion of Worsley's total annual revenues, they could still account for a sizeable percentage of the returns from an individual manor. Expressed as a share of the money annually due to the Dean, conventionary rents amounted to between a quarter and 40% of the Dean's annual income from the manors where they are documented (roughly 40% at Belchamp St. Paul, 20% at Norton Folgate, about 27% in the soke, 23–40% at Ardleigh). In reality, however, the importance of fixed rents may have been rather greater than these figures suggest, as their full payment was more reliable than that of the demesne farms. Thus, from 1487 onwards they regularly accounted for about 40% of the money received from the soke in Essex, whereas they should have made up less than 30% had all of Worsley's revenues there been paid in full. This, however, was not invariably the case. Occasional difficulties in levying amercements from the courts aside, the process of administering the revenues due from conventionary tenants was a labour-intensive process, and it is thus perhaps not surprising that the ministers charged with performing this duty fell into arrears. In the summer of 1493 the bailiff of the soke of St. Paul's not only owed £6 4s. 4½d. of the perquisites of the courts, but also £34 4s. 8d. of the rents. Over the course of the following year he was able to almost halve the outstanding court profits and the rents in arrears fell to £23 6s. 7d., but in 1496 more than £50 of rents were once more owing. By the summer of that year, an attempt had been made, with some success, to gain control of affairs. The profits of court were paid in full, and the bailiff was allowed various rents, causing his arrears of rents to drop to £31 8s. 6d.

In addition to the revenue from his estates, Worsley also annually received further sums of money by virtue of his spiritual functions in his various benefices. These monies left little trace in Radcliff's accounts, as they were often paid directly to the Dean by the local ecclesiastical officials. From the deanery of London, fines for corrections were paid to Worsley or his receiver, by the Dean's commissary or his deputy. Worsley's archdeaconries of Nottingham (1476–99) and Taunton (1493–96) returned revenues for the induction of clerics and chevage. The archdeacons were also responsible for the collection of Peter's Pence within their jurisdiction, and would keep a share for themselves.[124]

[124] R. N. Swanson, *Church and Society in Late Medieval England* (Oxford, 1989), pp. 220–21. Income from spiritualities at the higher - episcopal - level, and the difficulties in calculating them, are discussed by *idem*, 'Episcopal Income from Spiritualities in Later Medieval England: The Evidence for the Diocese of Coventry and Lichfield', *Midland History*, xiv (1988), 1–20; *idem*, 'Episcopal Income from Spiritualities in the Diocese of Exeter in the Early Sixteenth

For the periods when he was in residence at London or Hackney and not attending to his other benefices elsewhere in the kingdom, Worsley was also entitled to payments of commons, a weekly cash allowance, from the cathedral's common fund. As a rule, these payments were simply subtracted from the greater sum the dean paid into the fund for the common estates that he held to farm from the cathedral chapter. They were however allocated at various times over the course of the year, as the bills made out for them between the Dean's receiver and the cathedral chamberlain indicate.[125] The sums that Worsley thus received were not specified, but the rate of 1s. per week which was in force in about 1300 may still have applied in his day.

Furthermore, the residentiaries of St. Paul's at the turn of the thirteenth century were entitled to twenty-one loaves and thirty gallons of ale per week from the cathedral bakehouse and brewery, liveries in kind which continued in the late fifteenth century, as Worsley's purchases of grain for the bakehouse show. As his commons were allocated on the customary occasions throughout the year, it is likely that the Dean also drew his allowance in kind, although there is no record of it in the receiver's accounts.[126]

The picture of the administrative structures of Worsley's estates given by the receiver's accounts is incomplete, showing only those officials who came into contact with the receiver or the Dean in the course of their duties. Alongside the receiver, two central officials, the auditor and the estate steward, are documented in the Dean's estate administration. All three were itinerant officers who annually rode from manor to manor to receive and check the farmers' accounts, to hold the Dean's courts and to supervise the maintenance of the holdings.[127] The office of auditor was held successively by John Hewyk (c.1480–85) and John Saperton (c.1487–97).[128] The two men had prior connections: Saperton was a tenant of Hewyk's, and later served as his executor. The supervision of the maintenance of the estates and the holding of the Dean's courts was mainly the responsibility of the estate steward. There may have been several stewards at any one time: only the steward who was responsible for the soke of the St. Paul's in Essex received an annual fee from the Dean and seems to have held higher status than other officials described as stewards documented at Heybridge and Norton Folgate.[129] As the judicial task

Century', *Journal of Ecclesiastical History*, 39 (1988), 520–30.
[125] Cf. e.g. documents 4, 5, 7, below.
[126] Edwards, pp. 41–43.
[127] For the duties and methods of medieval auditors and stewards see Davies, 'Baronial Accounts', 222; D. Oschinsky, 'Medieval Treatises on Estate Accounting', *Ec.H.R.*, xvii (1947), 52–61.
[128] Documents 2–9, 12, below.
[129] GL, MS 25287, rot. 15; document 5, below. The steward recorded at Heybridge in 1484–85 was a Master Marke, probably the bishop of London's receiver general who may have been employed on a temporary basis during a vacancy of the manor.

of presiding at manorial courts was central to their duties, the stewards were selected on the basis of their training in the law: Robert Forster, steward of the soke in the first half of the 1480s, was a Middlesex lawyer and royal clerk, but also had prior connections at St. Paul's, being brother of the archdeacon of London, Master John Forster. His successor as steward, William Clarkson, was a Lincoln's Inn lawyer. After the Warbeck conspiracy, the Dean appointed the King's henchman John de Vere, earl of Oxford, chief steward of his Essex estates, a purely nominal appointment, which the earl discharged by a deputy. This deputy, John Alyff, probably came from a family of lawyers from Hornchurch, another member of which had married Robert Forster's daughter.[130]

The soke of St. Paul's, a separate administrative unit since Anglo-Saxon times, in the later fifteenth century continued to have its own bailiff, who took responsibility for the collection of rents of assize and court profits, as well as overseeing repairs in his bailiwick.[131] In London, the Dean had his own rent collector, distinct from the chapter's officer, who on occasion also conveyed some revenues to Worsley. While several of these men were in holy orders, such as William Hill, a minor canon of St. Paul's, or John Farman, one of the Dean's chaplains, others, such as Henry Saunder, had trained in the common law. Occasionally, household officials took charge of collecting Worsley's rents. The steward of the household, Thomas Bunewell, for some years performed this function at Hackney and Ardleigh, and another member of the Dean's household, John Fuldon did the same in the latter manor in the mid 1480s.

Elsewhere, the Dean's farmers were called upon to perform basic administrative duties, a policy designed to reduce the costs of the estate administration. Thus, Geoffrey Dallyng and John Lindsey, successive farmers of Heybridge, acted as the Dean's rent collectors there. Similarly, the Dean's rents at Belchamp St. Paul were collected by the farmers there and at Wickham St. Paul, John Lokear, vicar of Belchamp, and Thomas Watson, one of Worsley's household chaplains.

The Dean's more important benefices had their own administrative structures, which only came into contact with the receiver when paying the revenues they had generated. As the judicial functions of the benefices' incumbents were a central source of their revenues, the administrations were heavily dominated by canon and civil lawyers. In London, the Dean and Chapter's jurisdiction was exercised by their commissary general, Robert Braddows, rector of Markshall, Essex, and later of St. Mary Woolnoth, London. He was assisted by the Dean and Chapter's notary and registrar, M. Nicholas Colles. The income from Worsley's archdeaconry of Taunton was paid to the receiver by Master Robert Godde, vicar of Kingston, Som., whose

[130] For biographical details of these men cf. appendix 2.
[131] *Visitations of St. Paul's*, p. xvii.

office within the archdeaconry administration is uncertain. Similarly, the officials from the archdeaconry of Nottingham who came into contact with Worsley's receiver included the Dean's kinsman Thomas Orston, a lawyer, the collector Richard Samesbury, the registrar Master John Kendale and a number of officials including Master Robert Colyngham, rector of St. Peter, Nottingham, and Master Robert Wilby, rector of Woollaton, Notts., as well as Richard Breych, probably a civil lawyer.

As noted above, the accounts edited in this volume do not represent Worsley's full income, but show only the revenue rendered to his receiver. This averaged between £500 and £600 per annum, but in 1495–96 came to as much as £844 4s. The bulk of this increase is accounted for by monies from Worsley's personal estate at Hackney and from his northern and south-western benefices, revenue which was usually paid directly to the Dean by the local collectors, and did not appear in the receiver's accounts.[132] Taken together, the accounts make it possible to gain an impression of the total sums of money which the estates and spiritualities were annually expected to return. If paid in full, the Dean's potential annual income should thus have amounted to over £760, and probably reached as much as £800.

More difficult to establish is the Dean's annual disposable income, after a string of regular financial commitments arising from the estates had been met. In the first instance, substantial sums fell due to the cathedral's common fund as farms for the manors the Dean held from the Chapter in addition to his own prebend and deanery. Over the course of Worsley's tenure up to the late 1480s this annual payment steadily increased, peaking at £246 1s. 4d. in 1488–89. Although there is no conclusive evidence of this, fluctuations in this annual figure were probably influenced by two factors other than economic change. On the one hand, the sum retained by the Dean on account of his residency was dependent on the number of days he actually spent resident at London or Hackney. On the other hand, no additional evidence (for example, accounts of the cathedral chamberlain) survives to show whether the payments made by Radcliff accounted for all monies passed to the chamberlain from Worsley's estates. In addition to the payments to the common fund, a quantity of grain was due to the cathedral's bakehouse every year, to provide for the residentiaries' livery of canonical loaves (cf. above, p. 27). From his manor of Heybridge the Dean annually had to find thirty-two quarters of wheat. As he no longer farmed the demesne himself, this grain had to be bought, or a cash payment made in lieu. A further larger sum was paid in cash to the clerk of the bakehouse every year, presumably in place of the grain due from Worsley's other manors.[133] As both of these payments were

[132] Cf. documents 6–8, below.
[133] For instance, in 1481–82 £15 3s. 4d. was paid for the 32 quarters and £74 3s. ¾d. for the remaining wheat: document 3, below.

dependent on the amount of time Worsley spent in residence at the cathedral, they fluctuated to some degree, peaking in 1488–89.

Smaller sums had to be paid annually as rents to other feudal lords from whom some of Worsley's estates were held. The sum of 19s. was annually due for Bowes and Polehouse which were held from the manor of Shingleford. This manor was in the hands of the Bourgchier earls of Essex until 1485, thereafter passing to Edmund, Lord Roos. When the latter was found to be unsuitable for his dignity, the custody of his lands was granted to Sir Thomas Lovell, to whom Worsley paid the 19s. in 1495–96. The Bishop of London received £1 13s. 4d. p.a. for property held from his manor of Chadsworth, and the same prelate was also annually paid £9 15s. for the lease of a marsh at Stepney. The sum of £1 2d. p.a. (20s. in 1480–81) for Bowes and Polehouse was paid to Sir Richard Charlton and, after his death in 1485, to his sister Agnes and her husband Sir Thomas Bourgchier.[134] Further payments were made to exempt the Dean from various feudal services, such as the suit he owed at the court of Edmonton, and homage owed to William Lawshull for lands in Rochford hundred, Essex.[135]

As distinct from the parliamentary taxation to which the farmers of the Dean's manors were subject (cf. above, p. 21), some of Worsley's benefices were liable to pay clerical taxes granted by convocation.[136] The most common grant made by convocation was a tenth on the value of benefices, based on an assessment made by Pope Nicholas IV in about 1291.[137] Six full tenths were granted during the period covered by the accounts, to Edward IV in 1481, to Richard III in 1484 and 1485 (although in the event the second half of the second grant did not fall due for collection until after Bosworth) and to Henry VII in 1487, 1489, 1492 and 1495.[138] Worsley's accounts record the payments due for the benefices he held directly: the rectory of Lambourn, for which a tenth came to £5 6s. 8d. and the prebend of Willesden, for which 8s. had to be rendered.[139] Payments from Willesden are recorded in 1481, 1484, 1487 and 1495, but not in 1485 or 1492. In 1487–88, 4s. was levied additionally for the 'grace' of the rectory of Willesden. The statutory payments from Lambourn appear in the accounts in 1481 and 1495.[140] Only in

---

134 Documents 1–10, below.
135 Documents 2, 7, 8, below.
136 For Worsley's membership of convocation see above, p. 10.
137 A. K. McHardy, 'Clerical Taxation in Fifteenth Century England: The Clergy as Agents of the Crown', in *The Church, Politics and Patronage in the Fifteenth Century*, ed. R. B. Dobson, 168–92, p. 169; Scarisbrick, 'Clerical Taxation', pp. 49–50; *Taxatio Ecclesiastica Angliae et Walliae auctoritate P. Nicholai IV. circa A.D. 1291*, ed. T. Astle, S. Ayscough and J. Caley (London, 1802).
138 McHardy, pp. 188–89.
139 PRO, E359/35, rot. 51; The *Taxatio* estimated the annual value of the church of Lambourn as £53 6s. 8d. and of the prebend of Willesden as £4 (*Taxatio*, p. 19).
140 Documents 2, 5, 6, 9.

1495–97 are payments recorded for St. Paul's itself, assessed at £11 16s. for a full tenth. Understandably, by Worsley's day circumstances had changed and as in the case of lay taxation, the Crown sought to find ways of increasing its revenue in a variety of ways. In the case of clerical taxation this involved the taxation of previously unassessed benefices and on one occasion – in 1489 – the grant of a specified sum of £25,000 in subsidy by convocation.[141] This subsidy came to nearly the value of two tenths, and consequently Worsley's contribution also came to twice the normal level. The payment of £5 6s. 8d. for half a subsidy is recorded at Lambourn, while Willesden paid 16s. with an additional levy of 8s. by hand of the farmer for the 'grace' of the rectory.[142]

The sums at Worsley's disposal after subtraction of such payments still regularly exceeded £300 p.a., and probably even came to over £400 p.a. This placed him among the very wealthiest of English clergy below the episcopal level. On the basis of the 1535 *Valor Ecclesiasticus*, Christopher Dyer has calculated that the seventeen members of the fifteenth-century English episcopate could expect an annual income of between £400 and £3500, but few other beneficed clerics could even expect £40 p.a. Including the laity, there were only two hundred households with an annual income of £300 or more in fifteenth-century England.[143]

The period covered by the surviving accounts is too short, and their topographical distribution too patchy, to make any meaningful statements about economic change. What seems clear is that Worsley's management of his estates followed patterns conventional in the south-east of England in the fifteenth century. At the same time, it appears that he did not always exploit his lands to their full potential. The tightening up of the administration and the consequent increase in revenues from almost all his estates, occurred only after the Warbeck episode, when cash was needed to satisfy the Crown.

III. *The Accounts* II: *The Dean's Household*

A large part of Worsley's income was annually consumed by his household, based at one of his two mansions. For much of his tenure at St. Paul's, the Dean's favoured residence appears to have been his house (perhaps the building later known as Brooke House) in Hackney. It may have formed part of the holdings in Hackney which Archbishop Booth had left the Dean in his will, or may have been constructed on Worsley's orders shortly after he succeeded to the Hackney lands.[144] When his responsibilities at the cathedral necessitated his presence in London, he had at his disposal the dean's traditional residence in the south-west of the cathedral precinct, a building used for this purpose since the twelfth century. In 1486–87, Worsley was additionally granted the canonical house in Paternoster Row, opposite the

[141] McHardy, p. 189; Jurkowski et al., pp. 122–24.
[142] Documents 7, 8, below.
[143] Dyer, *Standards of Living*, p. 32.
[144] *A Survey of London*, ed. Sheppard, vol. 28, pt. i, pp. 68–69; *VCH Middlesex*, x. 78.

postern door of the cathedral, which his fellow canon John Forster had previously inhabited and in which Laurence Booth had also lived during his time at St. Paul's.[145]

Unfortunately, little is known about the organisational structures of Worsley's household. It was headed by the steward of the household, an office which Roger Radcliff combined with that of receiver until his death in 1496. Subordinate to the receiver was another official, occasionally also described as steward of the household, who may have functioned as Radcliff's deputy with specific responsibility for the household. Below the steward, the household's departmental organisation is less clear, but it may be reflected to some degree in the paragraph headings in the expenditure sections of the receiver's accounts. Thus, Worsley's household had a buttery (wine, beer, ale),[146] while the pantry with its traditional responsibilities for bread and napery may have been merged with the kitchen, which took charge of all other victuals and spices.[147] The separate account heading for the Dean's apparel points to the existence of a wardrobe, and Worsley's stables were headed by the keeper of the horses, the only lesser household office of which there is concrete evidence, an office held in 1489–90 by one Thomas Morys.[148]

As in most secular households of the period, there were no female servants in Worsley's establishment. When a woman was required for certain tasks, such as the making of linen sheets in 1489–90, the wife of Thomas Shaa, one of the Dean's servants, was hired specially.[149] Shaa was one of a number of Worsley's servants connected with St. Paul's cathedral. Both he and John Haryngton, one of the Dean's chaplains, are likely to have been kinsmen of prebendaries there, Ralph Shaa and William Haryngton. Similarly, the steward Roger Radcliff was a kinsman of the former dean of the same name, and Robert Forster, steward of the soke in the early 1480s, was a brother of Master John Forster, the archdeacon of London. Other members of the

---

[145] CCR, 1476–85, no. 39; R. Macleod, 'The Topography of St. Paul's Precinct, 1200–1500', London Topographical Soc., xxvi (1990), 1–14, pp. 6–7; HMC 9th Report, appendix, pp. 10–11.

[146] Some fifteenth-century households had a separate cellar to look after wine, while the buttery retained responsibility for beer and ale. Although Worsley's accounts have distinct headings for the three commodities, it was probably too small to make such a distinction: C. M. Woolgar, The Great Household in Late Medieval England (New Haven, London, 1999), p. 17. For the departmental structure of a basic household see e.g. ibid. pp. 16–17, Dyer, Standards of Living, p. 51; Woolgar, Household Accounts, i. 23–24.

[147] The household of Dean Thomas Lisieux earlier in the century may have had a similar structure: in his will Lisieux remembered the steward of his household, his butler and his cook, but did not mention a separate pantler among the senior officials of his household: PRO, PROB11/4, fols. 56v–58r (PCC 8 Stokton).

[148] Document 8, below. Biographical details of these officials can be found in appendix 2.

[149] Document 8, below.

household were drawn from among the minor clergy of St. Paul's: Thomas Bromley was a chantry chaplain there, and both the chaplain William Roke and the rent collector William Hill were minor canons.

Worsley's personal religious household consisted of up to five chaplains retained at any one time. In July 1473 and August 1474 respectively he received papal indults to chose a confessor and to receive absolution from him at the time of his death.[150] This function may have been performed by William Roke, the most permanent member of the Dean's clerical entourage, who stood surety for him in 1495. Whereas Roke was recruited to Worsley's household from the ranks of the clergy of St. Paul's, other chaplains shared other roots with the Dean: Thomas Cartwryght was a vicar choral at Southwell, while at least four men (John Slade, Thomas Smith, Thomas Turnour and Thomas Watson), like Worsley, were graduates of Cambridge university.[151]

More difficult to glimpse than the relatively small numbers of household servants with defined responsibilities were the members of Worsley's wider circle who were not permanently resident in the household, who held no specific household office, or were simply retained by a grant of an annual fee or a livery.[152] One such man was Sir Thomas Montgomery of Faulkborn who drew an annual fee of £4 from Worsley in the 1480s.[153] After the Warbeck affair, Worsley retained the lawyer Peter Peckham as a councillor at a fee of £2 13s. 4d. p.a.[154] Other men were hired for occasional services. Thus, in 1480-81 John Morton and William Ford were paid for transacting Worsley's business at the Exchequer, while M. Thomas Matyn, auditor of the English hospital in Rome, was paid for securing letters of absolution from the Roman curia that same year.[155]

At various times, blood relatives of the Dean were in some way or another attached to the household: a kinswoman, Isabel, daughter of Otwell Worsley, in 1480 had £40 as part of her marriage portion of 300 marks paid by the Dean;[156] another kinsman, Thomas Orston, served the Dean in his archdeaconry of Nottingham;[157] the Dean's half-brother Ralph Langford was paid a weekly wage of 12d. in 1496-97;[158] and two further kinsmen, Philip Booth and Edmund Worsley, replaced the receiver, Radcliff, after his death in 1497.[159]

[150]   *CPL*, xiii, pt. i, p. 381, pt. ii, p. 548.
[151]   For biographical details of these men see appendix 2.
[152]   Dyer, *Standards of Living*, p. 53.
[153]   Documents 5, 6, below. For Montgomery see *The Commons 1439-1509*, ed. Wedgwood, pp. 605-6.
[154]   Document 9, below.
[155]   Document 2, below.
[156]   Document 1, below; PRO, C1/84/7.
[157]   Documents 1, 4, 9, 10, below.
[158]   Document 12, below.

The size of Worsley's permanent household can only be estimated. His retinue for the journey to the north, a kind of 'itinerant household' headed by the steward Thomas Bunewell, consisted of seven men, including a chaplain.[160] The resident household at Hackney was somewhat larger, and may have been of a size similar to that of Dean William Say, who in his will of 1468 remembered twenty-seven servants, arranged according to their four grades.[161]

Provisioning of the Household

As with other noble or great ecclesiastical households, one of the major tasks to be accomplished was its provisioning.[162] Meat of various kinds (beef, veal, pork and mutton), fresh and salt fish, spices and other provisions were bought when required and the expenditure noted daily in separate quarterly accounts, the sums from which were then included in the steward's annual account. Much of the bread that was needed could probably be drawn from the bakehouse of St. Paul's cathedral, the clerk of which was responsible for purchasing the necessary grain, although the price of a set quantity had to be delivered annually in cash or kind from the Dean's manors (cf. above, pp. 29–30).[163] Under the cathedral statutes all canons were entitled to twenty-one loaves and thirty gallons of ale per week, but while there is no further record of purchases of bread in the accounts, large quantities of drink had to be acquired every year.[164] In 1480–81 £26 5s. 3d. was expended on ale, as well as almost 50s. on beer. Whereas beer and ale were drunk by the household on a daily basis, the smaller quantities of malmsey, claret and Rhenish wine accounted for in the same year were probably intended for consumption by the Dean himself, as well as for the provision of hospitality. The dean of St. Paul's table was famous for the splendid hospitality it offered, and the austere Erasmus of Rotterdam noted with disapproval that, prior to the deanery's reform by John Colet in the early sixteenth century, 'hospitality had been an excuse for devotion to luxurious living'.[165]

An integral part of late medieval hospitality was the entertainment provided by visiting minstrels, otherwise attached to the royal and some noble households. Whereas these musicians could expect only limited fees from their parent households, their temporary hosts often paid them generous rewards. Such payments are recorded in Worsley's accounts on an annual basis, indicative of the regularity with which entertainment was

---

[159] Ibid.

[160] Document 2, below.

[161] PRO, PROB11/5, fos. 199v–200v (PCC 26 Godyn).

[162] Dyer, Standards of Living, p. 55.

[163] History of St. Paul's, ed. Matthews and Atkins, p. 60.

[164] Edwards, p. 43; Reg. Stat., pp. 35, 75, 173.

[165] Lupton, Life of John Colet, pp. 148–49; Collected works of Erasmus, ed. Mynors and Bietenholz, p. 235.

provided in the Dean's household.[166]

Generally, the markets of London provided what was needed for the household; the accounts record only one instance of ale being purchased from a Hackney-based brewer.[167] The household patronised a select number of merchants, who maintained their connection with Worsley's establishment for years. On occasion, goods might be brought from further afield. Thus, in 1479–80 fifty-one baskets of salt fish were purchased at Canterbury.[168] For fuel, cartloads of wood were regularly brought to the household. Only towards the end of the period covered by the accounts is there evidence of quantities of charcoal being bought from the farmer of Bowes and Polehouse. Between 1495 and 1497 a series of cartloads were taken from the holdings in Edmonton to the Dean's household and used there. The price of the purchase was allowed against the farm of the holding, and otherwise left no trace in the receiver's accounts.[169]

Like the buildings on the Dean's other estates, the edifices that housed his domestic establishment were frequently in need of maintenance. Large sums were expended almost annually on the repair of the Dean's city mansion next to St. Paul's, including in 1488–89 the making of 'bars' outside the door.[170]

Servants' Allowances

The servants' annual allowances fell into two categories: the cash wage and the livery. In accordance with Worsley's lesser rank, his servants were paid about one-third less than comparable officials of contemporary bishops, and the recorded wages of the Dean's men dropped even further in the mid-1480s. Thus, episcopal auditors and surveyors could expect about £5 *p.a.* By contrast, Worsley's auditor between 1480 and 1482, John Hewyk, drew only £3 6s. 8d. *p.a.*, and John Saperton, his successor after 1487, had only £2 *p.a.* Likewise, the steward of the soke of St. Paul's in Essex from 1480 to 1483, Robert Forster, was paid 40s. *p.a.*, whereas his successor, William Clarkson, from 1487 received only 26s. 8d. By comparison, the Bishop of Worcester's understewards could expect to receive between £2 13s. 4d. and £5, and his

---

[166] Woolgar, *Great Household*, pp. 26–27; Dyer, *Standards of Living*, p. 74. For an example of Richard III sending his minstrels to entertain an Imperial ambassador see *Reisebeschreibung Niclas von Popplau Ritters, bürtig von Breslau*, ed. Piotr Radzikowski (Kraków, 1998), p. 58. For minstrels and other entertainers in the later middle ages more generally see e.g. R. Rastall, 'The Minstrels of the English Royal Households', *Royal Musical Association Research Chronicle*, iv (1967), 1–41; J. Southworth, *The English Medieval Minstrel* (Woodbridge, 1989); idem, *Fools and Jesters at the English Court* (Stroud, 1998), esp. pp. 35–47.

[167] Document 9, below.

[168] Document 1, below.

[169] Document 12, below.

[170] Documents 3, 5–8.

other manorial officials between 10s. and £3 p.a., while Thomas Kemp, Bishop of London, paid £3 6s. 8d. to his estate surveyor and demesne steward. Lower in the administrative hierarchy these differences were less pronounced. Several of the Dean's servants received £1 6s. 8d. p.a., John Lokear, vicar of Belchamp St. Paul and farmer of Wickham St. Paul and answerable for the Dean's revenue there, was paid 40s. in 1480–81 (raised to 60s. by 1482–83), while his successor, Thomas Watson, annually received 40s. Again, the bishop's parkers, paid at a rate of 3d. per day, could expect an annual income of over £4. Of Worsley's three chaplains, two were annually paid £3 6s. 8d., whereas the third received £2 13s. 4d. from the manor of Norton Folgate. The wages of the lesser members of the Dean's household were accounted for collectively, making their individual assignments impossible to establish.[171]

Cloth liveries were distributed twice annually, in summer and winter, to the members of the household. On occasion, special events necessitated extra expenditure. Thus, a visit by the King's stepson, the Marquess of Dorset, in April 1481 led to the acquisition of a vast range of new cloth items,[172] and for the funeral of Edward IV in 1483 black livery was ordered for the household servants.[173]

Although the bulk of the Dean's responsibilities kept him at London, the household was not always stationary there. A pluralist, Worsley was obliged to visit his other benefices in person at least occasionally. Such journeys required a supply of cash both for their preparation and for prospective expenditure along the way. Thus, on 17 June 1481 the Dean received £80 in gold royals and nobles from Radcliff for his journey to Southwell for the visitation of that summer.[174]

The expenses of Worsley's household annually ranged from £158 to £209, averaging £181. The exception was the year 1480–81, when provisions for the Scottish expedition brought the year's outgoings to over £300. In an average year, the Dean could thus expect to have between about £150 and £250 of freely disposable money available to him. This meant that he could afford to make the annual payments to the King and his advisors required

[171]   Documents 1–10, below. Comparative figures from Worcester after Dyer, *Lords and Peasants*, p. 159; for London see PRO, SC6/1140/25–27.

[172]   Document 3, below.

[173]   Document 4, below. There is no other explicit record of Worsley's presence at King Edward's funeral: A. F. Sutton and L. Visser-Fuchs, 'The Royal Burials of the House of York at Windsor', *The Ricardian*, xi (1998), 366–407. The provision of black liveries was the usual custom on such occasions: cf. e.g. A. F. Sutton and L. Visser-Fuchs, with P. W. Hammond, *The Reburial of Richard Duke of York, 21–30 July 1476* (London, 1996), p. 7; H. Kleineke, 'The Reburial Expenses of Sir Thomas Arundell', *The Ricardian*, xi (1998), 288–96, pp. 291, 292, 294; A. F. Sutton and L. Visser-Fuchs, 'The Royal Burials of the House of York at Windsor: II. Princess Mary, May 1482, and Queen Elizabeth Woodville, June 1492', *The Ricardian*, xi (1999), 446–62, p. 451.

[174]   *Visitations of Southwell*, pp. 42–3; document 2, below.

after the Warbeck conspiracy, but they stretched his resources to the limit. The Dean's new chief financial officers, and perhaps Worsley himself, realised this, and consequently embarked on a concerted effort to maximise estate revenue.[175]

IV. *The Accounts* III: *The Manuscripts*

Three types of accounts have been included in this edition. The bulk of the material edited consists of accounts of Dean Worsley's receiver, Roger Radcliff. They represent the final stage in the accounting procedure and were designed to be presented to the Dean's auditor and, as the signature on several of the documents shows, to the Dean himself. As Radcliff combined the steward of the household's responsibilities for provisioning with the receiver's fiscal duties, large parts of the expenditure side of the accounts detail purchases for the household along with the cash liveries to the lord falling strictly into the receiver's remit.

When presenting his accounts for audit, Radcliff would produce the documentation kept in the course of the accounting year in support of his claims. At the most basic level this would consist of wooden tallies and paper or parchment bills and indentures made out by the Dean's officials or suppliers. Following the audit and passing of the accounts, there was no further need for these supplementary documents, and it is likely that they were discarded, which explains their failure to survive. For additional security, the receiver would enter particulars of receipts and expenditure in his books of receipts and expenses on a daily and weekly basis. The books themselves do not survive, but frequent references in Radcliff's accounts give an indication of their organisation. Their contents were carefully arranged in different categories. Purchases of cloth, spices and other necessaries would all be recorded on separate pages, as would payments for fees and liveries of servants, of which meticulous lists of names and particulars were kept. At the next level, and probably in order to facilitate the compilation of the annual account, certain transactions would then be entered into the 'quarterly paper'.[176]

The receiver's accounts survive from 1479–80, starting at Michaelmas following Worsley's institution as dean, to 1496–97. Their run is not complete, and no accounts survive for the years 1483–84, 1485–87, and 1490–95. The date of the final extant account is significant. It is a view of

---

[175] Cf. above, pp. 23–24.

[176] For these procedures see document 3, below. Neither the 'quarterly papers' nor Radcliff's books of particulars have survived, but similar books are referred to in the accounts of the bishop of London's receiver, George Chauncy, in 1509–10 (PRO, SC6/HenVIII/2109, rot. 5), and survive from Durham Priory in the 1530s (*The Durham household book: or The accounts of the bursar of the monastery of Durham. From Pentecost 1530 to Pentecost 1534*, ed. James Raine [London, Surtees Soc. 18, 1844]).

account drawn up after the death of Roger Radcliff, the Dean's first receiver, in late 1496, suggesting that the system of record keeping in operation in Worsley's household owed much to his personal efforts, and may have declined towards the end of his life.

Also included are two sets of ministers' accounts, documents drawn up on the occasion of the annual accounting of the farmers and other officials responsible for the Dean's revenue locally. The first of these sets, for 1493-94, is incomplete and accounts survive only for the Essex manors of Walton, Kirby and Thorpe, Heybridge, Runwell, and Caddington and Kensworth in Bedfordshire. The second set, dating from 1496-98, is more comprehensive, including the prebend of Willesden, Bowes and Polehouse, Ardleigh, Norton Folgate and the archdeaconry of Nottingham in addition to the above manors. A single surviving example is also included of an individual minister's account, separate from the two sets of accounts, albeit closely related, is the account of the Dean's collector of rents in the city of London and at Norton Folgate, John Clerk, for the year 1484-85.

In the same way as the terms of tenure varied locally, so did ministers' and farmers' accounting practices. Whereas the Dean's receiver always presented his account in the second half of July, the farmers and local officials were taken to account at different points in the year, varying according to local custom. Most commonly, the farmers accounted at the feast of St. Peter *ad vincula* on 1 August. This was the custom at Walton, Thorpe, Heybridge, Runwell, Bowes and Polehouse in Edmonton, Ardleigh and the 'grace' of Willesden. Earlier, at the feast of the Nativity of St. John the Baptist on 24 June, the farmers of the two Bedfordshire manors of Caddington and Kensworth presented their accounts. The officials in charge of collecting the Dean's rents in the soke of St. Paul's and the revenues in the archdeaconry of Nottingham, as well as the farmer of the prebend of Willesden accounted at Easter, while the farmer of the manor of Norton Folgate drew his account up at the feast of the Annunciation of the Virgin (25 March).[177]

The receiver's accounts consist of several sheets of paper sewn end to end, and using one side of the paper only. The 1493-94 set of ministers' accounts is made up of four sheets, and the 1496-97 set of six sheets of paper. Both sets are sewn together at the top; both sides of the paper are used. The rent collector's account is made up of two sheets, sewn end to end. The language of the accounts is Latin, although English words are often interjected for weights, measures and commodities. The receiver's accounting was generally accurate, with only occasional amendments by the auditors, although minor errors went unnoticed in most of the accounts. Blanks in the text show that the main body was compiled in advance, presumably based on the previous year's account, and only figures varying from the norm would be added later.[178]

---

[177]   Documents 11, 12, below.

We have only one certain representation of William Worsley. His tomb brass in St. Paul's cathedral was destroyed in the fire of 1666, but there is a drawing of it in Dugdale's *History of St. Paul's Cathedral*.[179] This drawing shows a relatively slight man, wearing a richly embroidered cope.

More problematic is the identification of the kneeling cleric shown in a wall painting in 'Brooke House' at Hackney, traditionally thought to be a depiction of Worsley.[180]

The heraldic shield painted above the main image displays the arms of Radcliff (*argent, a bend engrailed sable*), differenced by an escallop. This shield is flanked by the letter W on either side. A second shield, in a less prominent position, is of the Radcliff arms (without the escallop), impaling a probable representation of the Worsley arms (*argent, a chief gules, differenced by 4 annulets interlinked two and two*). This shield is flanked by the letter T, or possibly the cross of St. Anthony, which is also repeated in-between the roses on the main wall.[181] The roses on the main wall have a white centre on a blue outside. These roses could be either a badge or a religious symbol, but may alternatively be purely decorative. Further problems are raised by the bearded figure which towers over the kneeling cleric. The crossed keys held by this patriarch identify him fairly unambiguously as St. Peter, the patron saint of Westminster Abbey and of York Minster, but not of London's cathedral church. As the families of Radcliff, Booth and Worsley all had close ties with the province of York, it is still possible that the building that housed the painting of St. Peter was part of the property owned first by William Booth and later by William Worsley, but it is far less certain whether the kneeling cleric can with any degree of certainty be identified with the latter. Alternatively, it is possible that different elements in the painting are of varying date, and that Brooke house was the suburban house of the deans of St. Paul's, rather than part of Worsley's personal property.

---

[178] For examples of errors, amendments and insertions see the entries for Thorpe, Walton, Kirby and Wickham St. Paul in document 3, below.

[179] C. N. L. Brooke, 'The Earliest Times to 1485', in *A History of St. Paul's Cathedral and the Men Associated with It*, ed. W. R. Matthews and W. M. Atkins (London, 1957), plate 4; Sir William Dugdale, *The History of St. Paul's Cathedral, London* (London 1818), p. 53.

[180] For Worsley's connection with Brooke House, see p. 31, above.

[181] *A Survey of London*, ed. F. H. W. Sheppard (42 vols., London 1900–86), vol. 28, pt. i: Hackney: Brooke House, a monograph. For the identification of the Radcliff arms, cf. pp. 20, 54–5, 67.

PART 2: CALENDAR OF THE ESTATE AND HOUSEHOLD ACCOUNTS OF DEAN WILLIAM WORSLEY, 1479–1497

EDITORIAL METHOD

Calendaring: Translation and Transcription

In this edition, the accounts have been translated and calendared. The aim of the calendaring has been to remove repetitive and formulaic material, and make the text accessible to a modern audience, while retaining some of the original tone and distinctive aspects of the content of the accounts. A sample account (no. 3) has been rendered in full: it is characteristic of the other, abbreviated, documents. Certain sections in other accounts, where they are of particular interest, have also been translated in full. These are distinguished by quotation marks.

Middle English Words

Some of the more unusual or ambiguous Middle English words have been included as in the original accounts and italicised to distinguish them from calendared text. These are interpreted in the Glossary.

Dating

Years generally have been given in the modern form as A.D., except for the account translated in full, where the original (regnal) form has been retained. Term and feast dates have been retained as in the original throughout, and their modern equivalents are given in the Glossary.

Money

Sums of money have been rendered in Arabic numerals and £, s., and d. For the sake of a tidier appearance the denominations have not been italicised. Accounting errors have been noted in footnotes.

Abbreviations and Omissions

Text lost through damage to the MSS has been indicated by [...], while blanks left in the text by the original scribe are marked [–]. Where it has been possible to supply missing text, e.g. Christian names, from other sources, the text has been placed in square brackets.

41

Marginalia

Marginalia that are mere repetitions of parts of the text have been excluded. Marginalia that add new material are included in the footnotes.

Place and Proper Names

The spelling of place names has been modernised. Proper names have been standardised. Brief biographical details of all individuals mentioned in the text may be found in Appendix 2.

1. RECEIVER'S ACCOUNT 1479–1480

The roll is damaged at its head and consists of five sheets of paper 30 cm wide sewn end to end. There are no surviving returns from York, Nottingham, Norwell Overall, Bowes and Polehouse, London, Ardleigh, Runwell, or Hackney. Sheet one measures 32 cm in length and sheet four 37 cm. The remaining sheets are 41 cm long.

Receipts from Rents and Farms
[…]

[Caddington and Kensworth]
[…]
Total:[1]   £70 8s. 3½d.

Willesden
John More, farmer, in two payments, as shown on the first
folio of the quarterly paper: £12 1s. 4d.

Belchamp St. Paul
John Lokear, vicar, in three payments, as shown in [–] folio
of the quarterly paper: £17 14s. 8d.

Thorpe, Kirby and Walton in the soke
James Raderford, collector of rents of assize, for Michaelmas
term 1479, £18 15s.
For Purification term 1480:
John Carter, farmer of the rectory of Bancroft, in two
payments, £8.
Matthew Cook, farmer of Thorpe Hall, £9.
John Toose, farmer of Walton, £19 3s. 4d.
John German, farmer of the rectory of Kirby, £9.
Total: £63 8s. 4d.[2]

Wickham St. Paul
The vicar of Belchamp St. Paul, farmer of the rectory, for
Purification term 1480:   £10 0s. 0d.

---

[1]   Only the total of the return survives. The revenue rendered suggests that this
      amount issued from Caddington and Kensworth.
[2]   *Recte* £63 18s. 4d.

43

Heybridge
John Lindsey, farmer, for all rents and farms for Purification
term 1480, including 20s. received from John Candish for
part of the farm of the mill: £12 6s. 8d.

Sutton
From the improvement of rents and farms, as shown in the
declaration made thereof: £28 11s. 8½d.

Added to the account
From sale of a silver-gilt cup with an ostrich egg (*le grypege*),
£4 3s. 4d.
From Richard Breych, by the hands of Thomas Orston, and
Thomas Leyke, for the Archdeaconry of Nottingham, £20.
Total: £24 3s. 4d.

Total receipts   £560 14s. 4d.[3]

Expenditure

Rent
To the Bishop of London, £1 13s. 4d. quit rent to the manor
of Chadsworth, and £1 13s. 4d. paid for the creation and
installation of the Dean: £3 6s. 8d.

Daily Expenses
On beef, veal, pork and other victuals, stuffs and necessaries,
as shown in 41 folios of the first part of the quarterly paper,
where the particular daily and weekly sums were noted: £44 8s. 11½d.

The Chamberlain of St. Paul's
To William Steward for the manors, demesnes and lands held
in farm by the Dean, as appears by five bills: £172 7s. 7¾d.[4]

The Clerk of the Bakehouse
To Adam Friday, for wheat to make bread, as shown in
four bills: £17 3s. 2¾d.

The Clerk of the Bakehouse
To Thomas Skypwith, now clerk, £37 8½d., with another

---

3   If the missing sum of 10s. is included [see n. 2, above], this sum should read £561
     4s. 4d.
4   £179 6¾d. crossed out.

44

£8 16s. for 22 qr. wheat at 6s. per qr.:[5]   £45 16s. 8½d.

The Brewer

To John Essenwolde, brewer of London, for ale, as shown in
various bills and tallies, £11 17s. 5d.
To [Alexander] Berebrewer of London for beer, as shown by
a tally of 25 December 1479, £1 4s. 4d.
Total: £13 1s. 9d.

Payments by order of the Dean

To Isabella Worsley as her marriage portion on 1 May 1480, £40.
To Richard Lee on 13 July 1480, £50.
To the Dean in his parlour in the Deanery, £10.
Total: £100 0s. 0d.

Liveries

To William Bukke, draper of London:
On 11 July 1479, for woollen cloth bought for two liveries,
winter and summer, for the Dean's servants, as shown
in two bills, £17 8s. 6d.
To [–] for two horses bought from him, now in the Dean's
stable, £1 12s. 6d.
Total: £19 1s. 0d.

Necessary Expenses

To three people on the order of the Dean, £30.
To the Bishop of London for the acquisition of a marsh at
Stepney, according to an agreement made between certain
people and on the order of the King, £9 15s.
For fifty-one baskets of salt fish bought at Canterbury for the
household, £3 6s. 8d.
Total: £43 1s. 8d.

The Goldsmith

To Nicholas Flynte, goldsmith of London, for 22½ oz. silver at
3s. 4d. per oz. (75s.) used for repairing and making two salt-cellars;
also paid for the repair of two salt-cellars, (30s.), with 6s. 8d. paid
for silver by the oz. and for his work in burnishing the salt-cellars,
as shown in one paper bill, £5 11s. 8d.
To Thomas Fitzwarren for a gilded cup bought on 15 July 1480,
as shown in a bill, £3 13s. 4d.
Total: £9 5s. 0d.

---

[5]   The calculation is incorrect. Twenty-two qr. at 8s. instead of 6s. per qr. would
give £8 16s.

Carriage of wood

To Roger Frende, John Chalk, and the Prioress of Kilburn for the carriage of seventy-one carts of wood from [–] to London, at 12d. per cart, as shown by three tallies: £3 11s. 0d.

Necessary Expenses

For goods and stuffs bought for the household of the said Dean, as shown in twelve folios of the quarterly paper: £73 1s. 10½d.

Fees Paid

The accountant's fee, for the terms of Easter and the Nativity of St. John the Baptist, £1.
To Thomas Bunewell, Marmaduke Cressy, William Lokkey, servants of the Dean in part payment for their fees, for Easter term, each receiving 6s. 8d.
To Stephen Holt, servant of the Dean, in part payment of his fee, for Easter term, 9s. 2d.
To John Fuldon, servant of the Dean, in part payment of his fee, for the terms of Easter and the Nativity of St. John the Baptist, 13s. 4d.
Total: £3 2s. 6d.

Sum Total Paid **£547 8s. 0d.**
And he owes **£13 6s. 4d.**

Audit

He is allowed
Paid from a surplus he had at the last account, £17 12s. 2¾d.
Paid for a hood with a *liripipe* of velvet bought for the Dean, 8s. 6d.
Surplus carried forward. **£4 14s. 4¾d.**[6]

---

[6]   The correct balance, taking into account n. 2, is a surplus of £4 4s. 4¾d.

2. RECEIVER'S ACCOUNT 11 JULY 1480–18 JULY 1481

The roll is damaged at its head and consists of eight sheets of paper 30 cm wide sewn end to end. The returns from York, Nottingham, London, Bowes and Polehouse and Ardleigh are missing.[7] The entries for Runwell, Caddington and Kensworth and Hackney are damaged. Sheet one measures 27 cm in length, sheet five 26 cm, sheet eight 38 cm. The remaining sheets are 41 cm long.

Receipts from Rents and Farms
[...]

[Runwell]
[...]

Total: [8]	£36 10s. 0d.

Caddington and Kensworth
Edmund Counteys, for rents and farms in seven payments: £61 2s. 4d.

Hackney Nil

Willesden
John More, farmer, for a year ending at Michaelmas 1480,
£4 16s. 8d.
for part of his farm, for Easter term 1481,[9] as shown in two
folios of the quarterly paper, £2 8s. 4d.
Total: £7 5s. 0d.

Belchamp St. Paul
John Lokear, vicar, collector of rents of assize, in eight payments
for a year ending at Michaelmas 1480, and also for the farm of
the rectory and demesne lands for a year ending at the
Purification 1481: £53 2s. 8d.

Thorpe, Kirby, and Walton in the soke
James Raderford, collector of rents of assize, £28 18s. 4d.
John Carter, farmer of the rectory of Bancroft, in two

---

[7] Although the entry for London is also missing, note that the final audit (see p. 55) for this year includes sums of £4 7s. 9d. and £13 12s. 5½d., which are described as having been received from London and the Deanery.

[8] Only the total survives. The revenue rendered suggests that this amount issued from Runwell.

[9] Easter 1481 fell on 22 April.

payments, £17 6s. 6d.

Matthew Cook, farmer of Thorpe Hall, for the term of St.
Peter *ad Vincula* 1480, £9.

Thomas Smith, farmer of Thorpe Hall, for Purification term
1481, £9.

John Toose, farmer of Walton, in two payments, £38.

John German, farmer of the rectory of Kirby, in two
payments, £14.

John Kent, farmer of the rectory of Thorpe, in three payments,
£4 13s. 4d., of which £4 is full payment for a year at the term
of St. Peter ad Vincula 1480.

John Nayller, for a fine made for his lands and holdings in
Thorpe, Kirby and Walton, as appears in the court roll,
£16 15s. 4d.

Total:	£137 13s. 6d.

Wickham St. Paul

John Grene, farmer, in two payments for the terms of St. Peter
ad Vincula 1480 and Purification 1481: £19 13s. 4d.

Heybridge

John Lindsey, farmer:

For a whole year ending at St. Peter *ad Vincula* 1480
(£38 5s. 5½d.), and in part payment of his farm for
Purification term 1481, (£3 7s. 10½d.), in two payments,
£41 13s. 4d.

In issues of the court held on the Monday before the feast of
St. Matthew, viz. that of 20 September 1479 and that of
18 September 1480, £3 4s. 4d.

From Lindsey by the hand of John Hewyk, £1 6s. 8d.

John Candish, farmer of the mill, in part payment for a year
ending at St. Peter ad Vincula 1480, £4 15s. 5d.

Total:	£50 19s. 9d.

Sutton

Robert Nevyll and Thomas Thomas, farmers, in eight
payments, £31 7d.

Arrears of rent from the Bishop of Bath and Wells, 9s. 3d.

Total:	£31 9s. 10d.

Drayton

Edmund Prentesse, farmer of the manor, for Purification term
1481, £12.

Clement Cook, farmer of the mill, for Easter term 1481,

as shown in the quarterly paper, £2.

Total: £14 0s. 0d.

Norton Folgate
William Hill, farmer, for Christmas term 1480:   £3 6s. 8d.

The Deanery
From various people, as shown by several declarations
(including various tenants in London, £1 10s. 6d., William
Say for the farm of a tenement in Knightrider Street, £1 5s.,
and Richard Saddler for his farm for Easter term, 10s.), £14
4s. 6d.

John Bernard, procurator of the rectory of Chepyng
Lambourn, arrears £32 7s. 1½d., and profits for this year,
in three payments, £32 10s.

John Hewet, farmer of the mill of Ratcliff (£3 13s. 4d.
per term payable at Michaelmas, Christmas, and Easter,
beyond £3 13s. 4d. paid previously for the term of the
Nativity of St. John the Baptist), £10 13s. 4d.

Roger Frende, farmer of various pastures in Acton, for
a year ending at Michaelmas term 1480, including 3s. 4d.
for ½ qr. wheat flour and 4s. for oat flour called
otemayle, as laid down in his indenture, £5 14s.[10]

Various tenants in London and Stepney, as shown in a
bill, £7 5s. 9½d.[11]

Master Robert Braddows, commissary of the cathedral
church of St. Paul's, arrears £2 11s. 8d., and issues of his
office for this year, £3 8s. 4d.

John Clerk, collector of rents and farms of various tenants
in London and Stepney, as shown in a bill, £3 6s. 1½d.

Total: £112 0s. 10½d.

Added to the account
William Staveley on the 19 October, a debt to the Dean,
£4 13s. 4d.

Robert Hethe, by the hand of William Hill, collector of rents
of St. Paul's Cathedral, £4.

The sale of a grey horse called *Dyamande* at Smithfield,
£1 1s. 4d.

Total: £9 14s. 8d.

---

[10] For Frende's original lease see GL, MS 25342.

[11] This entry is repeated at the end of the returns from the Deanery, with an erasure
of the amount and the note *r[espice] supra*.

Added further to the account
Received by Roger Radcliff from the Dean: £1 7s. 6d.

Total receipts:[12]   £703 16s. 5½d.

Expenditure
Rent
Quit rent to the Bishop of London, to the manor of
Chadsworth: £1 13s. 4d.

Daily Expenses
Meat, victuals, stuffs and necessaries, as shown in [-] folios
of the first part of the quarterly paper: £52 4s. 10d.

The Chamberlain of St. Paul's
To William Steward for the manors, demesnes, lands and
tenements held to farm by the Dean, as appears by four bills: £183 9s. 3¼d.

The Clerk of the Bakehouse
To Thomas Smith and William Botery, executors of the will
of Adam Friday, late clerk of the bakehouse, in full payment
of all money owed by the Dean, £10 7s. 9d.
To Thomas Skypwith, now clerk of the bakehouse, for buying
wheat to make bread, as shown in six bills, £71 9s. 6½d.
To Thomas Skypwith, for 16 qr. wheat, at 6s. a qr., issuing
from the manor of Heybridge, and also for 16 qr. wheat at
6s. 8d.,£9 16s.[13]
Total: £90 18s. 7½d.[14]

The Brewer
To John Essenwolde, brewer of London, for ale bought for the
household:
Before the time of this account, as shown by a tally, £11 19s. 3d.,
On 29 January 1481, £3 16s. 6d., on 10 April 1481, £7 2s.,
on 2 July 1481, £3 7s. 6d., as shown by various tallies.
Total: £26 5s. 3d.

---

[12] £538 6s. 1d. is the total for the recorded receipts. The lost entries amount to £165
10s. 4½d.
[13] £8 5s. 4d. has here been amended by the accountant to £9 16s., but should read £10
2s. 8d., viz. a discrepancy of 6s. 8d.
[14] £80 17s. 9d. crossed out. The sum should, however, read £91 13s. 3½d. or, if the
6s. 8d. from n. 13 is included, £91 19s. 11½d.

Beer
To Sander Berebrewer at 'le Hermitage' for 31½ *kylderkyns*
of penny beer, as shown by a tally, £2 11s. and for 3 *kylderkyns*
of three-halfpenny beer, 8s. 8d.
Total: £2 9s. 8d.

Wine
From Charles [Vyntener]:
For arrears owing from last year, viz. for two casks of red wine,
(£12), one hogshead of claret wine (£1 10s.), and one *roundlet*
of *Malmsey* (18s. 1d.), as shown in the book of memoranda,
£14 8s. 1d. For two casks of red wine (£11), two barrels
Malmsey wine containing 36 gallons (£1 13s.), and one barrel
Rhenish wine containing ten gallons at 10d. per gallon (8s. 4d.),
bought from him this year, as shown in one bill, £13 1s. 4d.
Total: £27 9s. 5d.

Livery
From William Bukke, draper of London:
For woollen cloth bought last year for the livery of the Dean's
servants for the feasts of Christmas (£10 16s. 9d.), and the
Nativity of St. John the Baptist (£5 10s. 9d.), £16 7s. 6d.[15]
For russet-coloured woollen cloth, bought this year for the
servants for Christmas, as shown in the quarterly book, £11
18s. 9d. For woollen cloth of various colours bought for the
Dean's livery, viz. for 4½ virges of crimson in grain
provided on 25 March 1480 at 12s. per virge, £2 14s.
For 4½ virges of fine scarlet at 13s. 4d. per virge, £3.
For 4½ virges violet in grain at 11s. per virge, bought for
the livery of the Dean for Christmas 1480, £2 9s.[16]
For 8 virges of violet in grain for a long gown and a short gown
to be made for the Dean for Easter 1481, at 9s. a virge, £3 12s.
For 3½ virges of woaded black to make a tunic for the Dean
for Easter, price per virge 4s., 14s.
Total: £40 15s. 3d.[17]

Necessary Expenses
For goods and stuffs, including £4 8s. 5¾d. for spices and
£1 10s. 4½d. for shoeing the Dean's horses, as appears in three

---

[15]   17s. 6d. has been crossed out, and 7s. 6d. inserted.
[16]   *Recte* £2 9s. 6d.
[17]   *Recte* £40 15s. 9d.

folios of necessaries and one folio of spices in the quarterly
paper.
Total: £30 10s. 5¼d.[18]

Quit Rents
To Sir Richard Charlton, knight, 20s. for Bowes and Polehouse.
To the Earl of Essex, 19s. annually issuing from the various
demesnes of Bowes and Polehouse.
To William Lawshull, for respite of homage on certain of the
Dean's lands in Rochford hundred held from the honour of
Rayleigh, 13s. 4d.
Total: £2 12s. 4d.

Chaplains' Salaries
To Thomas Cartwryght and Thomas Turnour, arrears from
Christmas term 1479 and Easter term 1480, as shown in a
declaration, £3 6s. 8d.
To Thomas Cartwryght and Thomas Turnour, for the terms
of the Nativity of St. John the Baptist, Michaelmas and
Christmas 1480, and Easter 1481, as shown by an acquittance,
£6 13s. 4d.
To William Roke, at £2 13s. 4d. p.a. from the manor of Norton
Folgate, for the terms of Michaelmas and Christmas 1480 and
Easter 1481, as shown by an acquittance, £2.
Total: £12 0s. 0d.

Fees Paid
To Robert Forster, steward of the demesnes of Thorpe, Kirby
and Walton, £2.
To John Hewyk, auditor of all the Dean's lands and
tenements, £3 6s. 8d.[19]
To Master John Lokear, vicar of Belchamp St. Paul, (for his
fee £2 and for his livery 10s.), £2 10s.
Total: £7 16s. 8d.

Stipends of servants
For wages and rewards for the terms of Michaelmas and
Christmas 1480, and Easter and the Nativity of St. John the
Baptist 1481, as shown in the quarterly paper where the
names and particulars of the servants are noted: £23 10s. 2d.

---

[18]   £30 15s. 8½d. has been amended by the accountant to £30 10s. 5¼d.
[19]   Crossed out: 'fee of John Morton, Dean's attorney at the Exchequer, 20s.'

For a whole Tenth due from the church of Lambourn and the prebend of Willesden

To Edmund Wylly, deputy of John Wode and John Fitzherbert, receivers of a whole tenth granted to the King by the prelates and clergy in the last convocation of Canterbury, viz. from the church of Lambourn in Salisbury diocese (£5 6s. 8d.) and from the prebend of Willesden in the archdeaconry of Middlesex (8s.), as shown in a sealed acquittance and a bill signed by Edmund on 28 May 1481.
Total: £5 14s. 8d.

Repairs

For repairs to the mill of Ratcliff and to tenements in the city of London, including £9 15s. paid to the bishop of London for acquisition and rendering profitable of a certain marsh at Stepney, according to an agreement made between certain persons on the King's mandate, beyond £9 15s. allowed in Roger's account for the last year, as shown in the quarterly paper examined at the time of audit.
Total: £17 15s. 8d.

Purchases of Arms and Stuffs for the war against Scotland [20]

"And in money paid for various goods and stuffs bought and provided at various times from certain people when the aforesaid Master William Worsley was riding with the Lord King in northern parts against the Scots:

> for 2¾ virges black velvet for covering the briganders of the said Dean, 27s. 6d.;
> for one pair of briganders bought for Thomas Bromley, covered in velvet and with gilded keys, 53s. 4d.;
> to John Fox for making [–] a jack, eleven days at 5d. per day, 4s. 7d.,
> and to his servant for ten days at 4d. per day, 3s. 4d.;
> for a piece of fustian called *Fustyon de Osbernes*, 13s.;
> for a pair of briganders bought and delivered for Thomas Bunewell, 18s.;
> for another pair of briganders bought and delivered for Robert Stykeswolde 18s.;
> for another pair of briganders bought and delivered for Robert Robson, 18s.;
> for another pair of briganders bought and delivered for

[20]   The items under this heading have been translated in full.

Henry Chaddekyrke, 18s.;

for another pair of briganders bought and delivered for
Robert Bordeman, 18s.;

for another pair of briganders bought and delivered for
Richard Samesbury, 13s. 4d.;

for two white trotting horses bought from John Cotez,
58s. 4d.;

for a bay horse bought from the same John, 13s. 4d.;

for *blakechalk* bought for a doublet, 1d.;

for a reward given to John Grege for mending the
aforesaid jack, 2s. 1d.;

for a gray ambling horse bought from the aforesaid
John Cotez for Master Dean, and a sorrel trotting
horse with a white face, £8 2s.;

for a cart with six horses and their appurtenances,
viz. collars, halters, and other goods, £10;

for iron instruments ordered and bought for the cart,
4s. 4½d.;

for five *standardes de le mayle*, 5s. 4d.;

for ten bows bought from John Symsone, 2s. each, 20s.;

for twelve sheaves of arrows, 34s. 8d.;

for cord bought for tents and pavilions, 9s.;

for a black trotting horse, £6 10s. 10d.;

for a dozen arrow cases of red hide, 9s.;

for a dozen belts bought for the said arrows, 2s.;

for the making of a pair of briganders covered with
velvet and gilded keys, ordered for the said Master
Dean, 73s. 4d.;

for a chariot and a *barret*, 55s.;

for a lance with a tip of iron, 5s. 9d.;

for *lez conysaunces* 5s.;

for repairing a *barehedde* at Hackney (4d.) with four
boxes (3s.) bought in London for putting on the *salette*,
3s. 4d.;

for repair of a harness and an axehead, 2s. 9d.;

for two stone of tallow for the *barret* at Hackney, 11d.;

for a pavilion and a tent (*le hayle*) in which to put the
horse, bought from Thomas Bedmaker, £9 12d.;

for a large barrel for putting the harness in, 3s.;

for a saddle called a chariot saddle, 3s. 4d.;

for mending horse harness, 3s. 4d.;

and paid to John Armar on 25 June 21 Edward IV, as shown
in this account and examined by the auditor, £17 7s."

Total: £76 19s. 10½d.

Money paid to the Dean

By Roger at Hackney when making his declarations at
Christmas 1479, and at Easter 1480, £7 10s. 9¼d.
By Roger as part of the issues of his office, to the hands of
Thomas Bunewell, as shown in the quarterly paper, £1 16s. 9d.
By Roger at Hackney in royals and nobles for the journey to
Southwell on 17 June 1481, by the Dean's recognisance
without bill, £80.
Total: £89 7s. 6¼d.

Sum Total Paid: **£691 12s. 11¾d.**
And he owes: **£12 3s. 5¾d.**

Audit
Allowed for a surplus in the preceding account, £4 14s. 6¾d.[21]
Paid on the order of the Dean to various minstrels of the
King and other lords when staying with the Dean, as shown in
one folio of the quarterly paper, £2 17s. 6d.
Paid on the order of the Dean to the steward of Gray's Inn for
his pension of 3s. 4d. p.a., 1s. 8d.
Paid to John Morton for his work done in the Exchequer to
expedite certain matters for the Dean, as shown in the quarterly
paper, £1.
Paid to William Ford for his work done in the King's Exchequer,
3s. 5d.
Paid by Roger for the expenses of the steward, the auditor and
other officials riding through the demesnes of the Dean and
settling disputes between tenants, as shown in the quarterly paper,
£3 4s. 5d.
Paid to John Fuldon on the order of the Dean for the acquisition
of various corn and hay at Hackney, as shown in the last folio of
the quarterly paper, £3.
Paid to various other people as rewards on the Dean's orders,
5s. 8d.
Paid to Master [Thomas] Matyn on the orders of the Dean for
an absolution at the Roman curia, £1 4s.[22]

He has a surplus of £4 7s. 9d.
Afterwards charged with £4 7s. 9d. received from John Clerk,

---

[21] Radcliff's declared surplus in 1479–80 was £4 14s. 4¾d. (cf. above).
[22] Totalling £11 16s. 8d.

collector of rents in the city of London and the Deanery
of St. Paul's Cathedral, beyond £13 12s. 5½d.[23] received above
from John, as shown by an indenture made between them.

And quit.

---

[23] See n. 7, above.

3. A FULL TRANSLATION OF THE RECEIVER'S ACCOUNT, 11 JULY 1481–13 JULY 1482

This account is not calendared, but given in full translation.[24] *The roll is complete: the first membrane is endorsed in the same hand as the remainder of the document with a note that this is the account of Roger Radcliff, steward of the household from 11 July year 21 to 13 July year 22. The roll consists of eight sheets, 30 cm wide and sewn end to end. The first sheet is 34 cm long, the fourth 25.5 cm, the fifth 38.5 cm and the sixth 35 cm. The remaining sheets are 40–41 cm long.*

London.

The account of Roger Radcliff, steward of the household of Master William Worsley, Dean of the cathedral church of St. Paul's, of various sums of money received at various times from the demesne, farms and other offices, and paid by him on the expenses of the household of the Dean, from the 11th day of July, 21 Edward IV, until the 18th day of July, 22 Edward IV, i.e. for one year and seven days.

Nothing carried over from his account of the previous year, as shown at the foot of the preceding account.

Total: Nil

Receipts from Rents and Farms

Bowes and Polehouse

£26 13s. 4d. received by him from Edward Westby and John Fox, farmers there, in several payments, as more plainly shown in [–] folio of the said quarterly paper.

Total: £26 13s. 4d.

London

£12 13s. 9½d.[25] received by him from John Clerk, collector of the rents and farms there, at various times, as shown in [–] folio of the said quarterly paper.

Total: £12 13s. 9½d.

The manor of Ardleigh

£35 13s. 4d. received from the rents and farm of the manor there at [–] times, as shown in [–] folio of the said quarterly paper.

Total: £35 13s. 4d.

---

[24] See Introduction.
[25] 13s. 4d. crossed out.

Runwell

£36 10s. received from John Athey, farmer of the manor there, at four times, as shown in [–] folios of the said quarterly paper.
Total: £36 10s. 0d.

Caddington and Kensworth

£86 17s. 10½d. received from Edmund Counteys from the rents and farm there in the county of Bedford at [–] times, as shown in [–] folio of the said quarterly paper.
Total: £86 17s. 10½d.[26]

Rents and farms in Hackney

He does not answer for other money to be received by him from the issues, profits and revenues of the rents and farm of lands and holdings there at [–] times, because none of this money from the said rents and farms came to Roger's hand during the time of this account, by the oath of the accountant.
Total: Nil

Willesden

But £4 16s. 8d. received by him from John More, farmer of the manor there, for one whole year ending on the feast of Michaelmas 21 [Edward IV].
And [–] received by him from the same John for Easter term 22 [Edward IV], as shown in the quarterly paper.
Total: £4 16s. 8d.

Belchamp St. Paul

£49 8s. received by him from John Lokear, vicar there, at [–] times, in rents of assize paid for one whole year ending at the feast of Michaelmas 21 [Edward IV], and in [–] payment for his farm of the rectory and demesne lands for one year ending at the feast of the Purification of the Blessed Virgin Mary 21 [Edward IV].
Total: £49 8s. 0d.

Thorpe, Kirby and Walton in the soke

£103 13s. 4d. received by him from various persons as written below, viz. from James Raderford, collector of rents of assize there, £43 15s. 3¾d.
And from John Carter, from the farm of the rectory of Bancroft, £12 8s.
And from Thomas Smith, from the farm of Thorpe Hall, at one time, £9.[27]
And from John German, from the farm of the rectory of Kirby, at [–] times, £16.[28]

---

[26] 97s. 10½d. crossed out.
[27] £9 15s. crossed out.
[28] 40s. and £7 crossed out.

And from John Kent, from the farm of the rectory of Thorpe, 40s.
And from John Toose, from the farm of the manor of Walton, at [-] times as shown in [-] folio of the quarterly paper, £20 10s.
Total: £103 13s. 4d.

Wickham St. Paul

£20 received by him from John Grene, farmer there, at two times.
Total: £20 0s. 0d.

Heybridge

£14 received by him from John Lindsey, farmer of the manor there, as part of his farm for a year ending on the feast of St. Peter ad Vincula 21 [Edward IV].
And 7s. 3½d. received by him from the said John Lindsey from the issues of the profits of a court held there on the Monday before the feast of St. Matthew 21 [Edward IV].
And 30s. ½d. received by him from Robert Pere late farmer of the mill there in full payment of his farm, at the feast of the Purification of the Blessed Virgin Mary 21 [Edward IV].
And 20s. received by him from Thomas Chaterton, the price of wood sold to him, as shown in the said quarterly paper.
Total: £16 17s. 5d.[29]

Sutton

£29 5s. received by him from Robert Nevyll and Thomas Thomas, farmers there, at [-] times, as more plainly shown in the quarterly paper.
Total: £29 5s. 0d.

Drayton

£23 13s. 4d. received by him from Edmund Prentesse, farmer of the manor there, at [-] term.
And 40s. received by him from Clement Cook, farmer of the mill there, at [-] term.
Total: £25 13s. 4d.

Norton Folgate

£6 13s. 4d. received by him from William Hill, farmer there, for a year ending on the feast of the Nativity of St. John the Baptist 22 [Edward IV].
Total: £6 13s. 4d.

---

[29] 16s. and £16 inserted; 4d. crossed out and 5d. inserted.

The Deanery

£32 10s. received by him from John Bernard, procurator of the rectory of Chepyng Lambourn, at the term of the Annunciation of the Blessed Virgin Mary 21 [Edward IV], at [–] times as shown in [–] folio of the quarterly paper.

And £31 received by him from the same John Bernard, from the issues and profits of the same rectory, in the time of this account, as more plainly shown in the said folio.

And £18 6s. 8d. received by him from John Hewet, farmer of the mill of Ratcliff, as shown in [–] folio of the said quarterly paper.

And of [–] received by him from John Clerk, collector of rents and farms of the Deanery of St. Paul's in London and Stepney within the time of this account.

Total: £81 16s. 8d.

Added to the account

56s. 8d. received by him, the price of two horses sold by him at the recognisance of Roger.

And of 2s. 6d., received from [William] Hale, for an estreat as shown in one folio of the quarterly paper.

Total, 60s. 6d.[30]

Sum Total Received   £539 12s. 7d.[31]

And quit.

Expenditure

Rent

He also accounts for money paid to the Bishop of London for a certain quit rent, 33s. 4d., yearly to the manor of Chadsworth, and its appurtenances, viz. for its payment at the time of this account, 33s. 4d.

And in rent paid to Sir Richard Charlton, knight, yearly issuing from the demesne of Bowes and Polehouse, viz. in its payment at the time of this account, as in its payment in the preceding account, 20s. 2d.

And in rent paid to the Earl of Essex, issuing annually from the said demesne, viz. in payment at the time of this account, as in payment in the preceding account, 19s.

Total: 72s. 6d.

---

[30]   *Recte* 59s. 2d.
[31]   *Recte* £539 1s. 3d.

Daily Expenses

And in money paid by the said Roger to the steward of the said household, for beef, veal, pork, and other victuals bought and paid for within the time of this account, together with all other things and stuffs and necessaries provided and bought and used in the said household, as shown in [-] folios of part of the quarterly paper, where the particular sums are daily and weekly signed, noted and declared and on this account are shown and examined by the said Roger, £60 7s. 3d.

Total: £60 7s. 3d.

Payments made to the Chamberlain of the Cathedral Church of St. Paul's

And in money paid to the Chamberlain of the cathedral church of St. Paul's, London, for diverse manors, demesnes, lands, and tenements held to farm by Master William Worsley, Dean of the church, from the canons in the chapter besides certain other sums retained in his own hands as his portion on account of his residency at the same time, as shown in [-] bills made between the said Roger and the said Chamberlain, and presented at the time of this account and remaining among the memoranda of this account, £184 17s. 10¾d.

Total: £184 17s. 10¾d.[32]

Payments made to the Clerk of the Bakehouse

Money paid by him to Thomas Skypwith, clerk of the bakehouse there, various sums of money annually issuing from certain manors for the purchase of certain quarters of wheat to make bread, as shown in a bill presented at the time of this account and remaining among its memoranda, £74 3s. ¾d.

And in money paid to the said Thomas Skypwith, clerk of the said bakehouse, the price of 32 qr. of wheat annually issuing from the manor of Heybridge, bought by him at various prices within the time of this account as more plainly shown in the said book, £15 3s. 4d.

Total: £89 6s. 4¾d.

Paid to the Brewer for ale

Paid to Richard Prowell, brewer of London, the price of ale bought from him and used in the household of the Dean, as shown in various tallies made between the said Roger and Richard and in one folio of the book of particulars, presented at the time of this account.[33]

Total: £14 13s. 0d.

---

[32] £202 10s. ½d. crossed out.
[33] 'inter' crossed out.

Paid for Beer

And in money paid to Sander Berebrewer at 'le Hermitage', the price of 36½ *kylderkyns* of penny beer bought from him and used in the household of the Dean, as shown in two tallies made between Roger and Sander, and shown in the said book, 43s. 6d.[34]

And in money paid to the same Alexander Berebrewer, the price of four *kylderkyns* of three-halfpenny beer bought from him within the time of this account and used in the said household, 7s. 6d.

Total: £2 11s. 0d.

Purchase of Wine

And in money paid by Roger himself to Charles Vyntener, the price of two casks of red wine and claret, a *roundlet* of sweet wine containing 17 gallons, (14d., 20s. 5d.)[35] provided and bought by him within the time of this account, as shown in the said book presented at the time of this account, £14 7s. 1d.

Total: £14 7s. 1d.

Livery of M. Dean and his servants

And in money paid by Roger himself at this time to William Bukke, draper of London, the price of various pieces of woollen cloth of *musterdevelis* bought from him for the livery of the household of Master Dean at Christmas in the time of this account as shown in a bill presented at the time of this account and remaining among its memoranda, £12 13s. 11d.

And in money paid by him to the said William for the price of various pieces of woollen cloth bought for the summer livery of the servants within the time of this account, £4 6s.

And paid by him for the price of three gowns given to three farmers of Belchamp St. Paul and Wickham St. Paul, at 6s. 8d. each, as shown in the said book, 20s.

Total: £17 19s. 11d.

Necessary Expenses

And in money accounted by him for various goods and stuffs bought by him from various persons at various times and used in the household of the said Dean for the said time, including 36s. 1d. for the price of spices bought at various times, and used in the said household, as shown in three folios of necessities and one folio of spices of the said quarterly paper, where the names of these persons and their particular sums are noted and laid out, and presented at the time of this account, £11 10s. 11¾d.

Total: £11 10s. 11¾d.

---

[34] Scribal error: xliijs. vj li. instead of xliijs. vjd.

[35] Presumably at 14d. a gallon, totalling 20s. 5d. (*recte* 19s. 8d.).

Chaplains' salaries[36]

And in money paid to Thomas Cartwryght and Thomas Turnour, chaplains, in the name of salary at the terms of the Nativity of St. John the Baptist before the time of this account, and at Michaelmas, Christmas, and Easter within the time of this account, as shown in four acquittances returned at the time of audit, £6 13s. 4d.

And in money paid to William Roke, chaplain, receiving 53s. 4d. p.a. from the manor of Norton Folgate at the same terms, viz. at the term of the Nativity of St. John the Baptist before this account, and at Michaelmas, Christmas, and Easter within the time of this account, returned at the time of audit, 54s. 4d.

Total: £9 6s. 8d.

Fees Paid

And in fee paid to Robert Forster, steward of the lands of Thorpe, Kirby and Walton in the soke, receiving 40s. p.a., viz. in payment at this time, 40s.

And in fee paid to John Hewyk, auditor of various demesnes, lands, and tenements of the Dean, receiving 66s. 8d. p.a., viz. in payment at this time, 66s. 8d.

Total: £5 6s. 8d.

Stipends of servants

And in money paid by this account to the servants of the said Dean for their wages and rewards, viz. at the terms of Michaelmas and Christmas 21 [Edward IV], and at Easter and the Nativity of St. John the Baptist 22 [Edward IV], as is shown in the quarterly paper where the names of these servants with their payments are particularly noted and laid out as shown and examined on this account, £22 13s. 4d.

Total: £22 13s. 4d.

Necessary Expenses for the apparel of Master Dean and for various goods and stuffs bought on Master Dean's order

Paid by the accountant for various goods and stuffs ordered and bought for the apparel of the Dean and for various necessities bought on the Dean's order, as particularly shown below, viz. first;

> 4½ virges of russet at 10s. per virge, bought for a gown to be made for the Dean, 45s.;
> the making of the said gown in trimming with fur without lining (2s.) and its furnishing, 18d.;
> three skins (12d.) of *grey* bought for the said gown, price per skin 4d.
> the lining of the said gown, 8d.;

---

[36]   These salaries were one term in arrears.

one pair of shoes with points, 3s. 2d.[37];

a pair of unlined hose, 6d.;

a pair of hose, 9d.;

the repair of a purse of the Dean, 2d.;

the repair of a blue gown of the Dean, 4d.;

a hood bought for the Dean, 3s. 4d.;

the making of an *Agnus Dei* with the surplus of the same supplemented to the value of 3s. 6d., 7s.;

on the order of the Dean to John Grymston, for the memory of the souls of the parents of the Dean and all the faithful, to the hand of Robert Robson at the cross of St. Paul's, 12d.;

in part payment of £8 for the making of a silver cross remaining at Southwell, 22s.;

for a cope[38] of cloth of gold with a white linen cloth and a gold fringe (*orfrey*) of new work with the price of the *bockeram* and the making of the said cope and other expenses of the making of the cope, £14 4s.;

the price and the payment of a golden cope bought for Laurence Booth late Archbishop of York, 22s.;

a silk *corsse* of black colour bought for the Dean, 4s. 2d.;

a strap (*garth*) bought for the horse of Master Dean, 10d.;

a pair of linen sheets, 2s.;

a tablecloth of plain work, 20d.;

a pair of sheets, 2s.;

another pair of sheets, 20d.;

a pillow (*pyle*) with 8 ounces, 4d.;

two towels and two napkins, 8d.;

eight pillow cases, 2s.;

an iron fire rake, 6d.;

three sheets bought and remaining in the house of the Dean, 2s.;

another pair of sheets bought and remaining in the house of the Dean, 2s. 4d.;

three pairs of *fustyances* bought for the arrival of the Lord Marquess of Dorset on the Monday before the feast of St. George the Martyr, 40s. 8d.;

31½ virges of linen cloth for two pairs of sheets bought for the arrival of the said lord, price per virge 14d., 37s. 11d.;

a pair of linen sheets containing 12 virges, price per virge and the making 12d., 12s. 6d.;

---

[37] Shoes at this date, either with points, or punched. Cf. Absolon, the parish clerk in the Miller's tale who had 'poules window corven on his shoes', i.e. the shoes were punched to give a pattern reminiscent of the Rose window in St. Paul's. (Chaucer, *Canterbury Tales*, line 3318). See *English Medieval Industries*, ed. John Blair and Nigel Ramsay (Hambledon Press, London and New York, 1991), pp. 303, 310.

[38] *cape* erased.

two shirts containing 4¾ virges bought for the Dean, price per virge 12d., 4s. 11½d.;

on the order of the Dean for the repair of a silver and silver-gilt salt-cellar broken by Thomas Bunewell, mended at Hackney, 8d.;

linen cloth called *dyaper worke* containing 26 virges, price per virge 2s. 4d., 60s. 8d.;

twenty-three and a half virges of linen cloth called *dyaper worke* bought for making towels for the household of the Dean, price per virge 14d., 27s. 2d.;

two and a half virges of green cloth, price per virge 6s., for making a gown for Master Dean, 15s.;

five virges of *bockeram* bought for the said gown, price per virge 7d., 2s. 11d.;

one and three quarter virges of cloth bought for a cloth saddle for Master Dean, 2s. 8d. per virge, 4s. 8d.;

two and three quarter virges of black *chamelet* bought for the Dean, for making a doublet or jacket, price per virge 3s. 6d., 9s. 7½d.;

three quarters of *blanket* ordered for the said jacket, 8d.;

one ell of canvas, 4d.;

two pairs of hose bought for the Dean, 6d. per pair, 12d.;

the making of the green gown, 20d.;

making the said jacket of black *chamelet*, 2s.;

one feather-bed and one bolster bought for Master Dean from the executors of Laurence Damlet, 18s.;

two silver and partly silver-gilt cruets bought from the said executors, containing 15 oz., price 3s. 4d. per oz., 50s.;

to [–] Wylle for one pair of shoes with points for the Dean, 3s.;

one new saddle with repairs to it, 10s.;

one helmet bought for the Dean, 12d.

Total: £35 18s. 10½d.[39]

Repairs

And in money paid by him on various repairs made this year on the mill of Ratcliff and on various houses within this time, viz. on the mansion of the Dean in the city of London (£10 12s. ½d.), on the mill of Ratcliff (75s. 8d.), on the demesne of Ardleigh, (30s. 5d.), and on the marsh of Polehouse (13s. 4d.), as shown in various bills of repair and presented and examined at the time of this account and remaining among its memoranda, £16 11s. 5½d.

Total: £16 11s. 5½d.

---

[39]   *Recte* £35 17s.

Money paid

And in money paid to Master William Worsley, Dean of the cathedral church of St. Paul's, London, by the hand of the accountant from the issues of his office for this year, at the time of payment of 200 marks,[40] by recognisance of the same Roger over the account without bill.

Total: £20 0s. 0d.

Sum total money paid   £509 3s. ¼d.
And he owes: £30 9s. 6¾d.

Of which 75s. 2d. is paid by the said accountant on the order of the Dean to various minstrels of the King and other lords staying with the Dean at various times within this account and to those of other persons bringing the Dean gifts as shown more plainly in one folio of the said quarterly paper.

And paid by him £4 7s. 1½d. for the expenses of Robert Forster, John Hewyk, Roger Radcliff and other officials riding through the Dean's lands to hold court and settle matters between tenants, as particularly shown more plainly in another folio of the quarterly paper.

And 7s. 6d. paid by him to Edward Shuldham, doctor of law, official and collector of the rights of the archdeaconry of Huntingdon, for his portion of the vill of Ardleigh, as shown by one acquittance of the said official dated the 8th day of October 1481, presented at the time of audit and remaining among the memoranda of the account.

Total: £8 9s. 9½d.

And he owes: £21 19s. 9¼d.

Paid to William Worsley, Dean of St. Paul's.[41]

---

[40]   The sum of 200 marks has been inserted at the time of audit in a space previously blank. The context of this payment is obscure.

[41]   Account signed William Worsley, probably in his own hand.

4. RECEIVER'S ACCOUNT 18 JULY 1482-18 JULY 1483

The roll is complete and is endorsed in a contemporary hand with the date of the account on the first sheet. The roll consists of eleven sheets, 30 cm wide and sewn end to end. The second sheet is 20 cm long, the third 18 cm, the fifth 32 cm, the sixth 20 cm, the tenth 17.5 cm and the eleventh 15.5 cm long. The remaining sheets are 42 cm long.

Arrears: Nil

Receipts from Rents and Farms

York Prebend
Thomas Orston, receiver, on 10 November 1482:   £30 0s. 0d.

Bowes and Polehouse
Edward Westby, farmer, on 6 November 1482, £5 16s. 8d., on 16
September 1482, £2 10s., on 29 June[42] 1483, £2 10s. and £1 11s. 4d.
Total: £12 8s. 0d.

London
John Clerk, collector of the Deanery, in several payments,
£25 6s. 8d.
William Say, £1 5s., and John Bulman, £1 7s.
Total: £27 18s. 8d.

Ardleigh
William Frost, farmer of Wadende, £5 11s. 8d., (£1 6s. 8d. on
1 August 1482, and £4 5s. on 26 January 1483).
George Retford, farmer of the manor, on 7 February 1483,
£2 9s. 5d.[43]
John Fuldon, collector of rents of assize, £6
(on 1 August 1482, £2; on 18 February 1483, £4).
Total: £14 1s. 1d.

Runwell
John Athey, farmer, on 18 September 1482, £9, on
5 December 1482, £9 3s. 4d. and on 26 April 1483, £8 18s. 4d.
Total: £27 1s. 8d.

---

[42]   July crossed out.
[43]   8d. crossed out.

Caddington and Kensworth

Edmund Counteys and John Bray,[44] farmers, £38 5s. 2¼d.
(on 19 December 1482, £9 1s. 3¾d., £4 15s. 11½d. and 8s. 11d.,
on 3 February 1483, £19, and on 27 May 1483, £4 19s.)
And part of their farm, £15 9s. 5¾d.
Total: £53 14s. 8d.

Hackney

Nothing from Hackney lands and tenements because receipts
are shown in the account of John Fuldon, servant of the Dean
and *appruator* there: Nil

Willesden

William Northcote, farmer, in two payments: £4 8s. 4d.

Belchamp St. Paul

John Lokear, vicar and collector: £66 10s. 8d.[45]

Thorpe, Kirby, and Walton in the soke

James Raderford, late collector of rents of assize, part of his arrears, £17.
Thomas Bogas, now collector, £13.
John Carter, farmer of the rectory of Bancroft, £16 10s.
Thomas Smith, farmer of Thorpe Hall, in two payments, £18.
John German, farmer of the rectory of Kirby, in four payments, £18 10s.
John Kent, farmer of the rectory of Thorpe, £3.
John Toose, farmer of the manor of Walton, in four payments, £57.
Fines of various tenants from the court held on the feast of
St. Anne 1481, £4 13s. 4½d.
Total: £147 13s. 4½d.

Wickham St. Paul

John Lokear, chaplain,[46] and John Grene, farmer, in two payments:
                                                                      £20 0s. 0d.

Heybridge

John Lindsey, farmer, in five payments, £19.
Arrears from John Candish, late farmer of the mill, £1 13s. 4d.
Total: £20 13s. 4d.

---

[44]   At the time of audit another 103s. 10¼d. is received from Edmund Counteys and
       John Bray, see p. 72.
[45]   £48 2s. 10½d. crossed out.
[46]   'Farmer there' crossed out.

Drayton
Edmund Prentesse, farmer, in two payments, £24.
Clement Cook, farmer of the mill, on 7 December 1482, 20s.
Total: £25 0s. 0d.

Sutton
Robert Nevyll, farmer, on 1 December 1482, £6, on 4 July 1483,
£7, on 8 July 1483, £3.
Total: £16 0s. 0d.

Norton Folgate
William Hill farmer, in two payments. £6 13s. 4d.

The Deanery
John Bernard, procurator of the rectory of Chepyng Lambourn,
£41 13s. 4d. (on 13 October 1482, £11, on 18 April 1483,[47]
£20 13s. 4d.,[48] on 13 June 1483, £10).
John Jordan, for wood sold, 13s. 4d.
Roger Frende, farmer of Acton, on 12 December 1482, £4 1s. 6d.
John Hewet, farmer of the mill of Ratcliff, in two payments,
£7 8s. 2d.
Total: £53 16s. 4d.

Added to the account
A horse of the Dean sold to Master John Barthorn: 16s. 8d.
A pipe of old red wine sold on the order of the Dean to Charles
Vyntener: £2 6s. 8d.

Total Receipts: £529 2s. 9½d.

Expenditure
Rent
Quit rent to the Bishop of London to the manor of
Chadsworth, £1 13s. 4d.
To Sir Richard Charlton, knight, issuing from the demesne of
Bowes and Polehouse, £1 2d.
To the Earl of Essex, 19s.
Total: £3 12s. 6d.

---

[47]   '1 Edward V' crossed out.
[48]   £24 crossed out.

Daily Expenses
On beef, veal, pork and other victuals, stuffs and necessaries,
as shown in thirty-seven folios of the paper book: £73 10s. 3d.

The Chamberlain of St. Paul's
For the estates held to farm by the Dean, as shown in six
paper bills: £186 8s. 5¾d.

The Clerk of the Bakehouse
To Thomas Skypwith and Martin Jolyff, clerks of the
bakehouse, for wheat for bread, as shown in [–] paper bills,
£87 6s. 10½d., and for 32 qr. wheat issuing from the manor
of Heybridge, £18 16s. 4d.
Total: £106 3s. 2½d.

The Brewer
To Richard Prowell, brewer of London, for ale, as appears by
four tallies: £13 13s. 9d.

Penny Beer
To Alexander Berebrewer at 'le Hermitage', for 40 barrels and
one *kylderkyn* of penny beer, as shown in one tally.
Total: £2 1s. 0d.

Halfpenny Beer
To Alexander Berebrewer, for 14½ barrels of three-halfpenny
beer, as shown in one tally.
Total: £1 13s. 9d.

Livery
From William Bukke, draper of London:
Medley-coloured woollen cloth for the livery of the Dean's
servants at Christmas, £11 2s. 6d., as appears by one bill.
Black woollen cloth bought for the livery of the Dean's servants
for the burial[49] of King Edward IV, £4 9s., as appears by another
bill.
Three gowns given to three farmers of Belchamp St. Paul and
Wickham St. Paul, at 6s. 8d. each, totalling £1, as shown in
Roger's book.
Total: £16 11s. 6d.

---

[49] 9–19 April 1483 (see A. F. Sutton and L. Visser-Fuchs, 'The Royal Burials of the
House of York at Windsor', *The Ricardian*, xi (1997–99), no. 143, pp. 366–407).

Wine

To Charles Vyntener, £19 6s. 8d. for two casks (£16) and three
pipes (£1 6s. 8d.) of red wine and one hogshead (£2) of claret wine,
and £1 15s. for 35 gallons sweet wine called *Malmsey* at 12d. per
gallon.
Total: £21 1s. 8d.

Necessary Expenses

On goods and stuffs, including £3 2d. on spices, as appears by
three folios of necessaries and one folio of spices in the quarterly
paper.
Total: £9 7s. 5¼d.

Chaplains' Salaries

For the terms of the Nativity of St. John the Baptist 1482,[50]
Michaelmas 1482, Christmas 1482 and Easter 1483:
Thomas Cartwryght and Thomas Turnour, as shown in eight
acquittances, each receiving £3 6s. 8d., £6 13s. 4d.
William Roke, as shown in two acquittances, £2 13s. 4d. p.a.
Total: £9 6s. 8d.

Fees paid

To Sir Thomas Montgomery, knight, £4.
To Robert Forster, steward of the court of the demesnes of
Thorpe, Kirby and Walton, £2.
To John Hewyk, auditor of all lands and tenements of the
Dean, £3 6s. 8d.
To Master John Lokear, collector of Belchamp St. Paul
and Wickham St. Paul, £3.
Total: £12 6s. 8d.

Wages of servants

Wages and rewards at Michaelmas and Christmas 1482, and
Easter and the Nativity of St. John the Baptist 1483, as shown
in the quarterly paper.
Total: £27 0s. 0d.

Necessary Expenditure

For goods and stuffs for the Dean's apparel, as shown in two
folios of the quarterly paper.
Total: £7 13s. 7½d.

---

[50]   'Before the time of this account'.

Repairs

To the mill of Ratcliff, including the price of 4000 tiles (£1 2s.),
roof tiles, (2s.), and corner tiles, £3 11s. 10d.

In the manors of Belchamp St. Paul (£8 9s. 5½d.),[51] Wickham
St. Paul (£6 5s.),[52] and Ardleigh (£1), and to the mansion of the
Dean (2s. 2d.), as shown in four separate bills.

Total: £20 12s. 5½d.

Money paid to the Dean

To William Worsley on 20 December 1482, in royals.
Total: £7 10s. 0d.

Money paid to Thomas Bunewell

To Thomas Bunewell, for a claim he had at the end of his
account as steward of the household, at the time when the Dean
was riding to the soke and other demesnes in the county of
Essex, as is more fully told at the foot of his account.[53]
Total: 16s. 5d.

Sum total paid: £519 9s. 4½d.
And he owes: £9 13s. 5d.

Audit

Received from Edmund Counteys and John Bray, farmers of
Caddington and Kensworth, £5 3s. 10¼d.
And he owes: £14 17s. 3¼d.

Allowances:

Gifts to minstrels of the King and of other lords with the Dean,
as shown in one folio of the quarterly paper: £7 1s. 9d.

Expenses of Robert Forster, John Hewyk, Roger Radcliff and
other officials riding through the Dean's demesne lands to hold
court in the soke, settle matters between tenants, and supervise
repairs, as shown in the last folio of the quarterly paper: £2 11s. 10d.

And he owes: £5 3s. 10¼d.

Which is paid to William Worsley, Dean, before the auditor
without bill by the Dean's recognisance.

And quit.[54]

51 5s. crossed out.
52 10s. crossed out.
53 Margin: '*r[espice] Bounwell*', added at the time of audit.
54 Signed '*William Worsley, decanus Sancti Paule*' [*sic*], probably in his own hand.

5. RECEIVER'S ACCOUNT 1484–1485

This roll is damaged and incomplete. Returns for Norwell Overall and the Archdeaconry of Nottingham are missing, as are the returns from the estates of Bowes and Polehouse and London. The first, but damaged, return is from Ardleigh.[55] *This return contains the first legible references to the date of this account, viz. 'xv die Junii a[nn]o s[e]c[un]do regni dicti regis' and 'viij die July anno r[egni] r[egis] predicti iij'.*[56] *The roll consists of seven sheets, 31 cm wide. The undamaged portion of the first sheet is 15 cm wide and 15 cm long. The remaining sheets are 41–42 cm long.*

Receipts from Rents and Farms

Ardleigh
[...]
from ...St. John the Baptist last... £6 13s. 4d.
from William Frost farmer, five payments, £7 1s. 8d.
first 29 [...1484] £2 2s. 4d.
second time 20 January 1484, 20s.
third time 20 [...1484] ...6s. 8d.
fourth time 21 [...1484...]
fifth time 15 June 1484, 25s.
from John Fuldon, collector, £2 6s. 8d.
....August 1484 by his own hands 40s.
...2 Richard III by his own hands 6s. 8d.
from Thomas Bunewell, collector, £6 in three payments,
first on 22 April, £3.
second time 22 April [...]
third time 8 July 1485 [...][57]
Total: £35 8s. 4d.

Runwell
Received from John at [Hey] and John Herde: £26 1s. 0d.

---

[55] The total of £35 7s. 4d. is in line with other returns from Ardleigh. The name William Frost is legible and he appears in other accounts as a farmer of Wadende in Ardleigh. John Fuldon, collector for Ardleigh also appears. Thomas Bunewell contributed £6. These persons appear in the context of Ardleigh in accounts for other years.
[56] 15 June and 7 July 1485.
[57] Totalling £22 1s. 8d.

Caddington and Kensworth
John Bray and Edmund Counteys, farmers, in six payments: £55 0s. 0d.

Hackney
Nothing came to the accountant's hands: Nil

Willesden
William Northcote, farmer, in two payments, £4 16s. 8d.
Sale of wood, viz. of nine cart-loads of *dolwod* at 1s. 7d. per
cart (14s. 3d.), and for *bakens* sold by him in gross (8s.),
£1 2s. 3d.
Total: £5 18s. 11d.

Belchamp St. Paul
John Lokear, collector: £52 14s. 8d.

Thorpe, Kirby, and Walton in the soke
Thomas Bogas, bailiff, including £5 8s. 2d. in fines, £33 2s. 6½d.
John Carter, farmer of the rectory of Bancroft, in four
payments, £20 6s. 8d.
John German, farmer of the rectory of Kirby, in three
payments, £24.
Thomas Smith, farmer of Thorpe Hall, in two payments, £18.
John Kent, farmer of the tenement[58] of Thorpe, £5 6s. 8d.
John Toose, farmer of the manor of Walton, in eight
payments, £34 16s. 6d.
Total: £135 12s. 4½d.

Wickham St. Paul
John Lokear, farmer, in two payments: £20 0s. 0d.

Sutton
Robert Nevyll, farmer: £24 0s. 0d.

Drayton
Edmund Prentesse, farmer, £24.
Clement Cook, farmer, £2.
Total: £26 0s. 0d.

Heybridge
John Lindsey, £34 14s. 8d., and John Pere, £8 6s. 8d., from the
farms of the mill and manor, in eight payments.

---

[58] 'Rectory' crossed out.

Total: £43 1s. 4d.

Norton Folgate
William Hill, farmer, in two payments: £6 13s. 4d.

Deanery
John Bernard, procurator of the rectory of Chepyng Lambourn,
in five payments, £61 19s. 11d.[59]
John Hewet, miller of Ratcliff, in four payments, £14 13s. 4d.
Roger Frende, farmer of Acton manor, including allowances of
25s. for making a hedge and 6s. 8d. for a gown, £4 2s. 4d.
Total: £80 15s. 7d.

Total Receipts: £568 1s. 3½d.[60]

Expenditure
Rents
To the Bishop of London, quit rent, for the manor of
Chadsworth, £1 13s. 4d.
To Sir Richard Charlton, knight, for the manor of Bowes
and Polehouse as shown in one bill, £1 2d.
To the Earl of Essex, from the same manor, as shown in one
bill, 19s.
Total: £3 13s. 6d.

Daily Expenses
On meats, other victuals, stuffs and necessaries, as appears in
thirty folios of the paper book: £66 12s. 11½d.

To the Chamberlain of St. Paul's
For the estates held in farm by the Dean, as shown in three
bills: £208 10s. 4¼d.

The Clerk of the Bakehouse of St. Paul's
To Martin Jolyff, as shown in four bills, for wheat for bread,
£74 3s. 1d., and for 32 qr. wheat issuing from Heybridge, £7 19s.
Total: £82 2s. 1d.

The Brewer
To William Witheney, brewer of London, for ale, as shown by
three tallies: £15 1s. 9d.

---

[59]   This sum has been written over an erasure.
[60]   The sub total of the surviving entries is £511 5s. 6½d.

Beer
To Alexander Berebrewer, for 12½ barrels of beer at 2s. a barrel.
Total: £1 5s. 0d.

Wine
To Charles Vyntener, for two casks of red wine £10, for one
pipe of claret wine £2 15s., and for two *roundlets*, £1 16s.
Total: £14 11s. 0d.

Livery of servants
To William Hulme, draper of London, for:
Tawny-coloured woollen cloth for the livery of the Dean's
servants at Christmas, £11 10s. 10d.
One piece of *medley*-coloured woollen cloth for certain
servants on 14 July 1485, £4 8s.
Total: £15 18s. 10d.

Necessary Household Expenses
Goods and stuffs for the household, as shown in one folio of
the large paper book: £14 3s. 9¼d.

Expenses for the Dean's apparel
For various goods and stuffs for the Dean's apparel and other
necessities, as appears in one folio of the large book: £2 8s. 6d.

Chaplains' salaries
To Robert Combes and Thomas Turnour, each of them
receiving £3 6s. 8d. p.a., for the terms of the Nativity of St.
John the Baptist, Michaelmas, and Christmas 1484 and Easter
1485, as shown by eight acquittances, £6 13s. 4d.
To William Roke, as shown by four acquittances, £2 13s. 4d.
Total: £9 6s. 8d.

Fees Paid
To Sir Thomas Montgomery, knight, £4 p.a., as shown by an
acquittance.
To Robert Forster, steward of the court of Thorpe, Kirby and
Walton in Essex, £2 p.a.
To John Hewyk, auditor of all lands and tenements of the Dean,
at £3 6s. 8d. p.a.
To John Lokear, collector of Belchamp St. Paul and Wickham
St. Paul, at £3 p.a.
Total: £12 6s. 8d.

Stipends of servants

For wages and rewards at Michaelmas, Christmas, Easter and the
Nativity of St. John the Baptist.

Total: £27 8s. 4d.

Repairs to the mill at Ratcliff, as shown in four paper bills: £2 1s. 9½d.

Sum Total Paid: £475 10s. 2½d.

He owes: £92 11s. 1d.

Audit

Paid to minstrels of the King and other lords and to other
persons bringing gifts to the Dean, as shown in one folio of
the book, £2 12s. 8d.

For expenses of Robert Forster, John Hewyk, Roger Radcliff
and other officials riding through the demesnes of the Dean
to hold court, as shown in the large book, £2 1s.

Paid for spices, £2 3s. 5½d.

Paid for a pound of saffron bought at one time in gross, 13s. 4d.

Paid for four gowns bought for four farmers by the steward
according to the terms of their indentures on taking their farms,
all at 6s. 8d. each, viz. Master John Lokear as farmer of
Belchamp St. Paul, and as farmer of the rectory there, John
Grene, farmer of Wickham St. Paul, and Edmund Prentesse,
farmer of the manor of Drayton, £1 6s. 8d.

Paid on the order of the Dean for repairs to the Dean's mansion
in the tenure of Doctor Jane, as shown in two paper bills, 17s. 6d.

Paid for necessary repairs to the house of the Dean in the city of
London, as shown in one bill, 3s. 11d.

Paid to the collector of the King as a whole tenth for the King
granted at the feast of St. Martin[61] 1484 for the prebend of
Willesden, 8s.

Paid for the expenses of Roger (1s. 4d.) and of Robert
Stykeswolde riding to and from 'Wympill',[62] over two and a half
days, and for the expenses of Thomas Shaa (4d.) going to Eltham
on the order of the Dean, 1s. 8d.

Paid for his expenses for riding from London to
Heybridge in Essex, and remaining there for four days in
order to hold a court and receive money for the Dean, 8s. 4d.

---

[61]   11 November 1484.
[62]   'Wikampaule' crossed out. Possibly Wimpole, Cambs., which belonged to the
        Charltons.

Paid for the expenses of Master Marke, and of his men and other tenants there, for a court on the Monday before Michaelmas 1484, 7s. 11d.

Paid for the fee of Master Marke as steward of Heybridge, 8s. 4d.

Paid for expenses and costs incurred for mowing and reaping of corn at Heybridge and for various arrears from Heybridge in the time of John Lindsey, as shown in one bill, £2 5s. 4d.

Paid for expenditure on the storage of grain, as shown in one bill, £1 6s. 6d.

Paid for shoeing the horses of the Dean and his servants before this account 13s., and within this account 16s. 2d., as shown in four tallies, £1 9s. 2d.

And he owes: £75 17s. 3½d.

Paid to the Dean at Hackney.

And quit.

6. RECEIVER'S ACCOUNT 20 JULY 1487–20 JULY 1488

The roll is complete, and the first sheet is endorsed with the date of the account in a contemporary hand. The roll consists of eight sheets, 30 cm wide and sewn end to end. With the exception of sheet seven, which measures 23 cm in length, the sheets are 40–42 cm long.

Arrears: Nil

Receipts from Rents and Farms

York prebend
Nothing, as the revenues were paid directly to the Dean: Nil

Archdeaconry of Nottingham
Nothing answered for at this time: Nil

Norwell Overall with the rectory of Eakring, Notts.
Nothing, as the Dean took the revenues himself: Nil

Hackney
Thomas Bunewell, collector, part of the issues of this year
and of arrears from last year.
Total: £1 11s. 2d.

Sutton
Robert Nevyll, farmer: £30 14s. 9½d.

Tillingham
Edmund Shaa, farmer: £33 15s. 0d.

Bowes with Polehouse
Edward Westby and John Fox, farmers: £19 4s. 6½d.

London and part of the Deanery
John Clerk, collector: £27 10s. 6d.

Ardleigh
George Retford, farmer of the manor, £20.
William Frost, farmer of Wadendé, £8 10s.
Thomas Bunewell, collector, £9 16s. 8d.
Total: £38 6s. 8d.

Runwell
John Bek, farmer: £30 13s. 4d.

Caddington and Kensworth
John Bray and Edmund Counteys, farmers: £61 15s. 2d.

Willesden
William Northcote, from the prebend (£2), William Swete from
the farm of the grace (£8), and £1 3s. from the sale of wood.
Total: £9 3s. 0d.

The Deanery
Thomas Garrard, procurator of the rectory of Chepyng
Lambourn, £60.
William Hewet, farmer of Ratcliff mill, £11 6s. 10d.
Joan Frende, farmer of Acton, £5 7s. 4d., in full payment for
the farm [–], beyond 6s. 8d. allowed for a gown for the said
Joan as farmer there.
Nicholas Colles, part of the issues proceeding by virtue of his
office as scribe of the commissary of the Deanery of London,
for three years, £5 9s. 2d.
Total: £82 3s. 4d.

Belchamp St. Paul
Geoffrey Downing, farmer of the manor, £20.
Thomas Watson, farmer of the rectory, £13 6s. 8d. and as
collector of rents of assize, £22 2s. 6d., in six payments.
Total: £55 9s. 4d.[63]

Thorpe, Kirby and Walton in the soke
Thomas Bogas, bailiff, issues of office and farm of the rectory
of Kirby, £46.
John Carter, farmer of the rectory of Bancroft, £8 6s. 8d.
Robert Orreys, late farmer of Thorpe Hall, in full payment
of his arrears, and John Percy, farmer now, £10 13s. 4d.
John Kent, (40s.) late farmer of 'Kent's tenement', and John
Saver, in two payments, £6.
John Toose, farmer of 'Walton Hall', £22 3s. 4d.
£13 15s. 3½d., fines and amercements from a court of tenants
held in Kirby, 1485–86.
Total: £106 18s. 7½d.

---

[63] *Recte* £55 9s. 2d.

Norton Folgate
Richard Ballard, farmer of the grace, part of his farm for a
year to St. Peter ad Vincula 1487:   £5 5s. 6d.

Wickham St. Paul
John Grene, farmer: £20 0s. 0d.

Barling
Richard Bower, farmer, for Purification term 1487:   £1 9s. 0d.

Heybridge
Geoffrey Dallyng, farmer of the manor and collector of rents
of assize, £32.
John Pere, farmer of the mills, £3 12s. 6d.
Total: £35 12s. 6d.

Drayton
Edmund Prentesse, farmer of the manor, £24 and Clement
Cook, farmer of the mill, 20s.
Total: £25 0s. 0d.

Total receipts: £584 12s. 5½d.

Expenditure
Rent
To Michaelmas 1488:
To the Bishop of London, £1 13s. 4d.
To the heir of Sir Richard Charlton, knight, for the same
term, to the manor of Bowes and Polehouse, £1 2d.
To Edmund, lord Roos, from Bowes and Polehouse to
Edmund's manor of Shingleford, Essex, 19s.
Total: £3 12s. 6d.

Daily Expenses
On meat, victuals, stuffs and necessaries, as shown in
twenty-three folios of the paper book: £48 11s. 6d.

The Chamberlain of St. Paul's
To Martin Jolyff, chamberlain, for the estates held to farm
by the Dean, as shown by [–] bill: £240 6s. 10d.

The Clerk of the Bakehouse
To Martin Jolyff, clerk of the bakehouse, for wheat to make
bread, £95 18s., and 32 qr. wheat issuing from the manor of

Heybridge, £9 15s. 8d.
Total: £105 13s. 8d.

The Brewer
To the [–] brewer of 'le Herteshorne',[64] London, for ale, as
shown by three tallies: £14 0s. 0d.

Beer
To [Alexander] Berebrewer for various barrels of beer bought
from him at various times, as shown by a tally: 9s. 0d.

Wine
To Charles Vyntener for:
Two casks of red wine at £6 13s. 4d. per cask.
One *tercion* of red wine at £1 2s. 3d. per *tercion*.
Three hogsheads claret wine at £1 13s. 4d. per hogshead.
One *tercion* claret wine at the price of the above red wine.
One hogshead white wine, £1 13s. 4d.
Two *roundlets* of sweet wine, holding altogether 33 gallons and
one potell,[65] at 12d. per gallon.
Of which, two casks of red wine, three hogsheads of claret wine,
one hogshead of white wine and two *roundlets* of sweet wine to
the Dean's household at London, and two *tercions* of red wine
and claret to the household at Hackney.
Total: £22 18s. 0d.[66]

Livery
To [William] Bukke, draper of London:
'Sad medley'-coloured woollen cloth, for the livery of the
Dean's servants at Christmas, £8 18s.
Tawny-coloured woollen cloth, for the summer livery,
£4 8s. 6½d.
Total: £13 6s. 6½d.

Necessary Expenses
On goods and stuffs for the household, as appears in one folio
of the large book: £12 7s. 6¾d.

Necessary Expenses for the Dean's apparel
Goods and stuffs for the dean's apparel, and other necessities,

---

64   A brewhouse near the Tower of London.
65   In this case, ½ gallon.
66   £23 18s., in fact the correct figure, is amended to £22 18s.

as appears in one folio of the large book: £3 14s. 7½d.[67]

Chaplains' Salaries

For the terms of the Nativity of St. John the Baptist,
Michaelmas, Christmas, and Easter:
Robert Combes, as shown by an acquittance, £3 6s. 8d.
John Farman, as shown by an acquittance, £3 6s. 8d.
William Roke, as shown by two acquittances, £2 13s. 4d. from
the manor of Norton Folgate.

Total: £9 6s. 8d.

Fees Paid

To Sir Thomas Montgomery, knight, £4.
To William Clarkson, steward of the court of the demesnes of
Thorpe, Kirby and Walton, £1 6s. 8d.
To Thomas Watson, chaplain, collector of Belchamp St. Paul
and Wickham St. Paul, £2.
To John Saperton, auditor of all the lands and tenements of
the Dean, £2.

Total: £9 6s. 8d.

Stipends of servants

Wages at the terms of Michaelmas, Christmas, Easter and the
Nativity of St. John the Baptist: £21 12s. 0d.

Repairs

On defects of the Dean's mansion next to St. Paul's, £1 1d.
Repairs made by John Hey and John Herde late farmers of the
manor of Runwell in 1485–86, as shown in a bill, 14s. 6½d.

Total: £1 14s. 7½d.

Sum Total Money Paid £506 19s. 8¼d.

And he owes £77 12s. 9¼d.

Audit

Paid 8s. to John, abbot of the monastery of St. James the
Apostle at Walden, collector of a whole tenth in the archdeaconries of London and Middlesex, granted to the King by
the clergy in 1486–87, viz. for the prebend of Willesden at
the feast of the Nativity of St. John the Baptist 1487, and at

---

[67]　72s. 6½d. crossed out.

the feast of St. Andrew the Apostle,[68] 1487, as appears by two acquittances sealed with the abbot's seal of office.

Paid to Robert Frende, collector, by William Swete on 7 February 1488 for the grace of the rectory of Willesden, as shown by another acquittance, 4s.

Paid for spices bought for the household, £1 4d.

Paid on the order of the Dean as gifts to mimes and minstrels of the King and other lords and others bringing gifts to the Dean, as shown in one folio of the book of payments, £2 17s. 6d.

Paid for the expenses of Roger Radcliff, William Clarkson, and John Saperton, riding to the demesne of Thorpe, Kirby and Walton and to other parts of the demesnes of the Dean to hold court and receiving revenue, £1 9s. 10½d.

Paid for four gowns at 6s. 8d. each given to four farmers on taking up their farms, viz. to the rent-collector of Belchamp St. Paul, to the farmer of the rectory there, to John Grene, farmer of Wickham St. Paul, and to Edmund Prentesse, farmer of Drayton, £1 6s. 8d.

Paid to the collector, John, prior of Hurley, of half a tenth lately granted to king, payable at the feast of St. John the Baptist 1487, and the feast of St. Andrew the Apostle 1487, as shown by two acquittances, £5 6s. 8d.

Paid for shoeing the horses of Roger Radcliff, William Clarkson and John Saperton, for their riding at this time, 5d.

Paid to Arnold Arnoldson for a lock bought for a door of his tenement, 3d.

Paid for 2½ qr. wheat bought for the bakehouse of St. Paul's, 10d.

Paid for two keys bought for two locks for the dwelling house at London, 7d.[69]

And he owes: £64 17s. 7¾d.

Paid to the Dean at Hackney, 19 July 1488.

And quit.

---

[68]   30 November.
[69]   Totalling £12 15s. 1½d.

7. RECEIVER'S ACCOUNT 20 JULY 1488-7 AUGUST 1489

The roll is complete and the first sheet is endorsed with the date of the account in a contemporary hand. The roll consists of seven sheets 30 cm wide and sewn end to end. With the exception of the first sheet, which measures 28 cm, and sheet five which measures 37 cm in length, the sheets are 40–42 cm long.

Arrears: Nil

Receipts from Rents and Farms

York Prebend
Nothing, as the revenues were paid directly to the Dean: Nil

Archdeaconry of Nottingham
Nothing rendered to Roger's hands: Nil

Norwell Overall with the rectory of Eakring, Notts.
Nothing received, as the issues and revenues were paid directly to
the Dean: Nil

Hackney
Nothing received of annual revenues of £16, because Thomas
Bunewell, collector, had all issues and profits and must answer
to the Dean: Nil

Sutton
Robert Nevyll, farmer: £26 0s. 0d.

Tillingham
John Shaa, farmer: £45 0s. 0d.

Bowes and Polehouse
Edward Westby and John Fox, farmers: £27 13s. 4d.

London with a part of the Deanery
John Clerk, collector, and by the hands of various tenants: £35 5s. 0d.

Ardleigh
George Retford, farmer of the manor, £20.
William Frost, farmer of Wadende, £4 12s. 8½d.
Thomas Bunewell, collector, £9 10s.

Total: £34 2s. 8½d.

Runwell
John Bek, farmer: £35 17s. 0d.

Caddington and Kensworth
John Bray, £33 15s. 8d., and Edmund Counteys, £8 10s.
Total: £42 5s. 8d.

Willesden
William Northcote, for the prebend, £3 13s. 4d.
William Swete, farmer of the grace, £12.
William Swete, from the sale of wood, £1 5s.
Total: £16 18s. 4d

The Deanery
Revenue, including 16s. received from the correctors of the
Deanery by the hand of Master Nicholas Colles: £88 0s. 0d.

Belchamp St. Paul
Geoffrey Downing, farmer of the manor, £20.
Thomas Watson, farmer of the rectory, £13 6s. 8d., and as
collector, £22 2s. 6d.
Total: £55 9s. 4d.[70]

Thorpe, Kirby and Walton in the soke
Thomas Bogas, bailiff, and farmer of Kirby rectory, £46 9d.
John Carter, late farmer of Bancroft rectory in Walton,
£12 6s. 8d.
John Percy, farmer of Thorpe manor and rectory, £8.
William Saver, junior, farmer of 'Kent's tenement' in Thorpe,
£4.
John Toose, farmer of Walton, £38 11s.
Fines and amercements, £6 9d.
Total: £114 19s. 2d.

Norton Folgate
Edmund Hill, farmer, by the hand of John Saperton at the time
of audit.   £1 6s. 8d.

Wickham St. Paul
John Grene, farmer: £20 0s. 0d.

---

[70]   *Recte £55 9s. 2d.*

Barling
Richard Bower, farmer, in one full payment: £11 0s. 0d.

Heybridge
Geoffrey Dallyng, farmer of the manor and the mills: £51 13s. 4d.

Drayton
Edmund Prentesse, farmer of the manor, and Clement Cook,
farmer of the mill: £26 0s. 0d.

Total Receipts £631 10s. 6½d.

Expenditure

Rent to Michaelmas 1488.
Quit rent to the Bishop of London, to the manor of
Chadsworth, by an acquittance, £1 13s. 4d.
To the heir of Sir Richard Charlton, knight, for the manor of
Bowes and Polehouse, by an acquittance, £1 2d.
To Edmund, Lord Roos, for the manor of Bowes and
Polehouse, by an acquittance, 19s.
Total: £3 12s. 6d.

Daily Expenses
On meat, victuals, stuffs and necessaries as shown in twenty-six
folios of the paper book: £60 19s. 0d.

Necessary Household Expenses
On goods and stuffs, as shown in one and a half paper folios.
For carriage of fuel, £5 5s. 11d.
For ditching and hedging of a wood at Willesden, and for the
keeping and guarding of osier beds in the wood, £1 6s. 1½d.
Total: £16 7s. 3¾d.

Necessary Expenses
Goods and stuffs for the Dean's apparel and other necessities, as
shown in one folio of the large paper book: £7 1s. 6d.

Stipends of servants
Wages and rewards at the terms of Michaelmas, Christmas,
Easter and the Nativity of St. John the Baptist.
Total: £21 1s. 8d.

Livery, from [William] Bukke, draper of London:
For russet-coloured woollen cloth bought for the livery of the
Dean's servants at Christmas, £9 5s. 4½d.
For medley-coloured woollen cloth bought for the summer
livery of certain servants, as shown in a bill, £4 16s. 4½d.
Total: £14 1s. 9d.

The Brewer
To the brewer of 'le Herteshorne' of London, and to a brewer at
Hackney for ale bought, in allowance to him until Relic Sunday,
as shown in divers tallies.[71]
Total: £17 11s. 6d.

Wine
Purchased from Charles Vyntener:
Two and a half casks of red wine, (£5 6s. 8d. per cask), £13 6s. 8d.
Three hogsheads of claret wine and one hogshead of white wine,
amounting between them to one cask, £5 6s. 8d.
Three *tercions* of red wine and claret sent to the household of
the Dean at Hackney, at 17s. 9¼d. per *tercion*, £1 15s. 6½d.
Two *roundlets* of sweet wine containing 38 gallons and one
potell, price per gallon, 12d.
Total: £22 7s. 4½d.

Spices: 18s. 6d.

The Clerk of the Bakehouse
To Martin Jolyff for:
Wheat for making bread, £101 3s. 1¼d.
Thirty-two qr. wheat issuing from the manor of Heybridge,
£10 4s. 6¾d., in payment for 32 qr. for this year, and
for ½ qr. and 3 bs. of wheat, arrears from last year.
Total: £111 7s. 7¾d.[72]

The Chamberlain of St. Paul's
To Martin Jolyff, chamberlain, for the estates held in farm
by the Dean, as shown in four bills: £246 1s. 4d.

---

[71]   12 July 1489.
[72]   *Recte* £111 7s. 8d.

Chaplains' salaries

for the terms of the Nativity of St. John the Baptist,
Michaelmas, Christmas and Easter:
Robert Combes, by an acquittance, at £3 6s. 8d. p.a.
John Farman, by an acquittance, at £3 6s. 8d. p.a.
William Roke, by an acquittance, at £2 13s. 4d. p.a.

Total: £9 6s. 8d.

Fees Paid

To Sir Thomas Montgomery, knight, at £4 p.a., by an
acquittance.
To William Clarkson, steward of the court of the demesnes of
Thorpe, Kirby and Walton, at £1 6s. 8d. p.a.
To Thomas Watson, collector of Belchamp St. Paul and
Wickham St. Paul, at £2 p.a.
To John Saperton, auditor of all the lands and tenements of
the Dean, at £2 p.a.

Total: £9 6s. 8d.

Repairs

On defects of the mansion of the Dean next to St. Paul's,
including 3s. for making and positioning of the bars outside
the door of the said mansion, as shown in a bill: £1 3s. 1½d.

Sum total paid: £541 6s. 6½d.
He owes: £90 4s. 0d.

Audit

To John, abbot of St. Peter, Westminster, collector of the
first half of a subsidy granted to the King in the last
convocation by the prelates and clergy, viz. for the prebend
of Willesden, by an acquittance made on 20 March 1489, 8s.
To the collector of the King for the grace of Willesden by
the hand of William Swete, farmer of the grace, by an
acquittance, 4s.
Gifts by the order of the Dean to mimes and minstrels of the
King and other lords and to various other persons, as shown
in one folio of payments, £2 16s. 8d.
To the King for a fifteenth for the manors of Bowes and
Polehouse at the terms of St. Martin in Winter and St. John
the Baptist, 13s. 4d.
To the lord of Edmonton for release of a suit of court (12d.)
and for money called Peter's Pence (4d.), 1s. 4d.

For the expenses of the accountant, William Clarkson and John Saperton, riding to and from Thorpe, Kirby and Walton and other parts of the Dean's demesne at the feasts of St. Anne 1488 and 1489 to hold court and collect money, £2 3s. 6d.

For the expenses of Roger and John riding from London to Caddington and Kensworth in Bedfordshire at the feasts of St. Peter ad Vincula 1488 and 1489 to receive money and to supervise the good state of the demesnes, together with 7d. for their expenses riding to the mansion of Master Lovell in Enfield upon the Dean's business, 6s. 2½d.

Paid for shoeing the Dean's horses, as shown by a tally, 5s. 7d.[73]

For five gowns at 6s. 8d. each, granted by the Dean to five farmers on the taking of their farms, viz. to the collector of rents of assize at Belchamp St. Paul, to the farmer of the rectory there, and to the farmers of Wickham St. Paul, Drayton, and Willesden, £1 13s. 4d.

The price of a gown for Thomas Morys, not paid for in the livery at the term of the Nativity of St. John the Baptist in the preceding year, as shown in a bill, 4s. 8½d.

Paid to William Clarkson for his fee as steward of the soke for a whole year ending on the feast of St. Peter ad Vincula 1489, £1 6s. 8d. [74]

He owes: £80 0s. 8½d.[75]

Paid to the Dean at Hackney, 7 August 1489.

And quit.

---

[73] 5s. 6d. crossed out.
[74] The total of the sums allowed at the audit is £10 3s. 4d.
[75] *Recte* £80 8d.

8. RECEIVER'S ACCOUNT 1489-1490

The roll is damaged at the head, but is apparently complete. It consists of seven sheets 28cm wide. The first (badly damaged) sheet is about 31 cm long and the seventh sheet 24 cm long. The remaining sheets measure 37–38 cm.

Arrears: Nil

Receipts from Rents and Farms

Prebend of York
Nothing received, because all to the Dean's hands: Nil

Archdeaconry of Nottingham Nil

Prebend of Norwell Overall with the rectory of Eakring
Nothing received, because the Dean received all revenues: Nil

Hackney
Thomas Bunewell, collector, received all issues and profits, worth
£16 p.a., and must answer to the Dean: Nil

Sutton
Master Odeby, one of the residentiaries must answer, for he
received all issues and profits: Nil

Tillingham
John Shaa, farmer: £45 0s. 0d.

Bowes and Polehouse
Edward Westby and John Fox, farmers: £18 8s. 2d.

London with a certain parcel of the Deanery of London
John Clerk, late collector, and William Trent, now collector: £28 0s. 3d.

Ardleigh
George Retford, farmer of the manor, £13 6s. 8d.
William Frost, farmer of Wadende, £7 2s. 3½d.
Thomas Bunewell, collector rents and farms, £10 13s. 4d.[76]
Sale of wood, £2 9s. 5½d.
Total: £33 11s. 9d.

---

[76]   ½d. crossed out.

Runwell
John Bek, farmer: £32 0s. 0d.

Caddington and Kensworth
John Bray, £38 15s. 4½d.
Edmund Counteys, £11.
Total: £49 15s. 4½d.

Willesden
William Northcote, for the prebend, £3 15s.,[77] including a parcel
of £1 13s. 4d.
William Swete, for the farm of the grace, £12.
William Swete, for the sale of wood, 6s.
Total: £16 1s. 0d.

The Deanery
Issues, including £2 15s. 3d. from the correctors of the Deanery,
by the hand of Master Nicholas Colles: £71 15s. 11d.

Belchamp St. Paul
Geoffrey Downing, farmer, £20.
Thomas Watson, farmer of the rectory, £13 6s. 8d.
Thomas Watson, as collector of rents of assize, £22 2s. 8d.
Total: £55 9s. 4d.

Thorpe, Kirby and Walton in the soke
Thomas Bogas, bailiff and farmer of Kirby rectory, and
appruator of the rectory of Bancroft in Walton, £57 1s. 9d.
John Percy, farmer of Thorpe manor and rectory, £19.
William Saver junior, farmer of 'Kent's tenement' in Thorpe, £4.
John Toose, farmer of Walton, £48 2s. 11d.
Fines and amercements, £5 1½d.
Arrears of John Carter,[78] £4 15s. 4d.
Total: £138 0s. 1½d.

Norton Folgate
Edmund Hill (£1 6s. 8d.), John Stephens (£1 6s. 8d.), farmers
there, by the hand of John Saperton at the time of audit
without bill: £2 13s. 4d.

Wickham St. Paul
John Grene, farmer: £20 0s. 0d.

---

[77]   61s. 8d. crossed out.
[78]   Late farmer of the rectory of Bancroft.

Barling

Richard Bower, farmer, in one payment: £16 9s. 9d.

Heybridge

Geoffrey Dallyng, farmer of the manor and mill: £13 6s. 8d.

Drayton

Edmund Prentesse, farmer of the manor, £24.

Clement Cook, farmer of the mill, £0 20s. 0d.

Total: £25 0s. 0d.

Total Receipts: **£565 11s. 8d.**

Expenditure

Rent

To the Bishop of London, a quit rent for a year ending
at Michaelmas 1489, to the manor of Chadsworth, by
one acquittance, £1 13s. 4d.
To the heir of Sir Richard Charlton, knight, for the manor of
Bowes and Polehouse, by another acquittance, £1 2d.
To Edmund, Lord Roos, for the manor of Bowes and
Polehouse, to Edmund's manor of Shingleford in Essex, by an
acquittance, 19s.

Total: £3 12s. 6d.

Daily Expenses

On beef, veal, pork and other victuals, stuffs and necessaries,
as shown in twenty-four folios of the paper book, from
7 August 1489 to 17 July 1490: £60 0s. 9½d.

Necessary Household Expenses

Goods and stuffs, as shown in one paper folio including £3 6d.
for making and carriage of fuel, 4s. 2d. spent on hedging and
ditching at Willesden to keep the woods there, and 16s. for a
hedge and its making.

Total: £10 11s. 2¾d.

Necessary Expenses for the Dean's apparel

Goods and stuffs for the Dean's apparel and other necessities,
as appears in half a paper folio of the large book: 18s. 1d.

Stipends of servants

Wages at Michaelmas, Christmas, Easter and the Nativity of
St. John the Baptist, as appears in the steward's book: £22 6s. 8d.

Livery
From [William] Bukke, draper of London:
For medley-coloured woollen cloth, for the livery of the Dean's
servants, as shown in Roger's book of payments, £9 5s.
For one medley-coloured woollen cloth, for the summer livery
of certain servants, as shown in a paper bill, £5 11s. 9d.
Total: £14 16s. 9d.

The Brewer
To the brewer of 'le Herteshorne', London, for ale, as shown by
various tallies: £18 7s. 9d.

Wine
From Charles Vyntener:
Two casks and one hogshead of red wine, at £7 per cask, £15 15s.
Three hogsheads claret wine, at £1 15s. per hogshead, £5 5s.
Two *roundlets* sweet wine called *Malmsey*, containing
36 gallons per *roundlet*, at 12d. per gallon, £1 16s.
Total: £22 16s. 0d.

Spices, as shown in the accountant's book: £2 0s. 9d.

The Clerk of the Bakehouse of St. Paul's
To Martin Jolyff, late clerk of the bakehouse, and to Laurence
Butler and John Farman, now clerks, for wheat for making
bread, £95 3s. 1d.
To Martin, for 32 qr. wheat, yearly issuing from the manor
of Heybridge, £8 1s. 10d.
Total: £103 4s. 11d.

The Chamberlain of St. Paul's
To Martin Jolyff, late chamberlain of St. Paul's, and to Laurence
Butler and John Farman, now chamberlains, for the estates
held in farm by the Dean, as shown in four bills of indenture: £230 3s. 6½d.

Chaplains' salaries
For the terms of the Nativity of St. John the Baptist,
Michaelmas, Christmas, and Easter, as shown by acquittances:
To Robert Combes, £3 6s. 8d.
To John Farman, £3 6s. 8d.
To William Roke, £2 13s. 4d.
Total: £9 6s. 8d.

Fees

To Sir Thomas Montgomery, knight, at £4 p.a., cancelled
because paid by the Dean himself.
To William Clarkson, steward of the court of the demesnes of
Thorpe, Kirby and Walton at £1 6s. 8d. p.a., cancelled because
allowed at the foot of the account of the previous year.
To Thomas Watson, chaplain, collector of Belchamp St. Paul
and Wickham St. Paul, £2 p.a.
To John Saperton, auditor of all lands and tenements of the
Dean, at £2 p.a.

Total:	£4 0s. 0d.

Repairs

To the mill of Ratcliff and the tenements annexed to the mill,
along with £5 for a mill-stone, as shown in four bills, £13 3s. 2d.
To various water-ditches leading from the Thames to the
mill, 382 rods at 18d. per rod, £28 13s.
To defects in the mansion of the Dean in London with
13d. spent on the repair of the tenement of Master Nykke
in Ivy Lane, as shown in one paper folio, £3 3s.

Total:	£44 19s. 2d.

Total Paid:	£547 4s. 9¾d.
And he owes:	£18 6s. 10¼d.

Audit

To Thomas, prior of Holy Trinity, London, collector of the
second half of a subsidy granted to the King in the last
convocation of prelates and clergy for the prebend of
Willesden, as shown by an acquittance made on 5 October
1489, 8s.
To the collector of the King by the hand of William Swete,
farmer of the grace of Willesden, by an acquittance, 4s.
To the abbot of Abingdon before 1 November, collector of
the second half of a subsidy granted to the King in the last
convocation of prelates and clerics, for the church of
Lambourn, by an acquittance, £5 6s. 8d.
To the lord of Edmonton for release of a suit of court and
for money called Peter's Pence, as shown in Roger's book,
16d.
Grant by the Dean to five farmers (6s. 8d. each, as in the
preceding account) on the taking of their farms, viz. to the
collector of rents of Belchamp St. Paul, to the farmer of the

rectory there, and to the farmers of Wickham St. Paul, Drayton, and Willesden, £1 13s. 4d.

To a certain smith for shoeing horses of the Dean, by a tally and at the recognisance of Thomas Morys, the keeper of the horses, before the auditor at the time of the audit of this account, 8s. 6d.

To William Wyle, hosier of London, for three pairs of shoes, (12d.) and for four pairs of socks (8d.), and three pointed *doss* (6d.), bought for the apparel of the Dean, as shown in a bill of particulars, 8s. 2d.

To Richard Milen, saddler of London, for mending saddles and other things and stuffs, as shown in another bill, 6s. 11d.

To the wife of Thomas Shaa for her work in washing linen sheets and other things for the Dean, as shown by a tally, 14s. 7d.

Gifts on order of the Dean to various mimes and minstrels of the King and other lords and to other persons bringing gifts, as shown in half a folio of Roger's book of payments, £1 8s. 8d.

On the order of the Dean the price of 3 qr. of woollen cloth bought to make a hood for John Slade, chaplain, 2s. 3d.[79]

And he owes: **£6 19s. 5¼d.** [80]

Paid to the Dean at Hackney on 17 July 1490, by the recognisance of the Dean, before the auditor, without bill.

[79] In margin: Total, £11 7s. 5d. and he owes £6 19s. 5¼d. The sums allowed at audit total £11 2s. 5d.
[80] *Recte £7 4s. 5¼d.*

9. RECEIVER'S ACCOUNT 10 JULY 1495 TO 21 JULY 1496

The roll is complete and has the date of the account inscribed on the back of the first sheet. It consists of six sheets, measuring 30 cm in width and 41–43 cm in length.

Receipts from Rents and Farms

Willesden
William Swete, farmer, £4 16s. 8d.
William Swete, farmer of the grace, for a year at
Annunciation 1496, £12.
Total: £16 16s. 8d.

Archdeaconry of Nottingham   Nil

Prebend of York   Nil

Prebend of Norwell Overall   Nil

Hackney
Nothing received. Thomas Bunewell, collector, received it all
and is answerable to the Dean: Nil

Foreign Receipts
From Thomas Orston[81] in several payments: £84 11s. 4d.

Archdeaconry of Taunton
Master Robert Godde, official of the Archdeaconry, in several
payments: £54 9s. 5d.

Deanery
Thomas Garrard farmer of the rectory of Lambourn, £83 6s. 8d.
Robert Frende, farmer of Acton, £11 8s.
[–] Hudson, farmer of the mill of Ratcliff, £22.
Total: £116 14s. 8d.

Belchamp St. Paul
Geoffrey Downing, farmer of the manor, £30.
Thomas Watson, farmer of the rectory, £20.

---

[81]   Acted for the Dean in Nottinghamshire and Yorkshire (cf. appendix 2).

Thomas Watson, collector of rents of assize, £33 4s.
Total: £83 4s. 0d.

Thorpe, Kirby and Walton in the soke
John Toose, farmer of the manor of Walton, £50 16s. 8d.
John Harnes, farmer of 'Kent's tenement', £4.
William Carter, farmer of Bancroft rectory, £15.
Thomas Bogas, bailiff and collector, £56 6s. 6d.
John Percy, farmer of 'Thorpe Hall', £9.
Total: £135 3s. 2d.

Norton Folgate
John Stephens, farmer, for part of his farm: £2 0s. 0d.

Wickham St. Paul
John Grene, farmer, in several payments: £30 0s. 0d.

Heybridge
Geoffrey Dallyng, farmer and collector of rents of assize and
farmer of the water mill, in several payments: £57 10s. 1d.

Drayton
The farm, £26 p.a., not answered for, because Master Audley, a
residentiary of St. Paul's, has the manor and appurtenances by
a grant from the Dean and Chapter, as in the previous account: Nil

Tillingham
Nothing received, because John Shaa, alderman of London,
holds the manor and appurtenances by a grant of the Dean and
Chapter, as in the previous account: Nil

Bowes and Polehouse
John Fox, farmer, in several payments: £36 13s. 4d.

London with a part of the Deanery
Henry[82] Sanders, collector of rents and farms, in several
payments: £27 3s. 4d.

Ardleigh
Thomas Bunewell, collector of rents of assize, £17 8s. 4d.
From Edmund Bardolf, farmer of the demesne lands, £29.
From William Frost, farmer of Wadende, £7 6s. 8d.
Total: £53 10s. 0d.[83]

---

[82] 'John' crossed out.

Caddington and Kensworth
John Bray (£47 6s. 8d.) and Richard Wynche (£51 2s. 4d.),
farmers, in several payments: £98 9s. 0d.

Runwell
John Bek, late farmer, £27 19s., and William Aleyn, now
farmer, £20:   £47 19s. 0d.

Total Receipts: £844 4s. 0d.

Expenditure
Rent
For a year to Michaelmas[84] 1495:
To the Bishop of London, quit rent, to the manor of
Chadsworth, £1 13s. 4d.
To the heir of Sir Richard Charlton, knight, for the manor
of Bowes and Polehouse, £1 2d.
To the bailiff of the heir of the said Richard Charlton for
respite of suit of court this year, 16d.
To the same bailiff for Peter's Pence, [also] called Romeshott, 4d.
To Sir Thomas Lovell, knight, to the manor of Shingleford,
for the manor of Bowes and Polehouse, by an acquittance, 19s.
Total: £3 14s. 0d.

Daily Expenses
On beef, veal, mutton, pork, salt and fresh fish, and other
victuals, stuffs and necessaries, from 5 June 1495 to 21 July 1496: £43 14s. 11d.

Necessary Household Expenses
Goods and stuffs bought from 5 June 1495 to 21 July 1496 with
£3 18s. 6d. for the provision and carriage of twenty-four carts
of fuel from Willesden to Hackney, and for the purchase of
five carts of coal:[85]   £8 4s. 3d.

Necessary Expenses for the Dean's apparel
Goods and stuffs for the Dean's apparel and other necessities: £1 5s. 4d.

Stipends of servants
Wages and rewards for a year to St. John the Baptist 1496:   £21 16s. 8d.

---

[83]   *Recte* 15s.
[84]   Easter term crossed out.
[85]   £5 15s. crossed out.

The Brewer

To the brewer of 'le Herteshorne' for ale bought between
Pentecost and October 1495, by two tallies, £4 14s. 9d.
To Richard Dene, brewer at Hackney, for ale bought from
5 June 1495 to 21 July 1496, by three tallies, £11 2s. 6d.
Total: £15 17s. 3d.

Wine

Two h[ogsheads] of red wine: £3 0s. 0d.

The Chamberlain of St. Paul's

To John Farman, chaplain, chamberlain of St. Paul's, for
the estates held in farm by the Dean for a year and a half
ending on Ascension Day 1496, as shown in six bills: £274 14s. 8½d.

The Clerk of the Bakehouse

To Laurence Butler:
On account of certain sums of money annually provided for
wheat for bread, beyond £1 10s. 9¾d. deducted for 23½ lbs. of
bread (at 10d. per lb.), viz., in payment of this money for a whole
year and a half ending on Ascension Day 1496, £91 17s. 10¾d.
And in part payment for 32 qr. wheat yearly issuing from
the manor of Heybridge, viz. for 22 qr. and 1 bs., beyond
25½ qr. 4 bs. paid to the same clerk from the Dean's
own wheat, viz., in payment for a whole year ending
on Ascension Day 1496, £4 5s. 10d.
Total: £96 3s. 8¾d.

Chaplains' salaries

For six terms, ending on the feast of the Annunciation 1496:
John Haryngton, at £3 6s. 8d. p.a., by an acquittance, £5.
John Farman, at £3 6s. 8d. p.a., for six terms, by six acquittances,
£5.
William Roke, at £2 13s. 4d. p.a., for six terms, by acquittances,
£4.
Total: £14 0s. 0d.

Fees

To Sir Reginald Bray, knight, at £10 p.a. for a year at the feast of
St. John the Baptist 1496, by an acquittance of Reginald
himself, testifying payment, £10.
To Sir Thomas Lovell, knight, at £10 p.a. granted to him for a
year ending at Christmas 1495, his fee for half a year, by an
acquittance, £5.

To Peter Peckham, gentleman, recently retained as of the
Dean's council, for a year ending at Christmas 1495, by a paper
bill testifying to the payment of the following sums, signed
with the sign manual of the Dean, £2 13s. 4d.
To Simon Digby, for a year ending at the feast of St. John the
Baptist 1496, by an acquittance, £5.
To John Alyff, deputy of the Earl of Oxford, chief steward
of all demesnes, manors, lands and tenements of the Dean in
Essex, for a year ending at the feast of St. Anne 1495, £1 6s. 8d.
To John Saperton, auditor of all the lands and tenements
of the Dean, £2.
To Thomas Watson, collector of Belchamp St. Paul and
Wickham St. Paul, at £2 p.a., £3.
Total: £29 0s. 0d.

Gifts and rewards
Gifts and rewards to certain people of the King's council and to
other lawyers on the Dean's orders, as shown in the
receiver's book of payments where names and sums are noted: £4 10s. 4d.[86]

Spices
As shown in the receiver's book of payments and by one bill of
particulars among the memoranda to this account: £2 10s. 4d.

Expenses of courts and riding servants
For the receiver, the auditor and stewards, two clerks and
servants riding from London to the soke and back in July,
and staying for the account etc., £1 4s. 8d.
For the auditor and receiver and two of their servants riding
from London to Caddington and Kensworth at the feast
of St. Peter ad Vincula 1495 to audit and settle the account of
the farmer, 3s. 8d.
For the receiver riding from London to Taunton and visiting for
19 days and the keeping of a horse for 19 days (7s. 8d.), £1 3s. 9d.
Total: £2 16s. 9d.[87]

Repairs
To Willesden manor, as shown in a bill, £1 13s. 3d.
To Ratcliff mill, as shown in several bills, [...].[88]
To the church of St. Paul's, paid to the hand of Thomas

---

[86]   £3 17s. 6d. crossed out.
[87]   *Recte* £2 12s. 1d.
[88]   The sum is illegible but should read £8 8d.

Smith, chaplain, £3 6s. 8d.

Total: £13 0s. 8d.

Paid to the procurator for the church of Ardleigh

To John Wryght, bachelor of decrees, and to William Stephens, licentiate of decrees, for two procurements[89] regarding the church of Ardleigh, in four payments over two years ending at Easter 1496, as shown by two acquittances sealed with the seals of his officials, attesting payment of the following sum: 15s. 0d.

First payment for a whole tenth

Paid at St. John the Baptist 1496:

To the abbot of Reading, collector of the King, for the first half of a whole tenth for the church of Lambourn, by an acquittance, £2 13s. 4d.

To Thomas Smith collector of the King for a first half of a whole tenth for the church of St. Paul's, by an acquittance, £5 18s.

To [John] Chace, deputy of [–], collector for a first half of a whole tenth for the church of Willesden prebend, 4s.

Total: £8 15s. 4d.

Necessaries and foreign payments

For expenses sailing from London to Sheen for certain matters of the Dean, as shown in Roger's book of expenses and in a bill of payments, 7s. 2d.

For beef and mutton, and various kinds of fish bought at various times to be sent to the Dean while in the Tower of London, as shown in a bill, £1 5s.

For expenses on the vigil of Holy Trinity 1496 for matins etc., 2s. 6d.

Payments to various ministers of the church for twenty-three days called feeding days ending on Relic Sunday[90] 1496, as shown in two bills, including one day not contained in the said bills, £5 6s. 8d.

For expenses of ministers of St. Paul's on Maundy Thursday 1496, 18s. 8½d.

Paid to the receiver concerning part of an order not paid at the time the Dean was staying in the Tower viz. 8 lb. sweetmeats (5s. 4d.) and one *kylderkyn* of ale (2s.), totalling 7s. 4d., taken by Robert Freman, chaplain.

To William Fox,[91] farmer of Bowes for one writ of

---

89   Payments to archdeacons.
90   10 July 1496.

replevin and other things thereto pertaining, 6s. 4d.
Total: £8 13s. 8½d.

To Peter Peckham, on the order of Master Dean

For all the money paid and spent by him to the use of the
Dean, as shown in three paper bills signed with the
Dean's sign manual, whereof one bill contains £3 6s. 8d.,
another £1 16s. 8d., and the third bill 4s.
Total: £5 7s. 4d.

To Master Bray, knight, for lands in Hackney

For the issues, lands, tenements and meadows late held
by the Dean in Hackney, now held by Reginald Bray,
for half a year ending at Christmas 1495, as shown
by an acquittance: £8 6s. 8d.

Board, while in the Tower

Paid to Simon Digby for the cost of the board of the Dean and
his servants in the Tower of London, for 16 weeks at 16s. 8d.
per week, by a paper bill signed with his sign manual remaining
among the memoranda of this year: £13 6s. 8d.

The cofferer of the King

To John Heron, by a bill made at Westminster, signed
with John's sign manual, 15 October 1495, £100.
To Sir Thomas Lovell, knight, by another bill signed with
Thomas's sign manual, made at London on 8 May 1496, £100.
To the King, by the hand of John Heron for all the money the
Dean owes the King upon a bond made on 28 June 1495, £35.
Total: £235 0s. 0d.

Paid to the Dean

At Hackney, immediately after the feast of St. Peter ad
Vincula 1495, in the presence of Thomas Bunewell: £10 0s. 0d.

Total Paid: £824 13s. 9½d.

And he owes: £19 10s. 2¼d.

---

[91]   *Recte* John Fox.

Audit

He is allowed:

For the gowns for six farmers on the taking of their farms, viz., the farmer of Acton for two years at Easter term 1496, the farmer of Ardleigh, the farmer of Willesden, and three farmers of Belchamp St. Paul and Wickham St. Paul, £2 6s. 8d.

Paid to a smith of Hackney for shoeing the horses and making one iron bucket, one pair of iron fetters and the piking of a staff of the Dean, as shown by a tally, 7s. 9d.

Roger asks to be allowed £3 18s. 10d. for his cash wages for the time when he stayed in his house at his own expense, viz. for 58 weeks and six days at 16d. per week.

For parchment bought and used, 6d.

For the expenses of the auditor staying in London for the settlement of this account, 2s. 8d.

He owes:

Paid to the Dean at Hackney on 21 July 1496 before the auditor.   £12 13s. 9¼d.

And quit.

10. VIEW OF ACCOUNT FOR THE ESTATES AND HOUSEHOLD, 1496–1497[92]

The roll is complete, but has no endorsement. It consists of two sheets, 30 cm wide and 43 cm long.

View of the account of Roger Radcliff, late the receiver of the Dean, of money received and paid or spent by him, from the 21 July 1496 until [–].

Receipts from Rents and Farms

Willesden
William Swete, farmer, for Michaelmas term 1496, £2 10d.
William Swete, farmer of the grace, for St. Peter ad Vincula 1496, besides the allowance for a gown, £5 13s. 4d.
Total: £7 14s. 2d.

Deanery
In three payments: £25 3s. 4d.

Thorpe, Kirby and Walton in the soke
Various officials, in seven payments: £104 19s. 9½d.

Norton Folgate
John Stephens, farmer, in part payment of the farm: £2 0s. 0d.

Belchamp St. Paul
The farmer, £36 in one payment, less 20s. for the fee of the collector and 20s. for three gowns, by a bill: £34 0s. 0d.

Heybridge
The farmer, in three payments: £15 12s. 2d.

Prebends of Southwell and York
Thomas Orston in two payments: £24 13s. 4d.

Archdeaconry of Taunton
In two payments: £48 6s. 7d.

---

[92]   Roger Radcliff died in December 1496: see appendix 2.

Bowes and Polehouse
The farmer, in two payments: £10 13s. 4d.

London
The collector, in two payments: £3 13s. 4d.

Ardleigh
Rents and farms in five payments: £16 12s. 11d.

Runwell
William Aleyn, farmer, for a year ending on the feast of St.
Peter ad Vincula 1496: £4 12s. 6d.

Caddington and Kensworth
The farmer, in four payments: £30 5s. 6d.

Total Receipts £328 6s. 11½d.

Expenditure

Daily Expenses
From 21 July to 23 December 1496, viz. for 22 weeks: £16 7s. 5½d.

Fee of the steward of the soke
To John Alyff, steward of the soke, at £1 6s. 8d. p.a. to the feast
of St. Peter ad Vincula 1496: £1 6s. 8d.

Salaries of three chaplains
By three acquittances: £2 6s. 8d.

Expenses of Necessaries: 19s.

Paid to the Dean
Paid in the presence of the auditor and Thomas Bunewell at
Hackney: £10 0s. 0d.

Ointment
1 oz., for the Dean's back: 2d.

Wages of the Household Servants
Wages for two terms at Christmas 1496: £9 8s. 4d.

Necessary Expenses
Expenses of the auditor, receiver and steward, including the
price of a horse: £3 11s. 3½d.

Money paid to the King
To the hand of John Heron in full payment of the annuity
of the King for half a year ending at Michaelmas 1496, £100.
To the King for a bond, £35.
Total: £135 0s. 0d.

Fee of Sir Thomas Lovell, knight
In part payment of his annuity of £10 p.a., viz. for half a year
ending on the feast of St. John the Baptist 1496, by an acquittance: £5 0s. 0d.

To Master Bray
For the issues of Hackney for the said half year: £8 6s. 8d.

To the Brewer
Richard Dene, for ale, by a bill dated 9 August 1497:   £11 2s. 6d.

Expenses of days called Feeding Days:
By one bill: £1 3s. 0d.

To the Clerk of the Bakehouse
For the terms of St. Peter ad Vincula and St. Martin in
Winter 1496, by two bills: £29 4s. 7½d.

To the Chamberlain of St. Paul's
For the same terms, by two bills: £79 8s. 3d.

Half a tenth
At St. Martin in Winter 1496:[93]   £5 18s. 0d.

A tenth
For the prebend of Willesden at St. Martin in Winter: 4s.

Roger Radcliff's Wages
22 weeks, at 16d. per week: £1 9s. 4d.

Allowed for a gown: 11s.

Total Paid: £321 7s. ¼d.[94]
And he owes: £6 19s. 11¼d.

---

[93]   11 November.
[94]   £327 crossed out.

11. ACCOUNTS OF MINISTERS ON CERTAIN ESTATES OF WILLIAM WORSLEY 1493-1494

The estates included in this account are Thorpe, Kirby and Walton, Heybridge, Runwell, Caddington and Kensworth. The manuscript consists of four sheets, 32 cm in width and 45 cm in length, inscribed on both sides of the sheet.

The Soke of St. Paul's, 1493-94
Walton manor
John Toose, farmer, for a year to the feast of St. Peter ad Vincula 1494.

Charges

Arrears:	£19 3s. 4d.
Farm of the manor:	£38 6s. 8d.
Total:	£57 10s. 0d.

Allowances and Payments

Part payment to Roger Radcliff of arrears from 1492–93:	£10 0s. 0d.
Issues of office for Purification term 1494:	£28 6s. 8d.
Carried Forward:	**£19 3s. 4d.**

Rectory of Bancroft in Walton
William Carter, farmer, for the same term.

Charges

Arrears:	£7 10s. 0d.
Farm of the rectory:	£15 0s. 0d.
Total:	£22 10s. 0d.

Allowances and Payments

Part payment of arrears:	£3 13s. 4d.
From arrears of the preceding year and from the issues of the farm:	£8 0s. 0d.
Carried Forward:	**£10 16s. 8d.**

Thorpe manor and rectory
John Percy, farmer, for the same term.

Charges

Arrears:	£43 6s. 8d.
Farm of the rectory and manor:	£18 0s. 0d.
Total:	£61 6s. 8d.

Allowances and Payments

Part payment of arrears:	£4 6s. 8d.
From arrears of the previous year:	£4 0s. 0d.
Carried Forward:	**£53 0s. 0d.**

'Kent's tenement' in Thorpe

John Harnes, farmer, for the same term.

Charges

Arrears:	£2 0s. 0d.
Farm of the tenement:	£4 0s. 0d.
Total:	£6 0s. 0d.

Allowances and Payments

Part payment of arrears:	£2 0s. 0d.
From the issues of the farm:	£2 0s. 0d.
Carried Forward:	**£2 0s. 0d.**

The office of bailiff and collector of rents in the soke

Thomas Bogas, bailiff and collector of rents of assize, Easter term 1493–94.

Charges

Arrears: £34 4s. 8d.

Rents of assize:
from Walton £6 13s. 7¾d.
from Kirby £12 4¼d.
from Thorpe £19 1s. 3d.

Total: £37 15s. 3d.

New rent:
At Thorpe, 4s.
From Thomas Bover[95] for a water mill newly built on a piece of land in Thorpe, 15 perches and 1 rod in length and 1 perch in width, 5s.
From William Thurston for ½a. of land in Thorpe, parcel of 'Hobbesdale', let to William in the court in 1485–86, 1s.[96]

Total:[97] 10s. 0d.

Total charges: £72 9s. 11d.

Allowances

Reductions in rent:
Tithes returned and decreases from lands and tenements in Walton, Thorpe and Kirby, £1 4s.
Tithes for the farm of the land called 'Frevelland', 1s.
Tithes for the lands of John Hykman, 8d.
Decreases in 6a. of land of John Toose in Walton, 4d.
Tithes for the previous year paid for the farm of a bakehouse formerly held by John Burgh and in the lord's hand this year

---

95 'Bower' crossed out.
96 '13s. 4d. from certain lands and tenements in Kirby taken into the King's hands for certain reasons after the death of Thomas Michell of Kirby' crossed out.
97 Margin: Memorandum of 1 pipe and 1 hogshead claret wine from a wreck at sea, which were not valued by the homage.

as in preceding years, 12d.

Decreases of the farm of a bakehouse in Walton, formerly
held in farm by the said John Burgh, this year in default of
a farmer, 6d.

Total:	£1 7s. 6d.
The stipend of the bailiff, £1 13s. 4d., and his reward, 6s. 8d.:	£2 0s. 0d.

Repairs:

To the manor, the pale of the park, the church chancel, and
houses of 'Kent's tenement' in Thorpe, £3 1s. 2d.

To the houses of the manor and to sea walls and earthworks
called the sea dyke in Walton, £1 14s. 8d.

Total:	£4 15s. 10d.

Payments

In part payment of arrears of the preceding year, on 24 October
£4, on 7 December £9, on 17 April £7, on 27 June £2, on

10 July £5, totalling:	£27 0s. 0d.
From the issues of the office:	£14 0s. 0d.
Total Allowances and Payments:	£49 3s. 4d.
Carried Forward:	£23 6s. 7d.

Thomas Bogas, as bailiff and collector of profits of courts

Charges

Arrears:	£6 4s. 4½d.

Profits of the court at Kirby held on the feast of St. Anne 1493:

Homage of Thorpe, (fines £3 3s. 11d., amercements 2s. 7d.)
£3 6s. 6d.

Homage of Kirby, (fines £3 3s. 6¾d., amercements 1s. 7d.)
£3 5s. 1¾d.

Homage of Walton, (fines £9 3d., amercements 7s. 4d.)
£9 7s. 7d.

Total of profits of court:	£15 19s. 2¾d.
Total charges:	£22 3s. 7¼d.

Payments

Fines from before the time of this account from John Hugh, John Cleydon, John Broke and John Rokes:	£5 12s. 2d.
Fines from the court held on the feast of St. Anne 1493 from various tenants:	£9 1s. 11½d.
Amercements from 1491–92 from various unfree persons:	8s. 8d.
From arrears of the previous year:	£4 0s. 0d.[98]
Carried Forward:	£3 0s. 9¾d.[99]

---

[98]   The total of allowances and payments is £19 2s. 9½d.
[99]   5s. crossed out.

Heybridge manor, including the farm of the mills
Geoffrey Dallyng, bailiff and farmer.
Charges
Arrears:	£28 0s. 0d.
Farm of the manor:	£43 0s. 0d.
Farm of the water mill and fulling mill:	£7 13s. 4d.
Total:	£78 13s. 4d.

Allowances and Payments
Repairs to the mill:	£5 19s. 0d.
Repairs to a bridge called 'Cowebryge':	8s. 8d.
Repairs on the manor:	4s. 4d.
Part payment by Robert Barlowe of arrears of the preceding year, by a bill made 29 August 1493:	£10 0s. 0d.
£18 from arrears and £16 from the issues of office:	£34 0s. 0d.
To the receiver:	£12 0s. 0d.[100]
Carried Forward:	**£16 1s. 4d.**

Runwell manor
John Bek, farmer.
Charges
Arrears:	£22 15s. 4d.
Farm of the manor:	£36 10s. 0d.
Total:	£59 5s. 4d.

Allowances and Payments
Repairs to the southern chamber of the manor house and others of its houses:	£3 10s. 7d.
Paid to Roger Radcliff (22 April 1493, £8, 23 December 1493, £6 13s. 4d., 29 January 1494, £4, 8 July 1494, £10):	£28 13s. 4d.
To the receiver:	£1 1s. 5d.[101]
Carried Forward:	**£26 0s. 0d.**

Kensworth
Richard Wynche, farmer, for a year to the Nativity of
St. John the Baptist 1494.
Charges
Arrears:	Nil
Farm of the manor, payable at Christmas and at the term of the Nativity of St. John the Baptist, including rents of assize, tithes of sheaves and half of all casualties:	£34 9s. 0d.
Sale of six oak shrubs from the wood:	5s. 10d.
Total:	£34 14s. 10d.

---

[100]   The total of allowances and payments is £62 12s.
[101]   The total of allowances and payments is £33 5s. 4d.

Allowances and Payments

From the issues of farm on two occasions (6 February 1494
£14 6s. 8d., 9 March 1494 £2 6s. 8d.): £16 13s. 4d.
Also to the receiver for the farm: £17 6s. 8d.
For repairs to the manor: 7s. 10d.
For a robe for the accountant granted to him in his indenture: · 6s. 8d.[102]
And quit

Caddington

John Bray, farmer.

Charges

Arrears: £16 18s. 6d.
Farm of the manor, payable at Christmas and at the term of
the Nativity of St. John the Baptist, including rents of assize,
tithes of sheaves of the rectory and all casualities: £34 9s. 0d.
Total: £51 7s. 6d.

Allowances and Payments

From the arrears and for the issues of his farm: £28 3s. 4d.
For the issues of his farm: £13 13s. 4d.
For a robe for the accountant: 6s. 8d.
To Roger Radcliff:[103] £3 0s. 0d.
Carried Forward: **£6 4s. 2d.**

---

[102] The total of allowances and payments is £34 14s. 6d., so the farmer owes 4d.
[103] The total of allowances and payments is £45 3s. 4d.

12. ACCOUNTS OF MINISTERS ON CERTAIN ESTATES OF WILLIAM WORSLEY 1495–1498

The estates included in this account are the three soke manors of Thorpe, Kirby and Walton, Heybridge, Runwell, Caddington and Kensworth, Bowes and Polehouse, Ardleigh, Nottingham, the Rectory of Winkburn and Offington, and Norton Folgate. It consists of seven sheets, 30 cm in width and 42 cm in length, inscribed on both sides of the sheet. There is no date or other inscription at the head of the first sheet and the seventh sheet is blank.

Walton manor
John Horward, farmer, for a year to St. Peter ad Vincula 1496.
Charges
Arrears, of John Toose, late farmer:	£19 3s. 4d.
Farm of the manor:	£38 6s. 8d.
Total:	£57 10s. 0d.

Allowances and Payments
Part payment of arrears to Philip Booth and Edmund Worsley, mercer of London, to the use of the Dean, witnessed etc. by Edmund 4 February 1497: £9 0s. 0d.

To Edmund Worsley, by John Horward and George Fitton, vicar of Kirby, 17 August 1497: £4 6s. 6d.

To the Dean, by hands of Thomas Shaa, from John Horward in full payment of arrears: £5 16s. 10d.

By hands of Thomas Shaa, the Dean's servant, from the farmer, in payment of his farm for Purification term 1497: £19 3s. 4d.[104]

Carried forward:[105] **£19 3s. 4d.**

The rectory of Bancroft in Walton
William Carter, farmer, for the same term.
Charges
Arrears of £3 6s. 8d. from Purification term 1496, and £7 10s. from the feast of St. Peter ad Vincula 1496: £10 16s. 8d.

Farm of the rectory, as in previous years: £15 0s. 0d.

Total: £25 16s. 8d.

Allowances and Payments
Part payment to Edmund Worsley, by George Fitton, vicar of Kirby, of arrears from the farmer, 7 April 1497: £4 6s. 6d.

To the Dean, by hands of Thomas Shaa, in full payment of the

---

[104] Total of allowances and payments, £38 6s. 8d.
[105] Margin: He promised to pay 100s. on the Feast of St. Martin in Winter next.

arrears and in part payment of the farm:	£10 13s. 6d.[106]
Carried Forward:[107]	**£10 16s. 8d.**

Thorpe manor with the farm of the rectory

Robert Palmer,[108] farmer, for the same term.

Charges

Arrears:	[–]
Farm of the rectory:	£18 0s. 0d.
Total:	[–]

Allowances and Payments

To Philip Booth and Edmund Worsley, in full payment of the farm for Purification term, on 16 November 1496:	£9 0s. 0d.
Carried forward:[109]	**£9 0s. 0d.**

'Kent's tenement' in Thorpe

John Harnes, farmer there, for the same term.

Charges

Arrears:	£2 0s. 0d.
Farm of the tenement:	£4 0s. 0d.[110]
Total:	£6 0s. 0d.[111]

Allowances and payments

To [–] Fourth of Oakley and John Felix, butcher of Kirby, on the feast of St. John the Baptist as first part of an aid to the King:	2s. 4d.
To Philip Booth and Edmund Worsley, to the use of the Dean, full payment of the farm for the term of St. Peter ad Vincula last, witnessed by Edmund 13 March 1496:	£2 0s. 0d.
To the Dean by the hand of Thomas Shaa:	£1 17s. 8d.[112]
Carried forward:[113]	**£2 0s. 0d.**

The office of the bailiff and collector in the soke

Thomas Bogas, bailiff and collector, for a year to Easter term 1497.

Charges

Arrears of £49 2s. 7½d., from the office of bailiff and collector, 18s. 8d. from profits of court:	£50 1s. 3½d.[114]

---

[106] Total of allowances and payments, £15.
[107] Margin: He promised to pay 66s. 8d. on the feast of St. Martin in Winter next.
[108] Cooke crossed out.
[109] Margin: He promised to pay 66s. 8d. on the feast of St. Martin in Winter next.
[110] 40s. crossed out.
[111] £4 crossed out.
[112] Total of allowances and payments, £4.
[113] Margin: he is to pay on the feast of St. Martin in Winter next.
[114] £49 2s. 7d. crossed out.

Rents:

from Walton:	£6 13s. 7¾d.
from Kirby:	£12 0s. 4¼d.
from Thorpe:	£19 1s. 3d.
from the new rent:	4s. 0d.
new rent of Thomas Bover for a water mill newly built on land in Thorpe, fifteen perches and one rod in length and one perch in width:	5s. 0d.
new rent from William Thurston for ½ acre of land lying in Thorpe, a piece of Hobbesdale, which was let to William by the court roll of the said year:	1s. 0d.
Farm of the rectory of Kirby:	£21 0s. 0d.
Total: [115]	£109 6s. 6½d.

Allowances and Payments

Tithes and decreases returned:

from Walton, Thorpe and Kirby, £1 4s., from the farm of 'Frevellandes', 1s.; from the decrease of the new rent of John Hykman, 8d., from six acres of the land of John Toose in Walton, 4d., and for last year from the farm of a bakehouse late in the tenancy of John Burgh, now in the lord's hand, 1s:	£1 7s. 0d.
The stipend of the bailiff, including 6s. 8d. for his reward for the year:	£2 0s. 0d.
Repairs in the manor of Thorpe, £3 13s., to the pale of the park, £1 7s. 10d. and in the manor of Walton £2 5s.:	£7 5s. 10d.
The expenses of Philip Booth and Edmund Worsley and three of their servants for one day and one night at the time of the settlement of this account:	4s. 0d.
To Roger Radcliff, late receiver, £3 on 22 October and £10 on 5 December 1496:	£13 0s. 0d.
To Philip Booth, and Edmund Worsley, to the use of the Dean, witnessed by Edmund Worsley, £9 on 3 February and £14 on 14 March 1497:	£23 0s. 0d.
The cost of one hundred ewes, at 16d. each,[116] paid to Robert Palmer, farmer of Thorpe manor, for the replenishment of stock lacking from the time of John Percy, late farmer:	£8 0s. 0d.
The cost of two oxen also bought to replenish the stock:	£1 6s. 8d.[117]
To the Dean by the hand of Thomas Shaa:	£20 0s. 0d.

Unleviable amercements from various people from the

---

[115] Blank, but in margin £109 6s. 6½d.

[116] 120 sheep at 16d. calculates at £8; 100 sheep at 16d. calculates at £6 13s. 4d.

[117] Margin: £55 3s. 6d. paid, £54 3s. ½d. owing (*recte*: £56 3s. 6d. paid, £53 3s. ½d. owing).

previous year:	1s. 5d.
Reduction in the farm of the rectory of Kirby charged above at £21 p.a., but this year charged at the lower rate of £19:	£2 0s. 0d.

Expenses of the steward, his clerk and his servant while at court at Kirby on the feast of St. Anne, and at court-leet on the morrow of St. Anne 1497.[118] The expenses also of the auditor, Thomas Shaa, and his servant staying there for the settlement of the account for three days and nights: 13s. 2½d.[119]

Carried forward: £31 8s. 6d.[120]

Thomas Bogas, as bailiff and collector of profits of Court Charges

Fines at court in Kirby on the feast of St. Anne 1496
– from Thorpe, £4 10s. 9d., from Kirby, £4 9d. and from
Walton, £3 3s. 3d.: £11 11s. 9d.[121]

Fines at court in Kirby on the Monday before St. Thomas
the Apostle 1497:[122] £2 5s. 0d.

Profits from a court-leet held there on the morrow of the
feast of St. Anne 1496: 7s. 1d.

Total: £14 3s. 10½d.

Allowances and Payments

Paid to the Dean, by hands of Thomas Shaa, part of the
fines of the first court, as appears in the estreats remaining
in the hands of Thomas Bogas: £9 9s. ½d.

Part of the fines of the second court: £2 1s. 3d.

Carried Forward £2 10s. 7½d.[123]

Arrears of fines and amercements of various tenants in
Thorpe: 4s. 9d.

Fines and amercements of various tenants in Kirby: £1 6s. 9d.[124]

From various tenants in Walton: 15s. 0d.

Amercements of various tenants (in Thorpe 2s. 6d.,
in Kirby 2s. 2d., in Walton 6½d.): 4s. 1½d.[125]

Paid to the Dean, by Thomas Shaa from a fine on three
acres of land in 'Hobbesdale', a parcel of 'Kent's tenement'
granted to him in the court roll of the soke held at Kirby
on the feast of St. Anne 1497: 6s. 8d.

---

[118] 26 and 27 July.
[119] These additional allowances and payments total £22 14s. 7½d.
[120] *Recte* £30 8s. 6d.
[121] Should read £11 14s. 9d.
[122] 18 December 1497.
[123] *Recte* £2 13s. 7d.
[124] 37s. 9d. crossed out.
[125] *Recte* 5s. 2½d. The sum 5s. 2d. has been crossed out.

And quit.[126]

Heybridge Manor

Geoffrey Dallyng farmer of the mill and manor, for a year
at the term of St. Peter ad Vincula 1497.

Charges

Arrears:	£34 6s. 0d.
Farm of the manor:	£43 0s. 0d.
Total:	£77 6s. 0d.[127]

Allowances and Payments

A millstone for a corn mill, bought from William Herdyng of Maldon at Easter term 1497:	£4 0s. 0d.
Repairs on various barns of the manor and on the mills:	£2 10s. 0d.
To Philip Booth and Edmund Worsley, by the farmer £6 on 4 February 1497, by Edmund Worsley £10 on 12 February 1497, and £15 on 9 July 1497:	£31 0s. 0d.
To the Dean, by Thomas Shaa, 29 July 1497:	£3 13s. 4d.
Carried forward:	£36 2s. 8d.

Heybridge mill

Robert Bette, farmer.

Charges

Arrears:	£2 12s. 6d.
Farm of the mill:	£7 0s. 0d.[128]
Total:	£9 10s. 6d.

Allowances and Payments

To Philip Booth in part payment of the farm:	£5 0s. 0d.
To the Dean by the hand of Thomas Shaa, on 29 July 1497:	£2 0s. 0d.
Repairs to the mill and its staddles:	£1 10s. 4d.
Carried forward:	£1 0s. 2d.

Caddington

John Bray, farmer, for a year at the term of St. John the Baptist
1497.

Charges

Arrears:	£18 0s. 0d.
Farm of the manor:	£34 9s. 0d.
Profits of court:	Nil
Sales:	18s. 5d.

---

[126] On the basis of the figures given in the account, the account would not be quit: 3s. 8d. would be carried forward. If the corrected figures are used in the calculation, then 1s. 10d. is carried forward.

[127] 10s. crossed out.

[128] 10s. crossed out.

Mesnalty, the price of a male sheep owing this year as
extraction of stock: 7d.
Total: £53 8s. 0d.

Allowances and Payments

A gown for the farmer: 6s. 8d.
To Roger Radcliff, late receiver, by a bill of 18 November 1496: £5 0s. 0d.
To Philip Booth and Edmund Worsley, by a bill of February
1497: £9 14s. 6d.
And by another bill of 18 February 1497: £6 13s. 4d.
To Edmund Worsley, by Thomas Bray, £3 5s. on 12 April and
£7 on 16 April 1497: £10 5s. 0d.
To the Dean, in subsidy for the church of St. Paul's, witnessed
by Thomas Smith, chaplain, before the auditor: £5 7s. 3¾d.
On 7 August 1497: £11 0s. 0d.
Repairs in the manor: £2 18s. 0d.
Paid to the Dean by the farmer: 10s. 0d.[129]
Carried forward: £1 13s. 2¼d.
Paid to the Dean[130] at Hackney.
And quit.

Kensworth
Richard Wynche, farmer, for a year at St. John the Baptist 1497.
Charges
Arrears: £3 0s. 0d.
Farm of the manor: £34 9s. 0d.
Half of the profits of the court held that year: [–]
Total: £37 9s. 0d.
Allowances and Payments
To Roger Radcliff, late receiver, now deceased, in a bill of
18 November 1496: £3 0s. 0d.
To Philip Booth and Edmund Worsley, receivers, in a bill of
3 February 1497: £17 4s. 6d.
To the Dean, part of the farm, by a bill of 19 July 1497: £12 0s. 0d.
For a gown for the farmer: 6s. 8d.[131]
Carried Forward: £4 17s. 10d.
Paid to the Dean.
And quit.

Willesden prebend and grace
William Swete, farmer, from Easter term 1496 to Easter term 1497.

---

129 The total of allowances and payments is £53 8s.
130 Hand here may be of William Worsley.
131 The total of allowances and payments is £37 9s.

Charges

Farm of the prebend:	£4 16s. 8d.
Farm of the grace at £12 p.a. (for the terms of St. Peter ad Vincula 1496, and Purification and St. Peter ad Vincula 1497):	£18 0s. 0d.
Wood valued at £20 from 'Deane Wodde' in Acton, and at £10 from wood in the same wood and hedges in the prebend and grace of Willesden, sold to the farmer by Edmund Worsley:	£30 0s. 0d.
Total:	£52 16s. 8d.

Allowances and Payments

A gown for the farmer:	6s. 8d.
19 score and 14 rods fencing wood from a certain wood called 'Deane Wodde' in Acton:	£1 12s. 10d.
For the safe keeping of the osier beds in the wood:	1d.
To Roger Radcliff, late receiver, £6 for the term of St. Peter ad Vincula and £2 8s. 4d. for Michaelmas term 1496:	£8 8s. 4d.
To Edmund Worsley £2 8s. 4d. for Easter term and £6 for Purification term 1497:	£8 8s. 4d.
In full payment of the sale of wood from Willesden:	£10 0s. 0d.
Wood from 'Deane Wodde' paid for by the farmer, £6 13s. 4d. at Michaelmas, £6 13s. 4d. at St. Martin in Winter, and £6 13s. 4d. at Easter:	£20 0s. 0d.
Received by the Dean at audit from the farmer:	£4 0s. 6d.[132]

And quit.

Bowes and Polehouse

John Fox, farmer.

Charges

Farm for the terms of the Ascension and St. Peter ad Vincula 1497 (at £26 13s. 4d. p.a., viz. £5 at St. Martin in Winter, £5 at the Purification, £5 at Ascension Day, £11 13s. 4d. at St. Peter ad Vincula):	£16 13s. 4d.
Profits of court:	[–]
Total:	[£16 13s. 4d.][133]

Allowances and Payments

For two and a half carts of charcoal bought from the farmer and used in the Dean's household between Christmas 1495 and St. Peter ad Vincula 1496, price per cart 10s:	£1 15s. 0d.
For four and a half bushels and another two bushels of coal bought from the farmer and used in the household between St. Peter ad Vincula and Christmas 1496:	£1 16s. 9d.

For five carts of coal bought from him and sold into the house-

---

132 The total of allowances and payments is £52 16s. 8d.
133 The sum of £16 13s. 4d. is given in the margin, but is left blank in the account.

hold between Christmas 1496 and St. Peter ad Vincula 1497: £2 2s. 0d.
For carriage and *le tallyng*, of eleven carts of wood called *tallwodde*
at 16d. per cart, and nine carts of wood called *pollewodde*
at 15d., carried to the household of the Dean at Hackney
between Christmas 1495 and the term of St. Peter ad Vincula 1496: £1 5s. 11d.
For *le tallyng* and carriage of eighteen carts of *tallwodde* and
four carts of *pollewodde*, priced as above, carried to the household
of the Dean: £1 9s. 0d.
For repairs to manors, lands and houses over two years ending at
the term of St. Peter ad Vincula 1497: £1 3s. 1d.
To the collector of the King for the first part of an aid on lands,
manors and tenements in Edmonton and Tottenham, granted to
the King in the last parliament held at Westminster:[134] 16s. 9d.
Peter's Pence paid on the feast of St. Peter ad Vincula 1497:[135] 4d.
A full tenth paid at the term of St. John the Baptist 1497 to the
collectors of the King, viz. 13s. 4d. to Thomas Ayskows
and John Turle, collectors of Edmonton and 6s. 8d. to
William, one of the collectors at Tottenham: £1 0s. 0d.[136]

Carried Forward: **£5 4s. 6d.**

Paid to the Dean, to his servant Thomas Dey, on 8 October 1497,
as written by the hand of the said Thomas Dey.[137]

And quit.

Runwell manor

William Aleyn, farmer, for a year at the term of St. Peter ad
Vincula 1497.

Charges

Farm of the manor and profits of court: £36 10s. 0d.
The cost of lopping wood from trees for repairs, as written
below: 6s. 0d.
Total: £36 16s. 8d.[138]

Allowances and Payments

For repairs in the manor: £21 10s. 8½d.
To Philip Booth and Edmund Worsley receivers there,
as shown in a bill given on 3 February 1497: £9 2s. 6d.
To the Dean by the hand of Thomas Shaa, the Dean's servant,
on 30 July 1497: £6 5s. 3½d.[139]

---

134 Parliament of 16 January–13 March 1497.
135 The total of allowances and payments at this point is noted as £10 8s. 10d. and the
 farmer is noted as owing £6 4s. 6d.
136 The total of allowances and payments is £16 13s. 4d.
137 This is in a different hand from the rest of the MS.
138 *Recte* £36 16s.
139 The total of allowances and payments is £36 18s. 6d.

Carried forward, a surplus: **2s. 6d.**

Cootes tenement in Wadende, Ardleigh
William Frost, farmer.
Charges
Arrears of the farm at £7 6s. 8d. p.a. from St. Peter ad Vincula
1496:   £9 6s. 8d
Farm of the manor, £3 13s. 4d. for Purification term and
£3 13s. 4d. for the term of St. Peter ad Vincula 1497:   <u>£7 6s. 8d.</u>
Total: £16 13s. 4d.
Allowances and Payments
To Edmund Worsley in part payment of £9 6s. 8d. arrears, by
a recognisance of the said Edmund and in front of [Thomas] Dey
and Thomas Bunewell, on the road from Hackney to London: £3 0s. 0d.
Balance of a debt of £4 owing to the Dean: £3 10s. 0d.
To the Dean, as part of the said £4:   10s. 0d.
Carried forward: £9 13s. 4d.

Ardleigh
Edmund Bardolf, farmer.
Charges
Farm of £6 13s. 4d. per term (£20 p.a.) for St. Peter ad
Vincula 1496, and for Purification, St. John the Baptist,
and St. Peter ad Vincula 1497:   £26 13s. 4d.
Ninety oak trees felled in the lord's wood called *le Parke* and
sold to Sir Robert Litton, knight, by Philip Booth and
Edmund Worsley at 2s. per tree: £9 0s. 0d.
Twenty-four oak trees felled for the reconstruction of half a barn
and other repairs in the manor, (out of a lot of 36 trees felled
on the orders of Philip and Edmund, the remaining 12 oaks
of which were used for the reconstruction work):   £2 16s. 0d.
Seven carts of wood from the areas where the trees were felled: <u>2s. 4d.</u>
Total: £38 11s. 8d.
Allowances and Payments
To Roger Radcliff late receiver, on 1 December 1496:   £5 6s. 8d.
To Edmund Worsley on 12 February 1497, in full payment for
the term of St. Peter ad Vincula 1496:   £1 6s. 8d.
By William Bardolf, brother of the farmer, on
16 February 1497, in full payment for Purification term 1497:   £6 13s. 4d.
For the reconstruction of half a barn and repairs on the manor: £3 10s. 8d.
To Edmund Worsley, in full payment for the above trees: £9 0s. 0d.
To the Dean at Hackney, in full payment for the farm for
the term of St. John the Baptist 1497:   £6 13s. 4d.[140]
Carried forward: £6 1s. 0d.

The Archdeaconry of Nottingham

Richard Samesbury, collector, from Easter 1497 to Easter 1498.

Charges

For chevage and Peter's Pence, £11 at Michaelmas term, and £58 at Easter:	£69 0s. 0d.
From inductions this year, to Master Robert Colyngham £2 6s. 8d., and to Simon Yates, deputy of Master [Robert] Wilby, 6s. 8d:	£2 13s. 4d.
Total:	£71 13s. 4d.

Allowances and Payments

Expenses at the time of visitation this year:	£2 5s. 5½d.
The fee of the official there this year:	£2 13s. 4d.
A gown for the said official:	13s. 4d.
A gown for his servant:	5s. 0d.
The fee of Master John Kendale, registrar there, for this year:	13s. 4d.
A gown for the registrar:	6s. 8d.
Cash wages of Ralph Langford, the brother of the Dean, at 1s. per week, and another 16d. for the year by the order of the Dean:	£2 13s. 4d.
The wages of the collector for the year:	£2 13s. 4d.
For two servants and two meals at Southwell at Michaelmas term and at Easter:	13s. 4d.
Paid to the Dean:	£10 19s. 3d.
Total: [£23 16s. 4½d.][141]	
Carried Forward:	**£47 16s. 11½d.**[142]

The Rectory of Winkburn and Offington

[...]

Charges

[...] at 6s. 8d. p.a. [...]

[...] for their synodal dues [...][143]

Issues of office of collector for this year: £46 17s. 7½d.

Total:	[...]

Allowances and Payments

[...] for the expenses of the collector riding from Southwell to London for the render of this account.	[...]
Total:	[...]
Carried forward.	**£46 12s. 7½d.**

Paid to the Dean at Hackney, May 1498.

---

140 Total allowances and payments: £32 10s. 8d.
141 MS damage. The total is given in the margin. *Recte* £23 16s. 1d.
142 MS damaged. This sum is given in the margin.
143 Synodal: an episcopal due representing a share in the cost of the bishop holding synods.

And quit.

Norton Folgate
Joan Stephens, the relict of John Stephens, late farmer there,
for a year at the Annunciation 1498.
Charges
Farm of the manor: £6 13s. 4d.
Allowances and Payments
The fee of John Saperton, auditor of the Dean: £3 6s. 8d.
Roofing various houses and barns of the manor over 12 days
at 2s. per day in straw, *le drawyng* of works of roofing, and
cash wages of two of his servants: £1 4s. 0d.
The work of two carpenters and one labourer for two days
on propping the houses in various places and on *le grondfillyng*
in the great chamber this year: 2s. 6d.
To the Dean, to his servant Thomas Bunewell, by John,
then farmer: £2 0s. 0d.
Total: £6 13s. 2d.
Carried Forward: 2d.

13. ACCOUNT OF THE RENT COLLECTOR OF THE DEANERY OF LONDON FOR SOME OF WORSLEY'S LANDS IN THE CITY OF LONDON AND IN NORTON FOLGATE, MIDDLESEX 1483–1484.

The roll is damaged at the head and consists of two sheets, 31 cm wide. The surviving portion of the first sheet is 38 cm long and the second sheet is 43 cm long. The first sheet is endorsed 'compotus John C... anno II Ric III'

Arrears:[144] £4 1s. 7½d.

Charges:
Ivy Lane
40s. for the farm of a tenement, paying at 4 terms a year [...]
13s. 4d. for the farm of another tenement there in the tenancy of Master Reynold for a year, paying at the same terms.
20s. for another tenement now held by [...] for a year paying at the said terms.
Total: £3 13s. 4d.

'Paules Cheyn'[145]
40s. for the farm of a tenement now held by Richard Saddler for a year.[146]
£7 6s. 8d. for the farm of a tenement called 'Powles Hede' held by Roger Forth, taverner, for a year.
£1 6s. 8d. for the farm of a tenement held by John Harlesley, for a year.
Total: £10 13s. 4d.

Knightrider Street
From the farm of Master Kent now held by William Say, paying at the customary terms of the Deanery in the city of London: 5s.

Norton Folgate
£1 12s. 6½d. rents of assize there for a year. And [...] for profits of a court held there at the feast of St. Peter ad Vincula.[147]
Total: £1 12s. 6½d.

[144] This first entry is damaged.
[145] A lane to the south of the cathedral precinct.
[146] See document 2, above.
[147] Margin: William Hale for the court roll.

Total including arrears: $£25$ 0s. 10d.[148]

Allowances and Payments
Repairs
On the holdings of Dr. Jane and 'Powles Hede' as laid out in
Roger Radcliff's paper, $£3$ 13s. 5d.
On the tenement called 'Powles Hede' formerly held by
Roger Forth, $£7$ 1s. 6½d.
Total: $£10$ 4s. 11½d.

Vacant tenements
For a tenement called 'Powles Hede', at $£7$ 6s. 8d. p.a., which
was empty and unoccupied for the term of Michaelmas within
the time of this account: $£1$ 16s. 8d.

Total Payments: $£12$ 1s. 7½d.
And he owes: $£12$ 19s. 2½d.

Whereof
To the prior of the hospital of St. Mary outside Bishopsgate,
for a quit rent of 9s. p.a. from the lands and tenements where
the grange was situated, for this year and arrears of the
three preceding years: $£1$ 16s. 0d.
To Ralph Kemp, for a quit rent at 16d. p.a. issuing from
certain lands, tenements and messuages of his lying between
the tenement of the prior of St. Mary and the tenement of
Alice Pomfret, widow, for this year and arrears of the
three preceding years: 5s. 4d.
To Alice Pomfret for a quit rent of 3s. 2½d. p. a. issuing
from a tenement lying between the tenement of Ralph Kemp
and the lands of the prioress of Haliwell, for this year and arrears
of the three preceding years: 12s. 10d.
To the Prioress of Haliwell, for a quit rent of 20d. p.a. from
a tenement called 'le Spaldynghouse' lying between the
tenement of Ralph Kemp and the land of John Cook, for
this year and arrears of the three preceding years: 6s. 8d.
To John Honyborne, for a quit rent of 4s. p.a. from five
messuages lying between the tenement of John Cook and
Moreland, for this year and arrears of the three preceding years: 16s.
To Ralph Kemp, quit rent 6s. 8d. p.a. from ten messuages
lying between Moreland and the lands of the Priory of Haliwell,
arrears for 3 years and this year: $£1$ 6s. 8d.

[148]   Total of surviving entries, $£16$ 12s. 6d.

To the Prioress of Haliwell, for a quit rent 16d. p.a. from a
tenement lying between the priory's lands and the messuage
of John Baldewyn, for this year and arrears of the
three preceding years: 5s. 4d.
[Total: £5 8s. 10d.][149]

Carried forward: **£7 10s. 4½d.**

---

[149]   The total is noted in the margin.

APPENDIX 1:
THE CHAPTER OF ST. PAUL'S AT WORSLEY'S ELECTION

Present:

M. Thomas Chaundeler	present, proxy for Thomas Hall
M. Thomas Jane	present, proxy for Audley, Byrd, Morton, Pevesey, Pykenham, Stanley
M. Richard Lichfield	possibly present[1]
M. Richard Luke	present, proxy for Audley, Byrd, Morton, Pevesey, Stanley
M. Richard Martyn	appears to be present[2]
M. John Sutton	presides
M. William Worsley	present, proxy for Audley, Byrd, Morton, Pevesey, Stanley
M. William Wylde	present, proxy for Pykenham

Present by proxy:

M. Edmund Audley	by Worsley, Jane, Luke[3]
Ralph Byrd	by Worsley, Jane, Luke[4]
M. Thomas Hall	by Thomas Chaundeler[5]
M. Robert Morton	2 prebends, by Worsley, Jane, Luke[6]
M. Robert Pevesey	by Worsley, Jane, Luke[7]
M. William Pykenham	by Thomas Jane and William Wylde[8]
James Stanley	by Worsley, Jane, Luke[9]

---

[1]   GL, MS 9531/7, pt. ii, fol. 13v.
[2]   *Ibid.*
[3]   *Ibid.* fol. 11v.
[4]   *Ibid.* fol. 10v.
[5]   *Ibid.* fol. 12r.
[6]   *Ibid.* fol. 11v.
[7]   *Ibid.* fol. 10r.
[8]   *Ibid.* fol. 9v.
[9]   *Ibid.* fol. 11r.

absent: [10]

M. John Bourgchier	absent unexcused
M. John Davyson	absent unexcused
William Kempe	absent unexcused
[M. Thomas Winterbourne	deceased][11]

unaccounted for: [12]

M. John Barville	St. Pancras
M. Walter Bate	Oxgate
M. Benedict Burgh	Archd. of Colchester
M. John Crall al. Sudbury	Holborn and Archd. of Essex
M. Walter Hert	Ealdstreet
John Isaak	Chamberlainwood
M. Walter Knightley	Treasurer
M. William Moreland	Ealdland
M. John Peese	Caddington Major
M. Ralph Shaa	Caddington Minor
M. Thomas Smith	Chancellor
M. John Tapton	Harleston
M. William Woodcock	Twiford

[10]   *Ibid.*, fol. 12v.
[11]   *Fasti*, vol. v, p. 63.
[12]   *Ibid.*, pp. 10, 14, 16, 19, 24, 26, 30, 34, 39, 41, 54, 55, 65.

APPENDIX 2:
BIOGRAPHICAL DETAILS OF INDIVIDUALS
MENTIONED IN THE ACCOUNTS

This appendix provides brief biographical information on the individuals mentioned in Worsley's accounts. It is not intended to give full biographies, and where published biographies are available elsewhere, only the briefest of details have been given and reference has been made to the relevant published works.

Abingdon, Berks, abbot of.
John Sant (d. 6 January 1495), elected abbot December 1469 following the resignation of his predecessor, William Asshendon. He came into contact with Worsley's household in 1489–90 as collector of a clerical tenth. In that same year – 1489 – Sant became guilty of a conspiracy against Henry VII, the so-called Abbot of Abingdon's Plot, an attempt to free the Earl of Warwick, which ultimately failed.[13]

Aleyn, William, of Runwell, Essex.
Aleyn was Worsley's farmer of Runwell from 1495, in succession to John Bek (q.v.). He is difficult to identify as there were several men of this name active in the south-east in this period, including a clergyman alive in Henry VIII's reign and a London baker.[14] However, the Dean's farmer was probably one of two more prominent men. He may have been the man who was alleged to have been a creditor of Laurence Damlet (q.v.) in a suit against Damlet's executors, brought in the London mayor's court by the London ironmonger Hugh Aleyn, who may have been a kinsman. This man, a London citizen and mercer, had married Barbara, widow of Robert Grene, but seems to have died childless in late 1519 or early 1520.[15] Another plausible candidate is William Aleyn of Rayleigh, an Essex landowner, who died in 1517, survived by his wife Anne and three sons. At some point between 1474 and 1485 this man was accused of an act of extortion by a priest, John Rome, whom he had had

---

[13] W. Dugdale, *Monasticon Anglicanum*, ed. J. Caley, H. Ellis, and B. Bandinel (6 vols. in 8, London, 1817–30), i. 509; *CPR*, 1467–76, pp. 119, 123; *VCH Berks*. ii. 62; Arthurson, p. 90; document 8, above.
[14] PRO, C1/114/17, 415/54.
[15] Documents 9, 10, 12, above; PRO, C1/64/689; PROB11/19, fols. 188–189v (PCC 24 Ayloffe).

imprisoned by the sheriffs of London.[16]

Alyff, John, of Essex.

In 1495–96 deputy of the Earl of Oxford (q.v.), then chief steward of the Dean's estates in Essex, the following year Alyff was described as steward of the estates in the soke of St. Paul's in Essex. He is likely to have been a kinsman of the William Ayloff who acted as an executor of the Dean's will.[17] Another putative kinsman, Thomas Ayloff, had married the daughter of Robert Forster (q.v.), brother of the archdeacon of London.[18]

Armar, John, of London.

An armourer by trade, Armar was the otherwise unidentified craftsman who supplied the apparel of the Dean and his retinue for their Scottish journey in 1480–81.[19]

Arnoldson, Arnold

In 1487–88 Arnoldson held an unspecified tenement from the Dean, for which a lock was bought at Worsley's expense. He died in December 1496 and was survived by his wife whom he had appointed his executrix.[20]

Audley, Master [Edmund], bp. of Hereford.

Son of James Tuchet, Lord Audley. Educated at Lincoln College, Oxford, Audley (d. 23 August 1524) soon assembled a number of benefices, including a canonry at St. George's, Windsor, and the prebend of Mora at St. Paul's, which he held from 1476 to 1480, also becoming archdeacon of Essex. A significant pluralist, he was absent from Worsley's election, but had appointed the future Dean, Thomas Jane (q.v.) and Richard Luke his proxies. In 1480 Audley was preferred to the see of Rochester, in 1492 translated to Hereford and in 1502 finally made bishop of Salisbury, at the same time becoming chancellor of the Order of the Garter. In 1495–96 Audley occurs in Worsley's accounts as tenant of Drayton, evidently having succeeded the Dean as the chapter's lessee.[21]

[16]   PRO, C1/66/104, 190/29; PROB11/18, fols. 252v–253v (PCC 32 Holder).
[17]   Documents 9, 10, above; PRO, C1/240/7–8.
[18]   PRO, C1/83/86.
[19]   Document 2, above.
[20]   GL, MS 9168/1, fol. 7; document 6, above.
[21]   G. L. Hennessy, *Novum Repertorium Ecclesiasticum Parochiale Londinense* (London, 1898), pp. 37, xxxix; Emden, *Oxford*, pp. 75–76; GL, MS 9531/7, pt. ii, fol. 11v; document 9, above; *The Coronation of Richard III. The Extant Documents*, ed. A. F. Sutton and P. W. Hammond (Gloucester, New York, 1983), pp. 305–6.

Ayskows, Thomas, of Edmonton, Mdx.

Not known to have been otherwise connected with the Dean, Ayskows occurs as one of the collectors appointed at Edmonton to collect the lay tenth granted to Henry VII in the 1497 Parliament. The original appointment shows that it was in fact his father, William Ayskows (d. 1499) of Edmonton, who was made collector that year. It is therefore probable, that Thomas served as his father's subcollector. Thomas died before 1523, and was succeeded by his son, Nicholas. His wife, Margaret, survived him and married Robert Wales. Elizabeth, the eldest of his six daughters, married Robert Page, two others, Margaret and Anne, married one David Jones and one Robert Vaughan respectively, and in 1532–33 the three were suing their father's executors for the marriage portions of £20 each which he had bequeathed to them in his will.[22]

Baldewyn, John, of London

In 1483–84 Baldewyn held a messuage adjacent to one of the Deanery's tenements. He may be the clergyman of that name who in June 1477 was pardoned his outlawry on account of a refusal to appear in court to answer for a debt of 50s. owed to a London embroiderer, John Lambe.[23]

Ballard, Richard, of Norton Folgate, Mdx.

Worsley's farmer at Norton Folgate in 1487–88, Ballard was probably a kinsman of M. Robert Ballard, the treasurer of St. Paul's 1474–78.[24] Likewise, he may have been related to, or even be the Richard Ballard of Romford, in the parish of Hornchurch, Essex, one of six siblings, who made his will on 26 July 1527.[25] Other Ballards, who were related to M. Thomas Kent, were resident in the parish of St. Katharine by the Tower, London, in the later fifteenth century.[26]

Bardolf, Edmund, of Watton, Herts.

Edmund was the eldest son of Henry Bardolf of Crowborough. Both Henry and his father, another Edmund, had died in rapid succession by July 1472, leaving Worsley's later farmer embroiled in a series of suits over both his paternal inheritance and his sister Elizabeth's marriage portion. Edmund died in late 1512 or early 1513, survived by his wife Elizabeth and his son Edmund, a minor.[27]

[22] GL, MS 9171/8, fol. 177v; document 12, above; PRO, C1/647/17–18, 687/2, 707/20; E179/241/365.
[23] Document 13, above; *CPR*, 1476–85, p. 26.
[24] Document 6, above; Hennessy, p. 11.
[25] PRO, PROB11/22, fols. 180–180v (PCC 23 Porche).
[26] PRO, PROB11/11, fols. 157–9 (PCC 19 Horne).
[27] Document 9, above; PRO, PROB11/6, fols. 43v–44 (PCC 6 Wattys); PROB11/17, fol. 79v (PCC 10 Fetiplace); C1/41/27–29, 128–130, 1337/60–61;

Bardolf, William of Ardleigh, Herts.
William Bardolf was the younger brother of Edmund Bardolf (q.v.), who in 1497 paid some of his brother's farm to the Dean's receivers. William Bardolf occurs in April 1497 as a petty constable or 'headborough' (*capitalis plegius*) at a view of frankpledge at Ardleigh. He died in April 1504, leaving three sons and a daughter, and survived by his wife Margaret who had previously been married to a member of the Halfched family.[28]

Barlowe, Robert of Heybridge, Essex.
A tenant or official at Heybridge in 1493–94, when he paid part of the preceding year's arrears to Roger Radcliff (q.v.).[29] He may have been the Colchester mercer of this name. This man's uncle Roger was a London tailor, and John Barlowe, a skinner of the London parish of St. Mary Colechurch, may have been another relative. Both Londoners mainperned for Robert's good behaviour in the aftermath of the Warbeck conspiracy in April 1495.[30]

Barthorn, Master John, of London.
Barthorn was one of the minor players in the vicious quarrel between Archbishop Morton and Bishop Hill of London (q.v.) in the first half of the 1490s. In April 1494 Hill had bills of excommunication against Thomas Percy, the prior of Holy Trinity Aldgate (q.v.), displayed in various prominent spots in the city, but the prior appealed against the bishop's actions to the primate. A proctor of the court of Canterbury, it fell to Barthorn to attempt to remove these documents while the appeal was pending. At the bishop's bidding he was arrested by the city authorities and imprisoned, and found himself forced to appeal to his master, the archbishop, in the latter's capacity as Chancellor of England to regain his freedom. In 1482–83 he occurs in Worsley's accounts buying a horse from the Dean.[31]

Bath and Wells, [Robert Stillington D.C.L.], **bp. of**
Son of John Stillington of Acaster near York, Stillington studied at Oxford where he was admitted to the degree of D.C.L. and served as principal of Deep Hall in 1442 and 1444. By August 1445 he served as chancellor of bishop Bekynton of Bath and Wells, and five years later he became archdeacon of Taunton and prebendary of Milverton at the bishop's cathedral. Further preferment and office were to follow: in 1458 he became Dean of St. Martin le

---

[28] *CFR*, xxii. 33.
Document 12, above; GL, MS 25301/1, m. 3; PRO, PROB11/14, fol. 71v (PCC 9 Holgrave).
[29] Document 11, above.
[30] PRO, C1/121/20–22, 323/32; C54/376, m. 18d.
[31] Document 4, above; C. Harper-Bill, 'Bishop Richard Hill and the Court of Canterbury, 1494–96', *Guildhall Studies in London History*, iii (1977–79), 1–12, p. 3; PRO, C1/117/64.

Grand, London, and in the summer of 1460 the Yorkists appointed him Keeper of the Privy Seal, an office in which he continued after Edward IV's accession. In 1465 he was preferred to the see of Bath and Wells and two years later he was appointed Chancellor. He continued in this office until 1473, only being replaced during Henry VI's readeption. He eventually fell out of favour with Edward IV and in early 1478 was placed in the Tower, having to pay a heavy fine for his release. Richard III's accession was advantageous for Stillington as he was close to the King, but when the tables turned in 1485 he was once more threatened with arrest and had to take refuge in Oxford. By the later 1480s he was growing increasingly old and frail and was dead by May 1491. The bishop held a tenement in Sutton from Worsley, for which arrears were owing in 1480–81.[32]

Bedmaker, Thomas
A clothworker, probably an upholder, by trade, Bedmaker supplied several items including a pavillion for the Scottish expedition.[33]

Bek, John, of Runwell, Essex.
Worsley's farmer of Runwell by 1487, Bek (or Bekke) continued to hold the farm until 1494–95, when he was succeeded by William Aleyn (q.v.).[34]

Berebrewer, Alexander, of London.
Alongside the ale supplied by a series of brewers based at London and Hackney, the Worsley household also consumed quantities of beer, which were for much of the period covered by the accounts bought from Alexander, resident at 'le Hermitage'. He supplied beer to the Dean's household as early as 1479 and continued to do so until at least 1484–85, but probably as late as 1487–88.[35]

Bernard, John, of Chepyng Lambourn, Berks.
Bernard was procurator at the Dean's church of Chepyng Lambourn between at least 1480 and 1485, but had been replaced by Thomas Garrard (q.v.) by 1487. He is likely to have been related to the John Bernard of Lambourn who acted as a feoffee for lands in Berkshire in 1429.[36]

---

[32] *Registers Stillington and Fox*, pp. viii–xix; Emden, *Oxford*, iii. 1777–79; document 2, above; W. E. Hampton, 'The Later Career of Robert Stillington', *The Ricardian*, iv (1976), 24–7, repr. in *Richard III, Crown and People*, ed. J. Petre (Gloucester, 1985), 162–65; *idem*, 'Bishop Stillington's Chapel at Wells and his Family in Somerset', *The Ricardian*, iv (1977), 10–16, repr. in *Richard III*, ed. Petre, 166–72.

[33] Document 2, above.

[34] Documents 6–9, 11, above.

[35] Documents 1–6, above.

[36] Documents 2–6, above; PRO, E326/1384.

Bocas or **Bogas, Thomas**, of Kirby-le-Soken, Essex.
Bogas succeeded James Raderford (q.v.) as bailiff and collector of rents of assize in the soke of St. Paul's in Essex in 1482 and continued in this office until at least 1497. From at least 1487 to 1489 he also held the rectory of Kirby to farm.[37]

Booth, Laurence, abp. of York.
A member of the prolific Booth family and a kinsman of Dean Worsley, Booth (d. 19 May 1480) was a younger and probably illegitimate son of John Booth (d. 1422) of Barton, Lancs. He was educated at Cambridge, where he became a fellow and subsequently master of Pembroke College. In March 1451 he was made chancellor of the household of Queen Margaret and in September 1456 Keeper of the Privy Seal. Less than two months later, he was elected Dean of St. Paul's, but within a year of his election he was preferred to the see of Durham (1457–1476). Despite his close links to Henry VI's government, he was appointed confessor to Edward IV in April 1461. Yet, for some years Edward did not fully trust him and only after the Nevilles' fall from grace, as a result of their involvement in the Readeption Crisis was he made archbishop of York (from 1476 to his death), as which he appears in Worsley's account of 1481–82. Two of his numerous kinsmen also rose into the episcopate: his brother William Booth (d. 12 Sept. 1464), Worsley's particular patron, became bishop of Coventry and Lichfield (1447–52) and archbishop of York (1452–d.) and his nephew John Booth (d. 5 April 1478) bishop of Exeter (1465–d.).[38]

Booth, Philip, esq., of Bergham, Suffolk.
Born in about 1455, Philip was son and heir of William, eldest son of Richard Booth (d. 1471) of Bergham by his wife Katharine, the daughter and sole heiress of the Suffolk esquire Philip atte Oke (d. 1421).[39] He married Margaret, daughter of Sir William Hopton (d. 1484), and they had a single daughter, Adriana, who married a son of Robert Litton (q.v.).[40] The connection of the Booths of Bergham with the main line at Barton is uncertain, but it is likely to have been a close one, for Philip's paternal uncle Robert (d. 1488) became Dean of York in 1477, a year after Laurence Booth's (q.v.) translation to the archiepiscopal see, and his father Richard had earlier also been associated with the later archbishop.[41] Also related to Worsley, he

37 Documents 4–8, 11, 12, above.
38 PRO, SC7/37/9, 9/10; document 3, above; *DNB*, ii. 849–50; Reeves, 'Lawrence Booth'. For an account of Booth's kinsmen cf. also Axon, 'The Family of Bothe'.
39 PRO, C139/52/68; *CFR*, xiv. 379; *CPR*, 1416–22, p. 400.
40 *The Visitation of Suffolk, 1561, made by William Hervy*, ed. Joan Corder (3 vols., London, Harl. Soc., n.s., 1981–84), pt. ii. 303; PRO, E150/640/6.
41 PRO, C140/60/22; C1/86/20; KB27/790, rot. att. 1; *Testamenta Eboracensa*, iv. 31–32.

appears in the Dean's household accounts in the aftermath of the Warbeck conspiracy. In 1495 he acted as one of the mainpernors for Worsley's future good behaviour, and his links within the London mercers' company, to which he had been admitted in 1494 on payment of £5, became crucial in raising securities for the Dean.[42] Yet, his relationship with the ageing Dean was a stormy one: Worsley brought suits for accounts against Booth and his fellow receiver Edmund Worsley (q.v.); Booth countered with a suit for securities for the bonds he had made on the Dean's behalf in 1495.[43] Within a few years Booth also took his place in the administration of his county. He was added to the Suffolk bench in July 1500, and, having been knighted in November 1501, at the wedding of Arthur, prince of Wales, served as sheriff of Norfolk and Suffolk in 1506–07.[44] He became close to Henry VIII, and was appointed knight of the body in 1516.[45] In 1523 he was appointed collector of a subsidy in Suffolk.[46] Booth died on 13 September 1528, leaving his grandson Robert Litton (b. c.1510) as his heir.[47]

Bordeman, Robert, ?of Lincolnshire.
Presumably a member of Worsley's household, he was equipped to accompany the Dean to Scotland in 1480.[48] A John Bordeman held lands in 'Gosberkirk', Lincs., in the right of his wife Margery, which by the end of Henry VII's reign had descended to their daughter Agnes, wife of William Cheell.[49]

Botery, William, of London.
By 1477 Botery was attached to St. Paul's cathedral as chaplain of the Dungeon chantry, and he continued in this position until at least 1488. He first occurs in Worsley's accounts in 1480–81 along with Thomas Smith (q.v.) as executor of Adam Friday (q.v.), clerk of the bakehouse of St. Paul's cathedral. The following year he was one of the executors of the deceased subdean, Laurence Damlet (q.v.), who sold certain items to Worsley. Along with his co-executor, Thomas Elys, a minor canon, he fell victim to the machinations of a London ironmonger, Hugh Aleyn, who sued them in the mayor's court of London for a debt of £20 supposedly owed by Damlet and caused them to be imprisoned.[50]

42 Document 12, above; *CCR*, 1485–1500, no. 863.
43 PRO, C1/186/74; C1/453/2–3.
44 *CPR*, 1494–1509, p. 660; *L&P Hen. VIII*, I.ii, p. 1544; II.i, no. 207; W. A. Shaw, *The Knights of England* (2 vols., London, 1906), i. 147; *CFR*, xxii. 871.
45 *L&P Hen. VIII*, II.i, no. 2735.
46 *L&P Hen. VIII*, III.ii, no. 3282, p. 1365.
47 PRO, E150/640/6; C1/1021/70–72.
48 Document 2, above.
49 PRO, C1/300/2.
50 GL, MS 25125/94–99; documents 2, 3, above; PRO, C1/64/689.

Bovour or **Bover, Thomas**, of Thorpe-le-Soken, Essex.
In 1493–94 Bovour took a newly built watermill at Thorpe to farm from Worsley and continued as farmer there until at least 1497. He may be the Thomas Bowar who by the early sixteenth century had married Joan, widow of Robert Willis of the parishes of St. Dunstan in the East and Allhallows in the Wall, London.[51]

Bower, Richard, of Barling, Essex.
Bower was Worsley's farmer of Barling between at least 1487 and 1490.[52]

Braddows, Robert, of Markshall, Essex, and London.
Braddows was rector of Markshall, Essex, and from 1484 until his death in 1493–94 rector of St. Mary Woolnoth, London. He occurs in Worsley's 1480–81 account as commissary general of the Dean and Chapter of St. Paul's. His responsibilities included the administration of the goods of persons dying intestate within the Chapter's jurisdiction and thus he was involved in acrimonious disputes in the courts on more than one occasion.[53]

Bray, John, of Caddington, Beds.
Worsley's farmer of Caddington from 1482–83, he was still farmer there in 1497.[54]

Bray, Sir Reginald kt., of Woking, Surrey.
Born in about 1440, Bray became steward to Lady Margaret Beaufort, Henry VII's mother, and he owed his subsequent exceptional advancement to Henry Tudor's accession. Knighted at the King's coronation, he was appointed chancellor of the duchy of Lancaster and Lord Treasurer in 1485, and although he was replaced in the latter office by John, Lord Dinham, in 1486 and thereafter served as undertreasurer, he is likely to have continued to be the more dominant of the two men. He had helped Dinham secure a pardon for his brother-in-law, Lord Zouche, from Henry VII in return for generous remuneration. His connection with Worsley was a similar one, for it cannot be doubted that the Dean's grant to Bray of his Hackney property and an annual fee was the price of his pardon in 1496. Bray died in 1503. His executors included Sir John Shaa (q.v.) and Simon Digby (q.v.).[55]

51 Documents 11, 12, above; PRO, C1/285/41.
52 Documents 6–8, above.
53 Document 2, above; Hennessy, pp. cxxxiii, 315; PRO, C1/61/371, 479.
54 Documents 4–9, 11, 12, above.
55 Documents 9, 10, above; PRO, PROB11/13, fols. 219–220 (PCC 26 Blamyr); *The Commons 1439–1509*, ed. Wedgwood, pp. 104–5; Condon, 'Ruling Elites'; *eadem*, 'Caitiff and Villain'; DeLloyd J. Guth, 'Climbing the Civil-Service Pole during Civil War: Sir Reynold Bray (c. 1440–1503), in *Estrangement, Enterprise and Education*, ed. Michalove and Reeves, 47–62.

Bray, Thomas, of Caddington, Beds.
A probable kinsman of John Bray (q.v.) he paid some of John's rents to
Edmund Worsley in April 1497.[56]

Breych, Richard, of Southwell, Notts.
An official of the archdeaconry of Nottingham in 1479–80 when he was
answerable to Worsley for the issues of this northern benefice. He may have
been a trained lawyer, for he later occurs as a mainpernor for members of the
Nottinghamshire gentry.[57]

Broke, John, of Essex.
Broke was one of Worsley's tenants in the soke in Essex in 1493–94 in which
year he paid a fine in the Dean's court there.[58]

Bromley, Sir Thomas, of London.
By 1477 Bromley was active at St. Paul's cathedral as chaplain of the chantry
of Gilbert de Brewer and he continued as such until at least 1488, but possibly
even into the sixteenth century. In 1480–81 he was to accompany the Dean on
his journey to Scotland and equipment was bought for him. He continued his
association with Worsley and in 1495 mainperned for his loyalty.[59]

Bukke, William, of London.
A London tailor, Bukke (d. 1501) annually supplied the cloth liveries for the
Dean's servants throughout the period covered by the accounts. Presumably
because of this supply activity the accounts regularly describe him as a draper.
He rose through the ranks of his profession to become master of the
Merchant Tailors' Company in 1488–89. Apart from his house in the parish
of St. Mary Aldermanbury, London, he also owned further property in the
same parish as well as a garden in St. Laurence Jewry. He had four sons and a
daughter and was survived until 1522 by his wife, who after Bukke's death
married Stephen Jenyns.[60]

---

[56] Document 12, above.

[57] Document 1, above; *CFR*, xxii. 78.

[58] Document 11, above.

[59] GL, MS 25125/94–99; document 2, above; *CCR*, 1485–1500, no. 863; E. A. New,
'The Cult of the Holy Name of Jesus in Late Medieval England, with special
reference to the Fraternity in St. Paul's Cathedral, London c.1450–1558' (unpubl.
Univ. of London Ph.D. thesis, 1999), p. 433.

[60] Documents 1–8, above. A short biography of Bukke can be found in *The Merchant
Taylors' Company of London: Court Minutes 1486–1493*, ed. M. P. Davies
(Stamford, 2000). The authors are grateful to Dr. Davies and Dr. Eleanor Quinton
for their comments on Bukke and his trade. Bukke's inquisition *post mortem*
which dates his death to 1502, but which was not taken until 1532, is wrong as the
evidence of his will shows: *Abstracts of Inquisitions post mortem relating to the City
of London*, ed. G. S. Fry (3 pts., London 1896–1908), i. 47–8; PRO, C142/54/87.

Bulman, John, of London.

In 1482–83 Bulman was paying rent for a Deanery tenement to Roger Radcliff (q.v.). By late 1484 he also held to farm from the Dean and Chapter a small mansion in Pope's Alley, part of the endowment of Pultenay's chantry. He continued as tenant there until at least 1489. He may be the same man who was preferred to a parsonage in Norfolk by May 1484, and later, described as a 'chaplain', became one of the executors of Walter Lihert, bishop of Norwich.[61]

Bunewell, Thomas, of Hackney, Mdx.

Alongside Roger Radcliff (q.v.) Bunewell was a prominent member of the Dean's household throughout the period covered by the accounts. Acting as rent collector at Hackney and Ardleigh in the late 1480s and 1490s, he was referred to as steward of the Dean's household in 1482–83, but under all circumstances appears to have been subordinate to Radcliff.[62]

Burgh, John, of Walton-le-Soken, Essex.

Burgh was the Dean's tenant of the bakehouse of Walton at some point prior to 1493–94.[63]

Butler, Laurence, of London.

In March 1473 Butler was presented by the mayor of London to the second of the three chantries of Sir John Pulteney and of the former archdeacons of Colchester, William Milford and John Plesseys. He resigned this benefice in mid-1488, presumably to concentrate on more administrative duties at the cathedral, for in 1489–90 he, together with John Farman (q.v.), took on the offices of chamberlain and clerk of the bakehouse of St. Paul's. He was still in office in 1495–96, by which date he appears to have been specialising in the latter position.[64]

Candish, John, of Heybridge, Essex.

Farmer of Heybridge mill 1479–83, Candish had previously in 1478 become involved in a violent quarrel with his neighbour Robert Pere (q.v.). The men beat each other and Candish was said to have drawn a dagger.[65]

---

[61] GL, MS 25125/96–99; document 4, above; PRO, C67/51, m. 29; *CPR*, 1485–94, pp. 2, 330.

[62] Documents 1–10, 12, above.

[63] Documents 11, 12, above.

[64] Documents 8, 9, above; *Calendar of Letterbooks: Letterbook L*, ed. R. R. Sharpe (London, 1912), pp. 191, 260; New, 'Holy Name', p. 433.

[65] Documents 1, 2, 4, above; GL, MS 25281/1, m. 12.

Carter, John, of Bancroft in Walton-le-Soken, Essex.
Carter, William
John Carter was farmer of Bancroft rectory between 1479–88. By 1493 he had been succeeded as farmer there by his putative son William. In 1458 a John Carter was churchwarden at Kirby, while the same man or a namesake held a similar post at Walton. In 1489–90 a man of the same name, probably another younger kinsman, occurs at Thorpe. A William Carter held lands at Gestingthorpe, Essex, until his death in 1498.[66]

Cartwryght, Thomas, of Southwell, Notts.
Cartwryght probably entered Worsley's service during his time at Southwell, where he served as a vicar choral from 1476. His conduct during his early years at Southwell was somewhat unorthodox, and he was one of a small group of vicars choral who were disciplined several times for wearing daggers, absenting themselves from divine service, staying in town until late, and taking their breakfast in town while prime was being sung at the minster. On other occasions he was said to have been playing at backgammon at times of service, and, even more seriously, boasted of his wrongdoing. In February 1479, Cartwryght and a fellow vicar, Robert Layn, were charged with having begun a fight in the churchyard, Cartwryght armed with a dagger, while his opponent wielded a cudgel. More interesting, however, were Cartwryght's musical talents. He appears to have been somewhat of an innovator, introducing a new form of harmonic plainsong to the choir. Such innovation did not meet with the approval of his fellows, who at visitations complained unanimously that Cartwryght had a singular and new-fangled way of singing, did not listen to the others and disturbed the chorus. Cartwryght only aggravated matters by boasting of his own ability and mocking his fellows' performance. It is interesting that Worsley nevertheless chose this man as one of his household chaplains in the early years of his Deanery, paying him an annual salary until c. 1483–84.[67]

Chace, [John], of Isleworth, Mdx.
In 1495–96 a man called Chace was deputy of the collector of the first half of a clerical tenth at Willesden. He was presumably the same man who acted as collector of a lay subsidy in Middlesex in 1489. This John Chace married Maud, daughter of Geoffrey Godelake, a servant of John Stafford, then bishop of Bath and Wells. Chace aquired much of his property in the parish of St. Clement Danes, as well as some in Isleworth from his wife's parents. They had a daughter Elizabeth, who married William Merston. Chace, however, failed to fulfil the marriage agreement reached with Merston, forcing his

---

[66] Documents 1–9, 12, above; *Visitations of Churches*, pp. 85, 90; PRO, PROB11/11, fol. 202.
[67] Documents 2–4, above; *Vis. & Mem. Southwell*, pp. 31–34, 40–50, 170.

son-in-law to sue for his wife's dowry.[68]

Chaddekyrke, Henry
A member of the Dean's entourage accompanying him towards Scotland in 1480–81.[69]

Chalk, John, ?of Walden, Essex.
In 1479–80 Chalk was paid for the carriage of a quantity of wood to the Dean's household in London. He may have been the Walden man who was connected with the Say family or a kinsman.[70]

Charlton, Sir Richard, kt., of Edmonton and Hillingdon, Mdx.
Born in about 1449 as eldest surviving son of a former Speaker of the Commons, Richard was a minor at his father's death in 1465. Having proved his age in 1470, he became close to the Yorkist court, and was knighted alongside the Prince of Wales at Westminster on 18 April 1475. In spite of this initial connection with Edward IV's son, Charlton served Richard III on a number of royal commissions and fought for him at Bosworth where he was killed. Posthumously attainted, some of his forfeited lands were subsequently restored to members of his family. Worsley's accounts record the payment of an annual rent to Charlton during his life and afterwards to his heirs. This rent was presumably derived from the manor of Edmonton, which after Sir Richard's attainder passed to his sister Agnes and her husband, who appear in the accounts simply as 'the lord of the manor of Edmonton' (q.v.).[71]

Chaterton, Thomas, of Heybridge, Essex.
Chaterton and Katharine his wife were Worsley's tenants at Heybridge, holding a cottage and a croft of 1½a. of land. He may be identical with the man who in 1502–3 was indebted to the London mercer Roger Bowecer and who around 1480 was dealing in large quantities of wood.[72]

---

[68] Document 9, above; *CFR*, xxii, no. 243; PRO, C1/150/98, 214/86.

[69] Document 2, above.

[70] Document 1, above; *CIPM Hen. VII*, i. 993.

[71] *Coronation of Richard III*, p. 321; documents 2–9, above; PRO, C140/35/64; BL, Add. MS 46,354, fol. 7; *CPR*, 1476–85, pp. 344, 394, 465, 490, 566; BL, Harl. MS 433, f. 330v; C. Ross, *Richard III* (London, 1981), p. 236; *The Ballard of Bosworth Feilde, Bishop Percy's Folio Manuscript* (3 vol., London, 1868), vol. iii, p. 257. The authors are grateful to Miss Jessica Freeman for these references. More detailed biographies of the Charltons will appear in J. Freeman, 'The county community of Middlesex in the fifteenth century' (Univ. of London Ph.D. thesis, 2002).

[72] GL, MS 25311, fol. 56; document 3, above; PRO, C1/260/4.

Clarkson, William, of Thorpe-le-Soken, Essex.
A Lincoln's Inn lawyer, Clarkson was steward of the soke of St. Paul's between at least 1487-90, in succession to Robert Forster (q.v.). He was probably the man who appeared in the manor court of Wickham St. Paul in 1482 to sue the clerk Robert Blakwalle for a debt of 6s. 8d.[73]

Clerk, John, of London.
By 1480 rent collector of the Dean, and probably also of the Chapter of St. Paul's, within the city of London, Clerk continued to serve in the same office until 1489, when he was succeeded by William Trent (q.v.).[74]

Cleydon, John, of Essex.
Cleydon was one of the Dean's tenants in the soke in Essex, and paid a fine in a court held there in 1493-94.[75]

Colles (alias Scholes), Master Nicholas of London.
Thought to have been an Oxfordshire man, Colles trained in the law to become a notary public and set up a London residence in a house near St. Paul's. By the summer of 1474 he was employed by Richard Martyn, one of the clerks of Chancery. By May 1477 he was acting as proctor at law of New College, Oxford, five years later he served Magdalen College in the same capacity. Admitted to Lincoln's Inn in 1479, by the 1480s he was also employed by the Dean and Chapter of St. Paul's as notary and registrar. In this capacity he took responsibility alongside the Chapter's commissary general, Robert Braddows (q.v.), for the administration of the goods of persons having died intestate within the Chapter's peculiar jurisdiction and occasionally had to defend their actions in the courts. Worsley's 1487-88 account describes him as scribe to the commissary of the Deanery of St. Paul's, but may be referring to his previous position. Between 1488 and 1490 he delivered the fines for corrections in the Deanery of St. Paul's to Roger Radcliff (q.v.). By 1490 at the latest, Colles can be found practising in the court of Canterbury. His precedent book survives to the present day in the library of Corpus Christi College, Cambridge.[76]

---

[73] Documents 6-8, above; GL, MS 25375/2, rot. 2d; *Records of the Honorable Society of Lincoln's Inn, vol. I: Admissions, A.D. 1420 to A.D. 1799*, ed. W. P. Baildon (London, 1896), p. 23.

[74] Documents 2-4, 6-8, 13, above.

[75] Document 11, above.

[76] Documents 6-8, above; Emden, *Oxford*, i. 465; PRO, C1/61/371, 479; CP40/856, rot. 340; J. H. Baker, *The Legal Profession and the Common Law: Historical Essays* (London, 1986), p. 88; M. R. James, *A Descriptive Catalogue of the Manuscripts in the Library of Corpus Christi College Cambridge* (2 vols., Cambridge, 1912), i. 381-90.

Colyngham, Master Robert B.Cn.L., of Notts.

A Cambridge graduate like Worsley, Colyngham was instituted as vicar of East Stoke, Notts., by 1470–71. He exchanged this for the church of Bishop's Wickham, Essex, but in June 1480 was re-admitted to East Stoke. About the same time he was also admitted to the vicarage of Mansfield, Notts., which he surrendered in June 1499. In the summer of 1486 he vacated East Stoke a second time in favour of the rectory of St. Peter's Nottingham, which he retained until his death. In 1496–97 Colyngham was an official of the archdeaconry of Nottingham. He was one of several men charged with receiving part of Worsley's income from inductions in the archdeaconry on behalf of the collector, Richard Samesbury (q.v.). He made his will in May 1499, asking to be buried in his church of St. Peter's and died within the next two months.[77]

Comber alias Combes, Robert

A chaplain in the Dean's household by 1484–85, Combes continued in this capacity until 1489–90.[78]

Cook, Clement, of Drayton, Mdx.

Cook held the mill of Drayton to farm of the Dean by 1480 and continued as farmer there until at least 1490.[79] A Clement Cook was granted a cottage and lands in Whitton, Mdx., in December 1465.[80]

Cook, John, of London.

In 1483–84 Cook held land next to a tenement of the Deanery's.[81]

Cook, Matthew, of Thorpe-le-Soken, Essex.

Cook was the Dean's farmer of 'Thorpe Hall' in 1479, but was replaced by Thomas Smith (q.v.) at St. Peter ad vincula the following year.[82]

Cotez, John

In 1480 Cotez sold a number of horses to the Dean for his journey towards Scotland.[83]

---

[77] Document 12, above; Emden, *Cambridge*, p. 152; *Testamenta Eboracensia*, iv. 163–64; *CPL*, xiii. 727.
[78] Documents 5–8, above.
[79] Documents 2–8, above.
[80] PRO, C146/469.
[81] Document 13, above.
[82] Documents 1, 2, above.
[83] Document 2, above.

Counteys, Edmund, of Caddington and Kensworth, Beds.
The Dean's farmer of Caddington and Kensworth by 1480, in 1482 Counteys surrendered Caddington (which was then farmed to John Bray (q.v.)), but continued as farmer of Kensworth until at least 1490. He was perhaps dismissed for allowing his farm to fall into arrears and by 1493 he had been succeeded as farmer by Richard Wynche (q.v.)[84]

Cressy, Marmaduke
A servant of the Dean in the first year of his Deanery.[85]

Dallyng, Geoffrey, of Heybridge, Essex.
Farmer of Heybridge by 1487, Dallyng later also served the Dean as rent collector there. In 1489 William Colman and Joan his wife surrendered a cottage at the end of the bridge of Heybridge to Dallyng's use.[86]

Damlet, Sir Laurence, of London.
A minor canon of St. Paul's, Damlet (d. 1481-82) was subdean of St. Paul's cathedral by 1468 and continued in office up to his death. In 1474 he acted alongside Worsley as a trustee of the London stationer Nicholas Sylverton. In 1481-82 Worsley bought number of items from Damlet's executors, Thomas Elys, a minor canon and later subdean, and William Botery (q.v.).[87]

Dene alias **Deyne, Richard**, of Hackney, Mdx.
Dene was a brewer based at Hackney, close to Worsley's main residence. He was one of a number of men of his trade to supply the Dean's household with ale and is recorded as doing this from 1495 to 1497.[88] He may have been related to the synonymous London skinner and Calais stapler who took John Fitzherbert's (q.v.) closes in Hackney to farm from him for 13 years in March 1502. This man died in the second half of 1519, survived by his wife Joan.[89]

Dey, Thomas, of Mdx.
One of the Dean's servants, who took charge of receiving some of his rents and farms in Middlesex in 1496-97.[90]

---

[84] Documents 2-8, above.
[85] Document 1, above.
[86] GL, MS 25311, fol. 59v; documents 6-9, above.
[87] Document 3, above; PRO, C1/64/689; New, 'Holy Name', p. 334; *CCR*, 1468-76, no. 1330.
[88] Documents 9, 10, above.
[89] PRO, E210/9639; PROB11/19, fol. 180 (PCC 23 Ayloffe).
[90] Document 12, above.

Digby, Simon, of Coleshill, Warwicks.
A younger son of Everard Digby of Tilton-on-the-Hill, Leics., Digby and his brothers fought for Henry VII at Bosworth and rose rapidly in the victorious Tudor King's service. Simon became deputy constable of the Tower of London, in which capacity he received payment from Worsley. He was well connected in Henry VII's inner circle, for his brother John became Marshall of the King's household. Simon himself became closely acquainted with Sir Reginald Bray (q.v.), and was to act as one of his executors. It was as a consequence of his connections that Worsley granted him an annual fee in 1495–96. Digby died on 24 February 1520, survived by his wife, Alice, and was succeeded by his son Reynold.[91]

Dorset, Thomas Grey, Lord Ferrers of Groby, **Marquess of**
Born in about 1451 as son and heir of John, Lord Ferrers of Groby (*alias* Sir John Grey), by Elizabeth, daughter of Richard Wydeville, 1st Earl Rivers (afterwards queen consort of King Edward IV). Thomas was consequently a stepson of Edward IV, and was created Earl of Huntingdon on 14 August 1471. He renounced this title, and on 18 April 1475 was made Marquess of Dorset, a title which Henry VII confirmed in 1486. He increased his landholdings substantially by his two successive marriages to wealthy noble heiresses, first to Anne, only daughter of Thomas Holand, Duke of Exeter, and secondly to Cicely, granddaughter of William, Lord Bonville (d. 1461). In 1481–82 the Marquess was entertained in the Dean's house, an occasion for which a substantial number of cloth items were specially acquired. He died in 1501.[92]

Downing, Geoffrey, of Belchamp St. Paul, Essex.
Downing held various lands in Belchamp St. Paul, including a garden called 'Hamondes' in a street called 'Mellegrene', as well as others in nearby Belchamp William and Belchamp Otton. By 1487 Downing also held Worsley's manor at Belchamp St. Paul to farm, and continued as farmer until at least 1495–96. Downing made his will in August 1503 and was dead within two months. He was survived by his second wife, Margery – the first, Alice, had died in his lifetime – and left a son, John, who was betrothed to Mary Carder, a widow. The provisions of his will included prayers for Thomas Watson (q.v.)[93]

[91] *CPR*, 1494–1509, pp. 65, 366; document 9, above; *VCH Warwicks.*, iv. 51; PRO, C142/35/61, 65, 94; E150/222/12, 623/1; PROB11/13, fols. 219–220 (PCC 26 Blamyr); PROB11/19, fol. 227 (PCC 29 Ayloffe).
[92] *CP*, iv. 418–19; document 3, above.
[93] Documents 6, 7, 9, above; PRO, PROB11/13, fols. 210v–211 (PCC 25 Blamyr).

Edmonton, Mdx., lord of the manor of

From 1488–90 Worsley's accounts record payments to the lord of the manor of Edmonton. Until his death in 1485 this manor had formed part of the estates of Sir Richard Charlton (q.v.). By virtue of Charlton's attainder the manor came into the King's hand, who on 7 March 1486 granted it to Charlton's sister Agnes and her second husband, Sir Thomas Bourgchier.[94]

Essenwolde, John, of London.

Son of the London brewer Robert Essenwolde, John took up his father's trade and became one of a number of men who supplied ale to the Dean's household. Worsley's accounts note payments to him between 1479 and 1481.[95]

Essex, Henry Bourgchier, Earl of

Born in about 1404 as son and heir of Sir William Bourgchier, afterwards count of Eu in Normandy, by Anne, daughter of Thomas, Duke of Gloucester, Earl of Essex. He succeeded his father as Count of Eu in May 1420, and was created Viscount Bourgchier in 1446, and Earl of Essex on 30 June 1461. He married before 25 April 1426 Isabel, daughter of Richard, Earl of Cambridge. He served as Lord Treasurer of England in 1455–56, 1460–62 and from 1471 until his death on 4 April 1483.[96]

Essex, Henry Bourgchier, Earl of

Born in about 1472 as son and heir of Sir William Bourgchier (*d.v.p.* February 1483), eldest son of Henry Bourgchier, Earl of Essex (d. 1483) (q.v.), by Anne, 3rd daughter of Richard Wydeville, Earl Rivers. He married Mary, elder daughter and coheiress of Sir William Say (q.v.) of Broxbourne and Essenden, and, having found significant favour under Henry VIII, died as a result of a riding accident on 13 March 1540, leaving a single daughter.[97]

Farman, John, of London.

A chaplain in Worsley's household from 1487, in 1489–90 Farman, together with Laurence Butler (q.v.), took on the offices of chamberlain and clerk of the bakehouse of St. Paul's. He was still in office in 1495–96, by which date he appears to have been specialising in the former position. At the same time, he appears to have assumed some duties as collector of the Dean and Chapter,

---

94 Documents 7, 8, above; *CPR*, 1485–94, p. 63; *L&P Hen. VIII*, I.i, no. 485(2). The authors are grateful to Miss Jessica Freeman for her comments on this point.

95 *Cal. Plea & Mem. Rolls, 1458-1482*, p. 177; documents 1, 2, above.

96 *CP*, v. 137–38; L. S. Clark, 'The Benefits and Burdens of Office: Henry Bourgchier (1408-83), Viscount Bourgchier and Earl of Essex, and the Treasurership of the Exchequer', in *Profit, Piety and the Profession*, ed. Hicks, 119–36.

97 *CP*, v. 138–39; *Coronation of Richard III*, p. 314.

an office which by 1501 had been assumed by Thomas Nutson.[98]

Felix, John, of Kirby-le-Soken, Essex.
A butcher by trade, Felix came from a family long-established at Kirby. Two kinsmen, Robert and William Felyx, were churchwardens in 1458. It was also there that he acted as a subcollector of the King's taxes in 1497.[99]

Fitton, George, of Kirby-le-Soken, Essex.
Fitton was vicar of Kirby in 1496–97 when he received some of the issues of Walton on behalf of Edmund Worsley (q.v.).[100]

Fitzherbert, John, of London.
Fitzherbert was born in about 1435 as son of Sir Nicholas Fitzherbert (d. 19 November 1473). He began his Exchequer career in 1464 as Clerk of the Estreats, subsequently serving as a teller (c.1472–85), Foreign Apposer (1474–85) and King's Remembrancer (1480–d.), with a brief spell as a Deputy Chamberlain during Richard III's reign. He married Joan (*fl.* 1528), daughter of Robert Babington, and they had at least one son and two daughters. As Fitzherbert's son Henry died in his father's lifetime, his eventual heir at his death on 18 November 1502 was his grandson Eustace (1491–1518). In 1481 he was appointed collector of a clerical tenth, in which capacity he occurs in Worsley's account for 1480–81. Holding lands as far afield as Derbyshire he also owned property in Hackney, including a house in Humblonstreet which he had bought, but he lived in a rented house in St. Bartholomew's close, West Smithfield. Fitzherbert's wider family also had links with Worsley's circle and family: in his will he mentioned his cousin Odeby, and his great-niece Dorothy later married a Ralph Langford.[101]

Fitzwarren, Thomas, of London.
A London goldsmith, Fitzwarren was not a regular supplier of the Dean's household, but is only known to have sold a gilded cup to Worsley in 1479–80. Nothing further is known of him, but he may have been related to a synonymous leatherseller of the parish of St. Benet with landholdings in Berkshire and Gloucestershire who died in 1499. Another possible kinsman of the same name was a verger of St. Paul's.[102]

---

[98] Documents 6–9, above; PRO, C47/10/28/39, 41; C146/3171; SP46/183, f. 92.
[99] *Visitation of Churches*, p. 85; document 12, above.
[100] Document 12, above.
[101] Document 2, above; PRO, E210/9639; PROB11/13, fols. 158–159 (PCC 18 Blamyr); *CIPM Hen. VII*, ii. 631; Sainty, pp. 44, 83, 90, 169, 229; *The Notebook of Sir John Port*, ed. J. H. Baker (London, Selden Soc. 102, 1986), p. xiii; *CFR*, xxi, no. 657. For Fitzherbert's earlier activity as a taxcollector see M. Jurkowski, 'Parliamentary and Prerogative Taxation in the Reign of Edward IV', *Parliamentary History* 18 (1999), 271–90, p. 281.

Flynte, Nicholas, of London.

A London goldsmith, Flynte's youth saw some unruly incidents, such as his quarrel with David Panter, whom he called a 'roughfooted Scot'. Henry VII appointed him controller, changer and assayer of the mint, and in 1487 also graver of the irons. In March 1490 Flynte was appointed surveyor and controller of the Irish mints and mines. He continued to hold his posts at the London mint until April 1495 when he was succeded by Henry Wyott, to be made royal pavillioner in April 1496.[103]

Ford alias **Forth, Roger,** of London.

A taverner, Ford held a tenement called 'Powles hede' from the Deanery until Michaelmas 1483.[104]

Ford, William

A servant of the Dean who, alongside John Morton (q.v.), transacted certain business at the Exchequer on his behalf.[105]

Forster, Robert, of Thorpe-le-Soken, Essex, and London.

By 1480–81 Forster served Worsley as steward of the soke of St. Paul's, and continued in this post until 1484–85, to be eventually replaced by William Clarkson (q.v.).[106] He should probably be identified with the lawyer Robert Forster of Islington and London, clerk of hell at the royal courts at Westminster, and brother of Master John Forster, the archdeacon of London. He held lands in Tottenham, Westminster and Hendon and died on 13 May 1485, leaving a 15-year-old son and three daughters.[107]

Fourth, [–], of Oakley, Essex.

Alongside John Felix (q.v.), one of the sub-collectors of the King's taxation at Kirby-le-Soken in 1496–97.[108]

Fox, John, of Edmonton, Mdx.

Fox was probably of low origins, for a man of this name recorded at Edmonton in 1469 was described as a 'husbandman'. Our John is first known to have been associated with Worsley in 1480–81, when he was paid for the making of a jack for the Scottish expedition. By 1481 he was, jointly with

---

[102] Document 1, above; PRO, PROB11/11, fol. 272v; C1/200/22.

[103] T. F. Reddaway, *The Early History of the Goldsmiths' Company, 1327–1509* (London, 1975), pp. 154, 201; PRO, E101/298/33; *CPR*, 1485–94, pp. 19, 96, 173, 299; *CPR*, 1494–1509, pp. 16, 60.

[104] Document 13, above.

[105] Document 2, above.

[106] Documents 2–5, above.

[107] PRO, C67/51, m. 11; C1/83/86; *CFR*, xxii. 6; *CIPM Hen. VII*, i. 133.

[108] Document 12, above.

Edward Westby (q.v.), farmer of Bowes and Polehouse, but he still occurs in this capacity in 1497. A reference to a *William* Fox as farmer in 1495–96 is probably the result of a scribal error.[109]

Freman, Robert, ?of London.
Freman was a chaplain connected with the Dean at the time of his imprisonment in the Tower.[110]

Frende, Joan, of Acton, Mdx.
Frende, Robert, of Acton, Mdx.
Frende, Roger, of Willesden and Acton, Mdx.
In 1460 Roger Frende (d. c.1483), originally a yeoman of Willesden, leased three fields and two crofts in Acton from Master William Say, then Dean, and the Chapter of St. Paul's. By 1480 at the latest, he was the farmer of Worsley's lands at Acton.[111] He was dead by 1483–84, when Joan, his widow, brought a suit in chancery for his landholdings. Three years later, in 1487–88, Joan herself accounted for the farm.[112] That same year Robert Frende, younger son of Roger and Joan, acted as a royal tax collector at Willesden. Robert subsequently went on to become farmer of Acton himself.[113]

Frost, William, of Wadende in Ardleigh, Herts.
By 1482–83 Frost held Wadende to farm from Worsley and continued as farmer there at least until 1497. He was probably the same man who served as *decennarius* (tithingman) in 1495–96 and as constable from 1496–98 at Ardleigh.[114]

Friday, Adam, of London.
Clerk of the bakehouse of St. Paul's cathedral in 1479–80, Friday died that same year, probably while still in office, and was succeeded by Thomas Skypwith (q.v.). Thomas Smith (q.v.), one of Worsley's chaplains and farmer of 'Thorpe Hall', and William Botery (q.v.) were appointed his executors.[115]

Fuldon *alias* **Fulledene, John**, of Hackney, Mdx.
Fuldon was an official of the Dean's receiving an annual fee of 13s. 4d. in 1479–80. The following year, Fuldon took charge of the acquisition of various types of grain and hay on his master's behalf. In 1482–83 and 1484–85 he also acted as the Dean's collector at Ardleigh, at the same time as acting as

---

[109]   PRO, KB27/831, rot. 6; documents 2–7, 9, 12.
[110]   Document 9, above.
[111]   Documents 1, 2, 4, 5, above; GL, MS 25342.
[112]   PRO, C1/65/126–127; document 6, above.
[113]   Documents 6, 9, above; C1/65/127.
[114]   Documents 4, 6–9, 12, above; GL, MS 25301/1, rots. 2–2d.
[115]   Documents 1, 2, above.

'*appruator*' at Hackney.[116]

Garrard, Thomas, of Chepyng Lambourn, Berks.
By 1487–88 Garrard had succeeded John Bernard (q.v.) as procurator of Chepyng Lambourn. He continued there for some years, and occurs again as farmer of the rectory of Lambourn in 1495–96, and continued in the farm until at least 1501. However, after the Dean's death he was forced to bring a suit in chancery against Worsley's executors who demanded payments of his farm which he claimed already to have made to Worsley and his successor, Robert Sherborne.[117]

German, John, of Kirby-le-Soken, Essex.
Worsley's farmer of the rectory of Kirby between 1479 and 1485, in 1458 German was executor of the will of Alice Poppes, who had bequeathed a cow to the church there.[118]

Godde, Master Robert B.Cn.L., of Kingston and Taunton, Som.
Descended from a westcountry family, Godde was instituted to the vicarage of Kingston at the presentation of the prior of Taunton in 1471. Some years later, in 1478, he acted as proctor for his brother, Master William Godde, at the latter's institution to the prebend of Warminster at Wells cathedral. When William died five years later, Robert acted as one of his executors and received a bequest of various books and garments. By 1495–96 Godde was an official of the archdeaconry of Taunton, who that year was charged with the collection of Worsley's revenue from the archdeaconry.[119]

Gray's Inn, London, steward of
At least in Worsley's early years at St. Paul's, the steward of Gray's Inn was paid an annual pension of 3s. 8d. by the Dean.[120]

Grege, John
In the course of the preparations for the Scottish expedition of 1480, Grege was paid for mending a jack.[121]

Grene, John, of Wickham St. Paul, Essex.
Worsley's farmer at Wickham St. Paul between 1480 and 1496, he may have been one of the two men of the same name who served as churchwardens

---

116 Documents 1, 2, 4, 5, above.
117 Documents 6–9, above; PRO, C1/240/7–8.
118 Documents 1–5, above; *Visitations of Churches*, p. 87.
119 *Regs. Stillington and Fox*, nos. 194, 653; *Fasti*, viii. 62; document 9, above; Emden, *Oxford*, ii. 776; PRO, PROB11/7, fols. 50v–51 (PCC 7 Logge).
120 Document 2, above.
121 Document 2, above.

there in 1458. One of the latter two, perhaps father and son, that year also acted as a surety that a new light or lamp would be found for the church. Grene, who also held lands at Gestingthorpe, probably resided in his house called 'Walshes' at Wickham. He made his will in February 1506 and died shortly afterwards. He left a daughter, Anne, who married George Reynew and was survived by his wife, Joan.[122] Grene may have been related or even identical with the synonymous stepson and apprentice of the mercer William Aleyn (q.v.).[123]

Grymston, Sir John, of London.

Grymston served as chapain of the Wendover chantry at St. Paul's from at least 1477 and continued in this capacity until about 1486-87 when he was replaced by John Rogers. In 1481-82 he received a payment for the memory of the souls of the Dean's parents. He may have been the chaplain who in 1450 was appointed one of the executors of the London draper William Bangore, and who as such was shortly afterwards sued by Bangore's next heir.[124]

Hale, William, of Norton Folgate, Mdx.

A servant of the Dean who first occurs in the 1481-82 account in connection with a payment for an estreat, Hale seems to have taken responsibility for holding the Dean's court at Norton Folgate in 1483-84. He may have been either the same man who was appointed a tax collector in Middlesex in 1492 as William Hale the younger, or his father. The younger man later became keeper of the London palace of Richard Nykke (q.v.), bishop of Norwich.[125]

Haliwell, Mdx., prioress of

Worsley held several tenements in London, including one called 'le Spaldynghouse', from the priory, for which annual quit rents of 3s. were paid in 1483-84. The name of the prioress at the time is uncertain, but either Elizabeth Prudde, elected 1472 and documented in 1474, or Joan Lynde, who had been elected by 1515, may have been in office.[126]

Harlesley, John, of London.

In 1483-84 Harlesley held a tenement at 'Paules Cheyn' to farm from the Dean.[127]

---

[122] Document 2-4, 6-9, above; *Visitations of Churches*, pp. 94, 97; PRO, PROB11/15, fols. 34-35 (PCC 5 Adeane).
[123] PRO, PROB11/19, fols. 188-189v (PCC 24 Ayloffe).
[124] GL, MS 25125/94-99; document 3, above; PRO, C1/19/317-23; C253/32/218.
[125] Documents 3, 13, above; *CFR*, xxii. 397; PRO, E179/141/109, p. 3.
[126] Document 13, above; *VCH Mdx*. i. 178.
[127] Document 13, above.

Harnes or Herneys, John, of Thorpe-le-Soken, Essex.
From at least 1493 John Harnes held John Kent's (q.v.) former tenement at Thorpe to farm of Worsley. He was still farmer there in 1496–97.[128]

Haryngton, John
One of the last chaplains to become attached to the Dean's household, his salary first occurs in the account for 1495–96.[129] He may have been a kinsman of William Haryngton, canon of St. Paul's and prebendary of Islington from 1497 to 1523.[130] Another contemporary putative kinsman, Dr. John Haryngton, was a canon lawyer and advocate in the court of Arches.[131]

Herde, John, of Runwell, Essex.
Joint farmer of Runwell with John Hey (q.v.) in 1484–86, they had themselves been replaced by John Bek (q.v.) by 1487–88.[132]

Herdyng, William, of Maldon, Essex.
In 1496–97 Herdyng sold a millstone for a grain mill to the farmer of Heybridge manor.[133]

Heron, Sir John, of Hackney, Mdx.
An Exchequer official close to Henry VII, Heron eventually became a chamberlain of the Exchequer in his son's reign, serving in the office from 1516 until his death on 15 June 1521. Under Henry VIII he rose to become Treasurer of the Chamber to the King. Like other members of Henry VII's inner circle, he received payments from Worsley after his pardon for his involvement in the Warbeck affair. At his death he was survived by his wife Margaret and left five sons and three daughters, one of whom married the illegitimate grandson of Henry VII's Treasurer, John, Lord Dinham.[134]

Hethe, Robert, of London.
Hethe served as rent collector of the Dean and Chapter in London and its suburb from about 1476–77. In 1480–81 he paid £4 to William Hill (q.v.), his successor in this office.[135]

---

[128] Documents 9, 11, 12, above.
[129] Document 9, above.
[130] PRO, E314/75/13–14; *Fasti*, v. 45.
[131] PRO, C1/205/42.
[132] Document 6, above.
[133] Document 12, above.
[134] *Officers of the Exchequer*, comp. J. C. Sainty (London, List and Index Soc. spec. ser. 18, 1983), p. 17; document 9, above; PRO, C1/679/55; C142/35/88, 40/113; PROB11/21, fols. 262–263 (PCC 33 Bodfelde).
[135] GL, MS 25125/92–95; document 2, above.

Hewet, John, of Ratcliff, Mdx.
Hewet, William, of Ratcliff, Mdx.
John Hewet held the mill of Ratcliff to farm from Worsley from at least 1480, and he was still farmer there in 1484–85, then described in the Dean's accounts as the miller. Two years later he had been succeeded by his putative son, William.[136]

Hewyk, John, of Chipping Ongar, Essex, and London.
John Hewyk served as auditor of the Dean's estates from at least 1480, and still held the office in 1484–5, but presumably surrendered the office when he was appointed King's auditor by Henry VII in December of that year. He held a number of tenements in Greenford, 'Merston', High Ongar and Stanford Rivers as well as a house in Chipping Ongar in which John Saperton (q.v.) lived. Hewyk appointed Saperton, who succeeded him as Worsley's auditor, one of his executors, and in his will left him and his wife his house in Chipping Ongar. Hewyk made his will in February 1491 and died on the following 3 April, survived by his wife Isabel (d. 1495) and five daughters.[137]

Hey, *alias* **At Hey, John,** of Runwell, Essex.
At Hey was the Dean's farmer of Runwell from at least 1481 to 1483. He was joined as farmer by John Herde (q.v.) in about 1484, but by 1487–88 they had been replaced by John Bek.[138]

Hill, Edmund, of Norton Folgate, Mdx.
Hill, William
Rent collector of the Dean and Chapter in 1480–81, William Hill held Worsley's lands at Norton Folgate to farm from 1480 to 1489. He was succeeded as farmer there by his putative kinsman Edmund. William, pardoned by Richard III in 1484, by which date he had been succeeded as rent collector by William Pope, was probably the same man, a former rector of St. Gregory by St. Paul's, who served as a minor canon and subdean at the cathedral after 1488, and became Master of St. Thomas of Acon in 1501.[139]

Holt, Stephen
In 1479–80 Holt was one of Worsley's feed household servants.[140]

---

[136] Document 2–6, above.
[137] Documents 2–5, above; PRO, PROB11/9, fols. 234–235 (PCC 29 Doggett); *CIPM Hen. VII*, i. 821; *CFR*, xxii. 45, 169, 368, 528; Sainty, p. 118.
[138] Documents 3, 4, 6, above.
[139] Documents 2–5, 7, 8, above; Hennessy, pp. 61, 427; PRO, C67/51, m. 17; New, 'Holy Name', p. 430.
[140] Document 1, above.

Holy Trinity Aldgate, London, Thomas Percy, prior of.

Prior of Holy Trinity Aldgate by 1489–90, Percy's conduct in office soon attracted the attention of his diocesan, Bishop Hill of London (q.v.). By 1491 he faced accusations of having wasted the goods of his monastery, of associating suspiciously with various women of questionable reputation, including one Joan Hodges for whom he secured the appointment for life as embroidress to his priory. The bishop's inquiry found the accusations to be true and Percy to be an adulterer, a perjurer and a simoniac and to have wasted the monastery's resources up to the huge sum of 3000 marks. The prior then appealed to the archbishop of Canterbury against bishop Hill's decision. This appeal triggered a full-blown quarrel between Hill and Archbishop Morton, in which Percy continued to play a colourful role. On 16 April 1494 the bishop himself appeared before the gates of Holy Trinity to remove Percy from office, but the prior refused him entry and held his house with armed men. Five months later, on 3 September, the bishop's men broke into the priory at night, dragged Percy out and imprisoned him. Yet, the intervention of some of the King's senior ministers and councillors forced Bishop Hill to submit to the archbishop, and as a consequence Percy was released on 22 November and reinstalled as prior on 3 December. The archbishop, however, also brought pressure to bear on the prior and Percy resigned again less than two weeks later. In compensation, he received one of the priory's most valuable manors as a pension from which he drew an annual income of £40, and was later also made vicar of Bexley. Ironically, towards the end of his life, in late 1506, Percy was for a second time elected prior of Holy Trinity and died in office.[141]

Honyborne, John, of London.

In 1483–84 Honyborne was paid a quit rent of 4s. p.a. from the Deanery. He may have been the same London citizen who on one occasion in the late 1450s was bound by statute merchant to pay 20 marks to a London butcher, William Stalon.[142]

Horward, John, of Walton-le-Soken, Essex.

In 1496 Horward succeeded John Toose as the Dean's farmer of Walton.[143]

Hudson, [–], of Ratcliff, Mdx.

In 1495–96 Hudson was Worsley's farmer of Ratcliff mill, a part of the Deanery of London.[144]

---

[141] Harper-Bill, 'Bishop Hill and the Court of Canterbury', pp. 2–3, 5–6; *Great Chronicle*, p. 440; *VCH London*, pp. 471, 474; document 8, above.

[142] Document 13, above; PRO, C1/26/574.

[143] Document 12, above.

[144] Document 9, above.

Hugh, John, of Essex.
In 1493–94 Hugh was one of the Dean's tenants in the soke of St. Paul's and in that year paid a fine in the court at Kirby.[145]

Hulme, William, of London.
A London draper, Hulme was not one of the Dean's regular suppliers, and only occurs in the accounts in 1484–85. Born in the parish of St. Nicholas Acon, he resided in the parish of St. Christopher le Stocks, where he asked to be buried, and where he held several tenements. He died in late October or early November 1495 and was survived by his wife Joan and a daughter, Mary, who had married Thomas Hertwell. A second daughter, Margaret, had predeceased him and had been buried at Woolwich, Kent.[146]

Hurley, Berks., **John** [Hilston], **prior of**
Head of Hurley Priory in Berkshire, a cell of Westminster Abbey, John Hilston had been elected abbot in early 1487 following the death of his predecessor, Thomas Preston, in the previous year. Soon after his election, he was one of the heads of religious houses appointed by the bishop of London in 1487–88 to collect the King's taxation in the diocese. He died in 1497 when he was succeeded by John Hampton.[147]

Hykman, John, of Essex.
From at least 1493–94 to 1496–97 Hykman was a tenant in the soke of St. Paul's in Essex, paying tithes to the Dean.[148]

Jane, Thomas, D.Cn.L. of London and Norwich, Norfolk.
Appointed a canon of St. Paul's and prebendary of Reculversland in 1471, Jane was one of the three important lawyers, including Worsley, who were chosen as proxies by most of the absentee prebendaries at the time of Worsley's election. He was translated to the prebend of Rugmere in 1480 and to that of Brownswood in 1487, becoming Archdeacon of Essex in July 1480. He became Dean of the Chapel Royal to Henry VII, and was preferred to the see of Norwich in 1499, but died in September 1500. In 1483–85 he held a mansion in London from Dean Worsley.[149]

Jolyff, Martin, of London.
A junior administrative official of the Chapter of St. Paul's, Jolyff served as clerk of the bakehouse of St. Paul's from 1482–83, in succession to Thomas

---

145   Document 11, above.
146   GL, MS 9171/8, fol. 100v; document 5, above.
147   Document 6, above; *Monasticon Anglicanum*, iii. 431; *VCH Berks.* ii. 76.
148   Documents 11, 12, above.
149   Document 5, above, 25168; *Fasti,* v. 11, 22, 58, 60; *CPR*, 1494–1509, p. 71; *DNB*, x. 681; Emden, *Oxford*, ii. 1013–14; PRO, PROB11/12, fol. 74v (PCC 10 Moone).

Skypwith (q.v.). From 1487 to 1489 he seems to have combined this office with that of chamberlain of St. Paul's. Even earlier he had officiated as 'Keeper of the Guild of Jesus' at St. Paul's and in 1489 he gave up both his administrative offices, presumably to concentrate on pastoral duties: in his will of 1493 he called himself 'prieste' and left a bequest of money to the London church of St. Bartholomew the Less. Indeed, he may have been ordained rather late in life, for his will mentions a son, Richard Jolyff, although his executors at his death in early 1496 were two Exchequer officials.[150]

Jordan, John, of Charlwood, Surrey.
A yeoman, Jordan held the manors of Gatwick (in Charlwood) and 'Salmans', which he acquired after a legal dispute with the Cobham family. In 1482–83 he made a payment to the collector of the Deanery of London for wood he had sold. He died in March 1512, survived by his wife, Alice, and leaving an under-age son and two daughters. In his will he asked that Master Henry Saunder, perhaps a kinsman of the synonymous collector of the Deanery, should assist his widow in its execution.[151]

Kemp, Ralph, of London.
Kemp was a London mercer, married to Margaret, the daughter of a fellow mercer, John Burton (d. 1460), whose apprentice he had been and who eventually was to appoint him one of his executors. Burton settled much of his property on his daughter Margaret, to the disinheritance of his own son, William. Kemp rose in his trade, and in 1470 and 1476 served as master of the London Mercers' Company. He died in October 1477 and was survived by his wife who had a life-interest in his estates, and his two sons John and Thomas to whom they passed thereafter. Several tenements in the Deanery were held from Kemp, for which he was paid quit rents of 8s. p.a., still recorded under his name in 1483–84, but by then presumably paid to his widow.[152]

Kendale, Master John, of Notts.
In 1496–97 Kendale was registrar of the archdeaconry of Nottingham, receiving an annual fee of 13s. 4d., as well as a robe worth 6s. 8d. for his office. He cannot be readily identified with any of the John Kendales known to have been active in the period, although he was certainly not Richard III's secretary

[150] Documents 4–8, above; PRO, C1/66/25; PROB11/10, fol. 248v (PCC 31 Vox).
[151] Document 4, above; PRO, PROB11/17, fol. 52v (PCC 7 Fetiplace); STAC1/1/31.
[152] Document 13, above; PRO, C1/27/1, 47–49; E13/147, rot. 4; PROB11/6, fols. 244–245; A. F. Sutton, 'Alice Claver, Silkwoman', in *Medieval London Widows*, ed. C. Barron and A. F. Sutton (London and Rio Grande, 1994), 129–42, p. 134; *Acts of court of the Mercers' Company 1453–1527* ed. L. Lyell and F. D. Watney (Cambridge, 1936), pp. 50, 52, 55, 76, 79, 86–94.

of the same name.[153]

Kent, John, of Thorpe-le-Soken, Essex.
Between 1481 and 1483, and perhaps as late as 1487 Kent held the rectory of
Thorpe to farm of Worsley. The lands attached thereto probably constituted
the holding there later known as 'Kent's tenement'.[154]

Kent, Master, of London.
Kent held a tenement in Knightrider Street, London, from Worsley at some
point prior to 1483–84, when it had passed to William Say (q.v.).[155] It is
possible, but by no means certain, that he was the William Kent who, having
been admitted to Cambridge university in 1474–75, from 1478 until his death
in 1485 was a fellow of Corpus Christi College.[156]

Kilburn, Mdx., **Prioress** of
Like Hurley, Kilburn Priory was a cell of Westminster Abbey. The names of
few of its heads are known and the identity of the lady who headed the house
in 1479–80 and appears in Worsley's account for that year is likewise
uncertain, but she may have been the same Katharine who was prioress in
1484.[157]

Langford, Ralph, of Southwell, Notts.
Langford was probably a half-brother of Dean Worsley, a younger son of his
mother by her first marriage to Sir Ralph Langford (d. 26 February 1432).
Described as Worsley's '*frater*', in 1496–97 he was paid a weekly wage of 12d.
by the Dean. He may have been the man who in November 1492 headed a
panel of 12 oathhelpers at Southwell. They were summoned to swear to the
innocence of two servants of Master William Talbot who were accused of
sodomy and fornication, as well as of robbing Thomas Orston (q.v.).[158] If so,
it is probable that he was the man who succeeded his brother Nicholas
(c.1419–81) at the latter's death and who was subsequently sued by Nicholas's
widow for her dower.[159]

---

[153] Document 12, above; A. F. Sutton, 'John Kendale: A Search for Richard III's
Secretary', *Richard III*, ed. Petre, 224–38.
[154] Document 2–6, above.
[155] Document 13, above.
[156] Emden, *Cambridge*, 336.
[157] Document 1, above; *VCH Middlesex*, i (1969), p. 182.
[158] Document 12, above; *Vis. & Mem. Southwell*, p. 57.
[159] PRO, C1/36/1213, 67/229, 363; C139/57/3; *CFR*, xxi. 614.

Lawshull, William, of Great Stambridge, Essex.
Lawshull held various lands in Great Stambridge from the bishop of Bath, some of which he appears to have granted to Worsley, for in 1480–81 he received money paid for respite of the Dean's homage for certain lands in Rochford hundred, Essex. He was still active as a feoffee in the county two years later, but died on 1 May 1485, leaving his 12-year-old son John as his heir.[160]

Lee, Richard, of London.
Lee was a London grocer with landholdings in Essex, Surrey, Sussex and Kent. He appears to have resided in a house in the parish of St. Stephen Walbrook which his father, another Richard Lee (d. 1472), had taken to farm from the dean and chapter of St. Paul's in 1457 for a term of 95 years. He made his will in 1494, asking to be buried in his parish church of St. Stephen Walbrook, London, but seems to have lived on until 1498. He was survived by his wife Joyce and several sons, the eldest of whom was called Richard like him.[161] He occurs in Radcliff's accounts in 1479–80 receiving a payment of £50, the nature of which is obscure. Alongside the dean he served as a feoffee of Richard Culpeper, first husband of William's kinswoman Isabella Worsley (q.v.).[162] In 1496 Lee was among the men to stand surety for William Sutton, rector of his parish of St. Stephen Walbrook, who had been arrested alongside Worsley for involvement in the Warbeck conspiracy.[163]

Leyke, Thomas, of Notts.
In 1479–80 an official of the archdeaconry of Nottingham who, along with Thomas Orston (q.v.), conveyed some of Worsley's income to Roger Radcliff (q.v.). He cannot be identified with certainty, as there were several men of this name active in Nottinghamshire in this period.[164]

Lindsey, John, of Heybridge, Essex.
In September 1479 John Lindsey and Joan his wife were admitted to a tenement of 6 acres called 'Mynhouyez'. In the same year Lindsey was acting as Worsley's receiver at Heybridge, where he also held the Dean's demesne lands to farm from 1480–85. By Michaelmas 1482 Lindsey had married a second wife, Alice, who was to survive him. He died c. 1496. His widow paid as a heriot a cow worth 6s. 8d. (paid in 1503–04). The John Lindsey senior and junior who held lands at Heybridge to farm in the early years of the sixteenth

---

[160] Document 2, above; *CCR,* 1476–85, no. 994; *CIPM Hen. VII,* iii. 611.
[161] PRO, PROB11/11, fol. 215v; C106/149; S. Thrupp, *The Merchant Class of Medieval London* (1949), p. 353.
[162] Document 1, above; PRO, C67/53, m. 4.
[163] PRO, C54/376, m. 19d.
[164] Document 1, above; *CFR,* xxii. 246; *CPR,* 1476–85, pp. 395, 400, 489, 569; *CPR,* 1485–94, pp. 241, 396, 496.

century were probably his descendants.[165]

Litton, Sir Robert, kt., of Stanwell, Mdx.

Litton (d. 1505) made his career in royal service at the Exchequer, which he entered in the reign of Edward IV, serving successively as Clerk of the Estreats (1474–85), teller (c.1482–85), and Treasurer's Remembrancer (1485–d.). In 1487 he replaced Sir Reginald Bray (q.v.) as Undertreasurer, holding the latter two posts until his death. In 1492 he was also appointed Keeper of the Great Wardrobe and in 1501–02 he served as Treasurer at War. Litton died in the first half of 1505, survived by his wife, Elizabeth, and leaving two sons and several daughters. One of his sons, between whom his lands were split, married Adriana, daughter and sole heir of Philip Booth (q.v.).[166]

Lokear, Master John, of Belchamp St. Paul, Essex.

Lokear was a Scotsman by birth, and only procured letters of denization as Anglo-Scottish relations rapidly deteriorated in the first half of 1480. From at least 1479 to 1485 he was vicar of Belchamp St. Paul and also took responsibility for the collection of the Dean's rents and farms there. At the same time, he also held the rectory of nearby Wickham St. Paul to farm.[167]

Lokkey, William

In 1479–80, a household servant of the Dean.[168]

London, Thomas Kemp B.Th., bishop of

Preferred to the see of London in August 1448, Kemp (d. 28 March 1489) held the bishopric for over 40 years. It was during his episcopate that Worsley was elected Dean.[169]

London, Richard Hill B.Cn.L., bishop of

Chosen as bishop of London in the summer of 1489 after Thomas Kemp's death, Hill held the see for seven years before his own death on 20 February 1496. Much of this time was taken up by an acrimonious quarrel with Archbishop Morton of Canterbury over the jurisdiction of the archiepiscopal and episcopal courts. The quarrel was triggered by Hill's measures against

---

[165] Documents 1–5, above; GL, MS 25311, fos. 52v, 54, 56, 62; *The First Book of the Churchwardens' Accounts of Heybridge, Essex, c. 1509–1532*, ed. W. J. Pressey (Heybridge, 1938), pp. 5, 6, 9.

[166] *CFR*, xxii, no. 807, *The Commons 1439–1509*, ed. Wedgwood, pp. 565–66; Sainty, pp. 54, 90, 199, 229; document 12, above; PRO, E150/640/6; PROB11/14, fols. 274–76 (PCC 35 Holgrave).

[167] Documents 1–5, above.

[168] Document 1, above.

[169] Emden, *Oxford*, ii. 1032–34; PRO, SC7/37/1; PROB11/8, fols. 226v–228v (PCC 28 Milles).

Thomas Percy, the corrupt prior of Holy Trinity Aldgate (q.v.).[170]

London, Thomas Savage D.C.L., bishop of

Bishop of Rochester (1492–96), Savage was translated to London after Bishop Hill's death in 1496. He did not remain there for long, for in early 1501 he was preferred to the archbishopric of York, which he held until his death six years later in September 1507.[171]

Lovell, Sir Thomas, kt., of Elsing by Enfield and Haliwell in Shoreditch, Mdx.

A prominent retainer of Henry Tudor, Lovell (d. 24 March 1524) was appointed chancellor of the Exchequer in 1485, when the Commons in Henry VII's first Parliament also chose him as their Speaker. The following year, Henry appointed him Treasurer of his household. It was by reason of his proximity to the King that Worsley granted him an annual fee after the conspiracy of 1494. Earlier, in 1488–89, the Dean's steward and receiver were paid for their expenses in riding to Lovell's mansion at Enfield on their master's business. After his accession, Henry VIII made Lovell steward of the Household and Constable of the Tower, but dismissed him from both offices in 1516.[172]

Marke, Master [Richard], of Heybridge, Essex.

In 1484–85 Marke acted as the Dean's steward at Heybridge. He may perhaps be identified with Richard Markes, receiver general of the bishop of London from the mid-1450s and surveyor of the bishopric estates. He was probably the same man who served as a bailiff, alderman and parliamentary burgess for the town of Colchester in the 1470s, 1480s and 1490s. In May 1480 and July 1483 Markes was appointed to royal commissions of sewers and on the Thames banks alongside Dean Worsley.[173]

[170] PRO, SC7/37/25; Emden, *Oxford*, ii. 934; Harper-Bill, 'Bishop Hill and the Court of Canterbury', pp. 1–12.

[171] Emden, *Oxford*, ii. 1646–47; PRO, SC7/37/14; *DNB*, xvii. 839; *Fasti*, iv. 24, v. 3, vi. 5; in the accts. 1482–96: documents 4, 5, 7–9, above.

[172] Documents 7, 10, above; PRO, PROB11/23, fols. 214–217v (PCC 27 Jankyn); Sainty, p. 38; *The Commons 1439–1509*, ed. Wedgwood, pp. 555–56; J. S. Roskell, *The Commons and their Speakers in English Parliaments 1376–1523* (Manchester, 1965), pp. 298–99, 358–59; *DNB*, xii. 175–76; Condon, 'Ruling Elites'. The most recent biography is Steven Gunn, 'Sir Thomas Lovell (*c.* 1449–1524): a New Man in a New Monarchy?', in *The End of the Middle Ages*, ed. J. L. Watts (Stroud, 1998), 117–54.

[173] Document 5, above; PRO, SC6/1140/23–27; *CPR*, 1476–85, pp. 215, 466. Richard Markes seems a more likely candidate for the Heybridge steward than M. Thomas Marke, archdeacon of Norwich 1477–83, Thomas Markes, Fellow of All Souls College, Oxford, 1487–99, and later rector of St. Pancras, Soper Lane, London, or either of the two other Thomas Markes educated at Oxford in the fifteenth

Matyn, Master [Thomas] D.C.L., of London and Rome.
After an unruly youth as a student at Oxford, Matyn successively served as principal of two halls there in the early 1460s. He was proctor in the chancellor's court from 1458, and still in 1470, but in 1468–69 he was granted grace for inception as a D.C.L. at Cambridge. By 1474 he was serving as auditor of the English Hospital of St. Thomas the Martyr in Rome. It was probably in the course of one of his journeys there in his official capacity that, in 1480–81, he acted for the Dean at the Papal curia and received payment for letters of absolution procured there. He also had other connections with St. Paul's, for by 1478–79 he held a tenement in the parish of St. Mary Magdalen in the Fishmarket from the Dean and Chapter.[174]

Michell, Thomas, of Kirby-le-Soken, Essex.
Until his death in about 1492–93 Michell held certain lands and tenements in Kirby from the Dean. As these were taken into the King's hand at his death, he may have been a tenant in chief.[175]

Milen, Richard, of London.
A saddler, Milen occurs among the Dean's suppliers in 1489–90, but is otherwise not known to have had any connection with the household.[176] He might be Richard Milard, a London saddler active around 1500.[177]

Montgomery, Sir Thomas, kt., of Faulkbourn, Essex.
Sir Thomas was a younger son of Sir John Montgomery of Faulkbourn (d. 1449), by Elizabeth Botiller, lady of Say, sister of Ralph, Lord Sudeley. Although he served Henry VI as Marshall of the Hall and Keeper of the Mint, he fought for Edward IV at Towton and was knighted after the battle. In favour with King Edward throughout his reign and generously rewarded, he also prospered under Richard III, who made him one of his counsellors, and under Henry VII. He judiciously avoided the battle of Bosworth, and managed to survive until 2 January 1495. In the same way as he amassed grants of office and rewards from successive Kings, as a result of his proximity to the Crown, he also attracted fees from members of the gentry and clergy, including Thomas Kemp, bishop of London (q.v.), and Worsley who retained him at least from 1482 to 1490 at an annual fee of £4, and from whom he held the manor of Landymer Hall, Essex.[178]

---

century: Emden, *Oxford*, ii. 1222; *idem, Cambridge*, p. 391.
[174] Document 2, above; GL, MS 25125/95; Emden, *Cambridge*, pp. 396, 680.
[175] Document 11, above.
[176] Document 8, above.
[177] PRO, C1/64/571, 378/9.
[178] Documents 4–8, above; PRO, C67/51, m. 29; PROB11/10, fols. 175–178 (PCC 22 Vox); SC6/1140/27, m. 2; *CIPM Hen. VII*, i. 1040; *The Commons 1439–1509*, ed. Wedgwood, pp. 605–6; W. E. Hampton, 'Sir Thomas Montgomery, K.G.', *The*

More, John, of Willesden, Mdx.
More was Worsley's first farmer of Willesden, where he was succeeded in 1482 by William Northcote (q.v.).[179]

Morton, John
In 1480–81 Morton acted as the Dean's attorney at the Exchequer.[180]

Morys, Thomas
Morys was attached to the Dean's household by 1488–89 and by the following year had been given specific responsibility for the keeping of the horses.[181]

Nayller, John, of Thorpe-le-Soken, Essex.
In 1480 Nayller was granted certain lands and tenements in the soke of St. Paul's by the Dean in return for a substantial fine. It is possible that he was the synonymous son of the London tailor Richard Nayler (d. 1483) and his wife Elizabeth, who in 1483 acted as his father's executor. This Nayler family held lands at Shingleford in Essex as well as in Kent.[182]

Nevyll, Robert, of Sutton, Essex.
Robert Nevyll was the Dean's farmer of Sutton by 1480 and continued to hold the farm until at least 1488–89.[183]

Northcote, William, of Willesden, Mdx.
In 1482 Northcote succeeded John More (q.v.) as farmer of the prebend of Willesden. He may have died in the first half of the 1490s, for by 1495 he had himself been succeeded by William Swete (q.v.), who had previously only held the 'grace' there to farm.[184]

Nykke, Master [Richard] L.L.D., of London and Norwich, Norfolk.
A Cambridge graduate, Nykke gained a doctorate from an Italian university. He assembled a series of benefices, including the rectory of Ashbury, Berks, and a canonry at Wells cathedral. In 1489–90 he held a tenement in Ivy Lane, London, from the Dean, which was subject to various repairs that year. Several further prebends, including one at Southwell, and the archdeaconries of Exeter and Wells followed, before Nykke was appointed Dean of the Chapel Royal in 1497 and eventually preferred to the see of Norwich in 1501 in succession to Thomas Jane (q.v.). He retained this see until his death in

---

Ricardian, iii (1975), 9–14, repr. in *Richard III*, ed. Petre, 149–55.
[179] Documents 1–3, above.
[180] Document 2, above.
[181] Documents 7, 8, above.
[182] Document 2, above; PRO, PROB11/7, fols. 52–52v (PCC 7 Logge).
[183] Documents 2–7, above.
[184] Documents 4–8, above.

Odeby, Master [Walter] D.Cn.L., of London.
A student at Cambridge by 1460, around the same time as Worsley, by the
end of the 1470s Odeby had assembled a number of benefices, including a
canonry at St. Stephen's Westminster and prebends at the cathedrals of Exeter
and Hereford. In November 1482 he also became rector of St. Margaret Moses
in London and three years later vicar of Stepney. In July 1485 he was collated
to the prebend of Harleston at St. Paul's cathedral and the following year he
was appointed a royal chaplain. He retained his London prebend until his
death in August 1498. He appointed John Fitzherbert (q.v.) as one of his
executors. He occurs in Worsley's accounts as a residentiary of St. Paul's who
received the issues of the manor of Sutton in 1489–90.[186]

Orreys, Robert, of Thorpe-le-Soken, Essex.
Otherwise unknown, Orreys appears to have succeeded Thomas Smith (q.v.)
as farmer of 'Thorpe Hall' in about 1485, but was himself succeeded by John
Percy (q.v.) within the next two years.[187]

Orston, Thomas, of Southwell, Notts.
A trained lawyer, Orston was a kinsman of William Worsley and maintained
links with both the Dean and his brother Thomas, who left him two books in
his will. From 1474 at the latest he was active at Southwell, regularly acting as
proctor at the installations of new canons. He is often found as an executor of
both the minster clergy and the local gentry, including two generations of the
Clifton family in whose wills he was remembered. Orston was closely
connected with the Dean by 1479–80 and serving as his receiver in the
archdeaconry of Nottingham. He upheld his links with Worsley throughout
the period covered by the accounts, acting for him in his various northern
benefices. In 1482–83 he acted as one of the executors of Thomas Byngham of
Nottinghamshire. The executors came into conflict with the law in some
form and in February 1484 successfully sued for a pardon from Richard III. In
1495 Orston was one of the Dean's mainpernors, but he died in 1499 around
the same time as the Dean himself.[188]

[185]   Document 8, above; PRO, SC7/37/30; *DNB*, xiv. 519–20; Emden, *Cambridge*, pp.
        430–31; *Fasti*, iv. 25.
[186]   Document 8, above; PRO, PROB11/11, fols. 233–233v (PCC 29 Horne); Emden,
        Cambridge, pp. 437–38; *Fasti*, ii. 38; v. 39; ix. 57.
[187]   Document 6, above.
[188]   Documents 1–4, 9, 10, above; PRO, C67/51, m. 9; PROB11/12 (PCC 21 Wattys);
        Testamenta Eboracensia, iv. 64, 68, 69, 70, 156; *CCR*, 1485–1500, no. 863; *CIPM
        Hen. VII*, i. 714, iii. 1036; *Vis. & Mem. Southwell*, pp. 57, 99, 112, 147–49.

Oxford, John de Vere, **Earl of**

Born on 8 Sept. 1442 as second son of John de Vere (1408–1462), Earl of Oxford, by his wife Elizabeth Howard, he was allowed to succeed his father despite the latter's execution for treason. Having joined the Lancastrian side at the Readeption, he was attainted in 1475 and imprisoned. He escaped, joined Henry Tudor in France, and returned to England with him. He was in great favour with Henry VII and served him as Lord Great Chamberlain and in other important offices. He continued to hold high office under Henry VIII. He died childless on 10 March 1513, survived by his second wife. In 1495–96 he occurs in Worsley's accounts as chief steward of the Dean's lands in Essex, an office that he executed by a deputy, John Alyff (q.v.).[189]

Palmer, **Robert**, of Thorpe-le-Soken, Essex.

In 1496–97 Palmer held the manor of Thorpe to farm from Worsley.[190]

Peckham, **Peter**, of London.

A clerk of chancery, Peckham was admitted to the London mercers' company in 1466. Within three years of his admission an acrimonious quarrel broke out between Peckham and his fellow mercer, the alderman John Tate, in the course of which Peckham publicly tore up his letters of freedom. Fined 100 marks by the mayor's court, he was committed to Newgate, and only the Chancellor's personal intervention succeeded in having his fine reduced to £20. Nevertheless, by the end of Edward IV's reign Peckham had risen to become Usher of the King's chamber. It was probably his earlier legal experience that led to his becoming Worsley's advisor after the Warbeck conspiracy. Peckham married Agnes, widow of John, son and heir of the wealthy London grocer Stephen Brown (d. 1463), who was buried in the church of St. Michael Bassishaw. Peckham acquired landholdings in Buckinghamshire, Oxfordshire, Middlesex and the city of London and was probably the same man who sued a series of men for debt in the 1480s and 1490s. In the reign of Richard III he himself appeared in court as a defendant, facing charges of forgery. He died in the early months of 1501 and was survived by his second wife Elizabeth and two sons and two daughters.[191]

Percy, **John**, of Thorpe-le-Soken, Essex.

By 1487–88 John Percy held the manor and rectory of Thorpe to farm, probably the same tenement otherwise known as 'Thorpe Hall'. He

---

[189] Document 9, above; *CP*, x. 239–44.

[190] Document 12, above.

[191] PRO, C67/46, m. 37; C67/51, m. 35; CP40/891, rots. 171, 174; CP40/896, rot. 35; KB27/896, rex rot. 7; C146/100; PROB11/12, fols. 124–125 (PCC 16 Moone); Baker, *The Legal Profession*, p. 81; document 9, above; *CPR*, 1485–94, p. 444; *CFR*, xxii. 688; A. F. Sutton, *A Merchant Family of Coventry, London and Calais: The Tates, c.1450–1515* (London, 1998), pp. 18, 20.

continued to hold this farm until late 1496.[192]

Pere, John, of Heybridge, Essex.
Pere, Robert, of Heybridge, Essex.
Two members of a somewhat unruly family, Robert (1481–82) and John Pere (1484–88) successively held the mill of Heybridge to farm of Worsley.[193] Both men made appearances in the manor court there for their riotous behaviour: on 1 November 1477 John Pere, son of John Pere, together with John Bray (q.v.) assaulted and maltreated Thomas Gawge,[194] and in 1478 Robert Pere was involved in a violent quarrel with John Candish (q.v.). They beat each other and Candish was said to have drawn his dagger.[195]

Pomfret, Alice, of London.
Like Ralph Kemp (q.v.), Pomfret, a widow, occurs in the London rent collector's account for 1483–84 as drawing a quit rent of 3s. 2½d. from the Deanery for a tenement in the city. As in Kemp's case, her name may simply have been copied from an earlier account and she may in fact have been dead by this date.[196]

Prentesse, Edmund, of Drayton, Mdx.
A Middlesex yeoman and Worsley's farmer of Drayton by 1480–81, Prentesse continued as farmer there until at least 1489–90. He was probably still farmer in 1497, when he provided a loan of 10 marks to the Crown. He made his will in August 1504 and died shortly afterwards.[197]

Prowell, Richard, of London.
A brewer by trade, Prowell was one of a number of men of his craft supplying ale to the Dean's household. Payments to him for such supplies are recorded between 1481 and 1483.[198]

Radcliff, Roger, of London and Hackney, Mdx.
Roger's place in the prolific Radcliff family is unclear, but it is clear that he was related to the Dean of St. Paul's of the same name. Dean Radcliff had a brother, Master Robert Radcliff, who acted as one of the younger Roger's executors. Roger Radcliff served Worsley at the head of his household and is described in the accounts as steward of the household or receiver. He held

---

192 Documents 6–9, 11, 12, above.
193 Documents 3, 5, 6, above.
194 GL, MS 25281/1, m. 12.
195 GL, MS 25281/1, m. 12.
196 Document 13, above.
197 Documents 2–8, above; PRO, E36/14, p. 288; PROB11/14, fols. 132v–133 (PCC 17 Holgrave).
198 Documents 3–4, above.

office from at least 1479 until his death and was the accountant in the majority of the Dean's surviving household accounts. As one of the last services he performed for his master, he stood surety for him in 1495 in the aftermath of the Warbeck conspiracy. Radcliff died unexpectedly and intestate around Christmas 1496. He was survived by his wife Alice, who, alongside her former husband's kinsmen Master Robert and John Radcliff, was entrusted with the administration of his affairs.[199]

Raderford, James, of Thorpe-le-Soken, Essex.
Raderford alias Ratherford alias Retford, George, of Ardleigh, Herts.
James Raderford served as the Dean's rent collector at Thorpe from the time of Worsley's appointment, but had retired or died by 1482–83. He may have been the same man who had earlier also served Dean Roger Radcliff and was remembered in his will.[200] A putative kinsman, George Raderford or Retford held the nearby manor of Ardleigh from 1482 to at least 1490.[201]

Reading, Berks., **abbot of**
The abbot of Reading in 1495–96, when he was appointed as a collector of a clerical subsidy, was John Thorne. He was abbot from 1486 to 1519, the second man of his name successively to head the abbey.[202]

Reynold, Master, of London.
In 1483–84 Reynold held a tenement in Ivy Lane, London, from the Deanery. He cannot be identified with certainty, but is likely to have been one of two men: a Thomas Reynold was a canon of Lichfield cathedral and died by August 1497. A second man, John Reynold, studied at Cambridge and rose to become Dean of King's College from 1472 to 1474. He later became a canon of Southwell, as well as being preferred to a prebend at York. In 1499 he became archdeacon of Cleveland, a benefice which he retained until his death on 4 December 1506.[203]

Ricas, Thomas, of Walton-le-Soken, Essex.
In 1495–96 Ricas was the Dean's bailiff and collector at Walton-le-Soken.[204]

[199] Documents 1–7, 9, 10, 12, 13, above; 9168/1, fol. 10; *CCR, 1485–1500*, no. 863; PRO, PROB11/6, fol. 34v (PCC 5 Wattys); PROB11/8, fols. 95–99 (PCC 12 Milles).
[200] Documents 1–4, above; PRO, PROB11/6, fol. 34v (PCC 5 Wattys).
[201] Documents 4, 6–8, above.
[202] Document 9, above; *VCH Berks.* ii. 73.
[203] Document 13, above; Emden, *Oxford*, iii. 1572; *idem, Cambridge*, pp. 478–79.
[204] Document 9, above.

Robson, Robert, of Hackney, Mdx.

Robson was a member of Worsley's household who accompanied him to the north in 1480. The following year he was entrusted with making a payment for the benefit of the souls of the Dean's parents to Sir John Grymston (q.v.). He was probably the Hackney man who made his will on 18 August 1496, leaving his wife Katharine as sole executrix, and may have died soon after.[205]

Roke, William, of London.

One of Worsley's longest serving chaplains, Roke drew a stipend in this capacity as early as 1480. He served in the household throughout the Dean's tenure. In the aftermath of the Warbeck conspiracy in 1495, he acted as a mainpernor for his future good behaviour. He was probably the same man who served as a minor canon by 1464 and chaplain of the chantry of Richard Foliot at St. Paul's from at least 1477. He held a tenement in the parish of St. Faith from the Dean and Chapter, annually paying 4s. in rent.[206] He may have been the son and heir of like name of another William Roke, an Oxfordshire man.[207]

Rokes, John, of London and Kirby-le-Soken, Essex.

In 1493–94, Rokes was one of the Dean's tenants in the soke in Essex who paid a fine in the court at Kirby-le-Soken. Although there is no certain evidence to this effect, he may have been related to the Dean's chaplain, William Roke (q.v.). A John Rokes, son of Thomas Rokes, a London goldsmith active in the late 1480s and early 1490s, inherited various shops and other buildings in Bridgestreet, London, leased from Sir Thomas Lovell (q.v.) by his father, and was still alive in 1515.[208]

Roos, Edmund, Lord.

Born in about 1455 as son and heir of Thomas, Lord Roos (1427–64), his father's attainder of 1461 was reversed after Henry VII's accession. However, as Edmund was found unsuitable for his dignity, so custody of his lands was granted to his brother-in-law, Thomas Lovell (q.v.). He died in 1508.[209]

Saddler, Richard, of London.

Between at least 1480–81 and 1483–84, Saddler was one of the Dean's tenants of a tenement belonging to the Deanery in London at 'Paules Cheyn'.[210]

---

[205] Documents 2–3, above; GL, MS 9171/8, fol. 132.
[206] Documents 2–9, above; GL, MS 25125/94–99; *CCR*, 1485–1500, no. 863; New, 'Holy Name', p. 431.
[207] PRO, C1/73/70–71.
[208] Document 11, above; PRO, C1/384/41–42.
[209] Documents 6–8, above; *CP*, xi. 105–7.
[210] Documents 2, 13, above.

Samesbury, Richard, of Southwell, Notts.

Samesbury was a member of the Dean's household early on in his career, accompanying him towards Scotland in 1480. He probably first came into contact with Worsley at Southwell where he was a chorister from 1475 to 1476. In 1496–97 he was Worsley's collector of his income from the archdeaconry of Nottingham. For this office he received an annual fee of 53s. 4d. and a robe worth 13s. 4d. By this date he resided at Southwell, where he served as keeper of the archbishop's park. There he owned a messuage, two tofts and two crofts, which after his death descended to his son Thomas.[211]

St. Mary without Bishopsgate, London, **prior of the hospital**

William Sutton was prior until replaced in 1484 by Richard Cressal, who found that his predecessor had allowed the hospital's London property to fall into disrepair. In 1483–84 the prior was paid a quit rent of 9s. for a tenement of the Deanery.[212]

Sanders, Henry, of London.

In 1495–96, Sanders was the Dean's collector of rents and farms in the city of London and in the London parcels of the Deanery.[213] He may have been the Henry Saunder of Ewell, Surrey, who died by February 1519 and asked to be buried in the Savoy, or one of his numerous kinsmen. A branch of the same family resided at Charlwood, Surrey, and one of their number, a Master Henry Saunder, occurs in the will of John Jordan (q.v.).[214]

Saperton, John, of Chipping Ongar, Essex.

John Saperton lived in a house in Chipping Ongar rented from John Hewyk (q.v.). Hewyk, who appointed him one of his executors, later bequeathed it to him and his wife Isabel. Saperton succeeded Hewyk as the Dean's auditor, holding the office from at least 1487 to 1497, and probably until Worsley's death. He was one of the Dean's most trusted servants and was appointed one of his executors.[215]

Saver or Saber, John, of Thorpe-le-Soken, Essex.
Saver, William, junior.

At some point in c. 1487 John Saver replaced John Kent (q.v.) as farmer of the holding at Thorpe known as 'Kent's tenement', but he may have died within

---

211   Documents 2, 12, above; PRO, C1/361/22; *Vis. & Mem. Southwell*, pp. 62, 187, 188.
212   *VCH London*, 534; document 13, above.
213   Document 9, above.
214   PRO, PROB11/19, fols. 116v–118v (PCC 15 Ayloffe); PROB11/17, fol. 52v (PCC 7 Fetiplace).
215   Documents 6–9, 12, above; PRO, PROB11/9, fol. 235 (PCC 29 Doggett); *Testamenta Eboracensia*, iv. 157.

the year, for in 1488–89 the tenant there was William Saver junior, perhaps his son. By 1493 he had in his turn been replaced as farmer by John Harnes (q.v.). John Saver may have been the same man to whom the chancellor of St. Paul's, Dr. Henry Saver, bequeathed two houses in his will of 1471.[216]

Say, William, of Broxbourne, Herts.
Probably William, son of Sir John Say (1420–78). He served as sheriff of Essex and Herts. in 1482–83 and sat in Parliament for Plympton Erle in 1472 and Herts. in 1491 and 1495. He married twice, firstly Genevieve, daughter of the Somerset landowner John Hill of Spaxton and secondly Elizabeth, widow of Sir Thomas Waldegrave and daughter of Sir John Fray. He died on 4 December 1529, survived by his daughter Mary who had married Henry Bourgchier, Earl of Essex (q.v.). In 1480–81 Say held a tenement in Knightrider Street to farm from the Dean and continued as a tenant there until at least 1483–84.[217]

Shaa, Sir Edmund, of Ardern, Essex.
Son of John Shaa of Dukinfield, Cheshire, Sir Edmund was farmer of Worsley's lands at Tillingham in 1487–88, but died in the course of that year on 20 April 1488. He had long been associated with St. Paul's, where his brother Ralph (d. 1484) was a canon, and in his will stipulated that restitution should be made for a sum of about £14, of which he had defrauded Roger Radcliff when Dean. Among the executors of this will was Sir Reginald Bray (q.v.), whom he described as his 'right especiall frend'. Shaa was survived by his wife, Juliana, until July 1494 and left a 22-year-old son, Hugh. When Hugh died only three years later, most of Sir Edmund's lands fell to his nephew John (q.v.), a London goldsmith.[218]

Shaa, Sir John, of Ardern Hall, Essex.
Son of John Shaa of Rochford, Essex, Sir John was nephew and ultimate heir of Sir Edmund Shaa (q.v.), to whom he was apprenticed. John was appointed a graver at the royal mint for life by Edward IV in 1482. In Henry VII's reign he was elected Prime Warden of the Goldsmiths' Company 1491–92 and Joint Master of the Mint by May 1492. He represented the City in Parliament in 1495, was elected an alderman in 1496, serving as sheriff the same year.

---

[216] Documents 6, 7, above; PRO, PROB11/6, fol. 19 (PCC 3 Wattys).
[217] Documents 2, 4, 13, above; *The Commons 1439–1509*, ed. Wedgwood, pp. 747–48. A new biography of Say will appear in *The History of Parliament, The Commons 1422–1504*, ed. L. S. Clark (forthcoming).
[218] Document 9, above; PRO, PROB11/7, fols. 70v–71 (PCC 9 Logge); PROB11/8, fols. 95–99 (PCC 12 Milles); PROB11/10, fols. 170–171 (PCC 22 Vox); CFR, xxii. no. 154; CPR, 1494–1509, p. 45; CIPM Hen. VII, i, 381, 985, iii, 677; *Coronation of Richard III*, p. 394. More extensive biographical details can be found in Reddaway, pp. 176–7, 306–7.

Probably through his offices at the mint he became associated with Sir Reginald Bray (q.v.) and acted as a co-feoffee when Bray acquired Worsley's lands in Hackney and Tottenham in 1496. For his services as sheriff of London in defending the city against the Cornish insurgents Shaa was knighted by the King at the bridgefoot on 17 June 1497. He subsequently continued his civic career, serving as an alderman until his death in 1503, as mayor and escheator of London 1501–02 and as auditor of the city 1501–03. He succeeded his uncle as farmer of the Dean's lands at Tillingham at least until 1490 and occurs again in Worsley's accounts as tenant of Tillingham in 1495–96.[219]

Shaa or Shaw, Thomas, of London.
Shaa was probably a junior scion of the important London family of the same name, and may indeed have been the youngest son of that name of Sir John Shaa (q.v.). By 1484–85 he had entered Worsley's household, and remained there as a servant, probably until the Dean's death. By 1489–90 Shaa's wife was also a member of the Dean's *familia*. Shaa was a trusted confidant of the Dean who appointed him an executor of his will.[220]

Shuldham, Edward D.C.L.
A fellow of Trinity Hall, Cambridge, in the mid-1470s, Shuldham's first benefice was the vicarage of Southoe, Hunts., which he vacated in 1477. In addition he was admitted to the rectory of Buckworth, Hunts., which he resigned in late 1479, having earlier that year become rector of Cranfield, Beds. He exchanged this church for the rectory of Therfield, Herts., in October 1485, which he retained until his death. He also acted as an official of the archdeaconry of Huntingdon, which had rights in the ville of Ardleigh, and in 1481 functioned as its collector there. In June 1488 he was collated a canon of Lincoln cathedral, but vacated his prebend in February 1490. Five years later, he was made a canon of Newarke College, Leicester, a final benefice which he also retained until he died. Shuldham made his will, one of the executors of which was Master John Wryght (q.v.), on 28 November 1499, but appears to have lived on for several more years, for it was not proven until August 1503.[221]

---

[219] *The Commons 1439–1509*, ed. Wedgwood, pp. 758–59; *CFR*, xxii. 720, 786; *CCR, 1485–1500*, no. 910; documents 7–9, above; PRO, PROB11/14, fols. 98v–100 (PCC 13 Holgrave). For other biographical details see Reddaway, pp. 307–8. A new biography of Shaa will appear in *The History of Parliament, The Commons 1422–1504*, ed. L. S. Clark (forthcoming).

[220] Documents 5, 8, 12, above; *Letter Book L*, p. 213; *Testamenta Eboracensia*, iv. 157; PRO, C1/240/7–8; PROB11/14, fols. 98v–100 (PCC 13 Holgrave).

[221] Document 3, above; Emden, *Cambridge*, pp. 526–27; PRO, PROB11/13, fols. 201v–202 (PCC 24 Blamyr); C1/370/69–70.

Skypwith, Thomas, of London.

Skypwith succeeded to the position of clerk of the bakehouse of St. Paul's in c.1479, and remained in office until about 1482–3, when he was succeeded by Martin Jolyff (q.v.). By this time he was one of the four chaplains of the perpetual chantry at the altar of the Holy Ghost at St. Paul's, and in August 1482 he was granted papal dispensation to hold an additional benefice. Earlier, in the second half of the 1470s, Skipwith had clashed and come to blows with a Dutch goldsmith, Simon Gerardson, who brought legal action against him in Chancery.[222] He may have been the same clerk who served a a feoffee of John Doreward and who by January 1491 had become Master of the Hospital of St. Mary Magdalen, Colchester.[223]

Slade, John

Probably the John Slade from the diocese of Coventry and Lichfield who was studying at Cambridge in January 1479 and ordained priest in September 1480. He drew a stipend as one of Worsley's chaplains in 1489–90 and had a hood made for him.[224]

Smith, Thomas, D.Th., of London.

In 1480–81 Smith, alongside William Botery, acted as one of the executors of Adam Friday (q.v.), the former clerk of the bakehouse of St. Paul's. It is likely that he was the man who served as chancellor of St. Paul's cathedral from August 1471 until his death in late 1488.[225]

Smith, Thomas, of Thorpe-le-Soken, Essex.

A man of this name held the tenement called 'Thorpe Hall' in Thorpe-le-Soken to farm from Worsley from the summer of 1480 to at least 1485, but he cannot with certainty be identified with the chancellor of the cathedral, for there were several prominent Essex men of that name in the period. A Thomas Smith, thought to have died in 1485, represented Colchester in the Parliament of 1478 and served several times as bailiff of that town, on one occasion alongside Richard Marke (q.v.). Another man served three terms as escheator of Essex and Herts. between 1488 and 1496.[226]

Smith, Thomas, of London.

Smith was one of the last clergy to join the Dean's private household as a chaplain, occurring in the accounts only in 1495–96. His origins are uncertain, but like the Dean himself he was probably a Cambridge graduate, admitted to

---

[222] Documents 1–4, above; PRO, C1/67/123; *CPL*, xiii, pt. ii, p. 746.
[223] *CIPM Hen. VII*, i. 631, 1144.
[224] Emden, *Cambridge*, p. 533; document 8, above.
[225] Document 2, above; *Fasti*, v. 19.
[226] Documents 2–5, above; *The Commons 1439–1509*, ed. Wedgwood, p. 778; *CFR*, xxii. 194, 325, 490, 537.

the university in 1465. He played a prominent part in the life of St. Paul's cathedral in 1495–96, acting as collector of a clerical tenth in the city of London that year and also receiving payments for repairs to the cathedral's property.[227]

Staveley, William, of Bignell and Burchester, Oxon.
Staveley, who on 19 October 1480 repaid a debt of £4 13s. 4d. to the Dean, was a landholder with estates in Oxfordshire, Yorkshire and Buckinghamshire. In Buckinghamshire he held the manor of Broughton, which he bought from Sir Thomas Tresham. He died on 10 October 1498 and was survived by his wife Alice. She subsequently married the later chief justice Sir Humphrey Coningsby. Staveley's heir was his son George, but he also left two other sons, William and John, and two daughters, Isabel and Mary, the latter of whom married Thomas Giffard the younger.[228]

Stephens, Joan, of Norton Folgate, Mdx.
Stephens, John, of Norton Folgate, Mdx.
Stephens, William, of Ardleigh, Herts.
In 1495–96, and perhaps as early as 1489–90, John Stephens held Worsley's lands at Norton Folgate to farm, but died in the course of 1496. He was survived by Joan, his putative wife. William Stephens, a canon lawyer who occurs at Ardleigh in 1495–96, may have been another member of the same family.[229]

Steward, William, of London.
By the mid-1470s Steward was one of the minor canons of St. Paul's and also served as chaplain of two united chantries there. In 1476 he also acquired the rectory of Wrentham in the diocese of Norwich. He did, however, pay a sum of money to the lay patron for the preferment and consequently had to obtain papal dispensation to absolve him from charges of simony. By 1479 he served as chamberlain of St. Paul's, in which capacity he occurs in Worsley's accounts until 1481. He was a minor canon at the cathedral until at least 1488 and held a tenement to the east of the house called 'la Sonne' in the parish of St. Bride Fleet Street at an annual rent of 66s. 8d.[230]

Stykeswolde, Robert
Stykeswolde was a member of the Dean's entourage on his journey towards the north in 1480. He was still in the household in 1484–85, when he rode to

[227] Emden, *Cambridge*, p. 536; document 9, above.
[228] Document 2, above; PRO, PROB11/11, fols. 210–210v; *CIPM Hen. VII*, ii. 388; *CFR*, xxii. 550, 619, 622.
[229] Documents 8–10, 12, above.
[230] Documents 1, 2, above; GL, MS 25125/94–99; Hennessy, p. 61; *CPL*, xiii, pt. i, p. 463, pt. ii, p. 514.

Wimpole with Roger Radcliff (q.v.).[231]

Swete, William, of Willesden, Mdx.
William Swete was one of Worsley's farmers at Willesden. Initially, from c.1487, he was farmer of the 'grace' there, but at some point before 1495 he succeeded William Northcote as farmer of the prebend.[232]

Symsone, John, of London.
Symsone sold ten bows to Worsley in 1480–81. He was a London citizen and bowyer resident in Fleetstreet. He was a parishioner of St. Bride, and may have been a member of the fraternity of Our Lady based in that church, to which he made a bequest in his will. He owned extensive lands at Lambeth (Surrey), Norton Mandeville (Essex), Plomstede and East Grenwich (Kent), as well as one called 'the Rose' in Turnmillstreet in the parish of St. Giles Cripplegate and a garden in Redcrossestreet. He was predeceased by his first wife, Maud, but married a second, Agnes, widow of John Baker, who survived him. Symsone died in late 1497 and was buried in the church of St. Bride Fleetstreet. He left a son, John (d. c. 1509), who later entered the mercery trade, and a daughter, Elizabeth, both under age at their father's death. A second daughter, Agnes, was a nun at Clerkenwell priory.[233]

Thomas, Thomas, of Sutton, Essex.
Along with Robert Nevyll (q.v.), Thomas was joint farmer of the Dean's demesne lands at Sutton between at least 1480 and 1482. He may be the man who in 1472 occurs as witness to a land transaction at Chiswick.[234]

Thurston, William, of Thorpe-le-Soken, Essex.
Thurston was Worsley's tenant at Thorpe in 1493–94, holding ½ acre in 'Hobbesdale'. He still held from the Dean in 1496–97.[235]

Toose or Toyse, John, of Walton-le-Soken, Essex.
One of William Worsley's longest-serving farmers, Toose held the manor of Walton by 1479 and continued as farmer until his death in about 1496.[236]

Trent, William, of London.
William Trent succeeded John Clerk (q.v.) as rent collector of the Dean in the city of London at some point in 1489, but by the mid 1490s may himself have

[231] Documents 2, 5, above.
[232] Documents 6–10, 12, above.
[233] Document 2, above; PRO, PROB11/11 fols. 95–96v (PCC 11 Horne); PROB11/16, fols. 121v–122 (PCC 16 Bennett); *CFR*, xxii. 593.
[234] Documents 2–3, above; *CCR*, 1468–76, no. 899.
[235] Documents 11, 12, above.
[236] Documents 1–9, 11, 12, above.

been superseded by John Farman (q.v.).[237]

Turle, John, of Mdx.
Not known to have been otherwise connected with the Dean, Turle was one of the collectors appointed at Edmonton, Mdx., to collect the lay tenth granted to Henry VII in the 1497 Parliament.[238]

Turnour, Thomas, of Nottingham and London.
Perhaps the Thomas Turner studying at Cambridge in 1470–71 and instituted as vicar of St. Mary's, Nottingham, in January 1477. He drew a stipend as Worsley's chaplain between 1480 and 1485, vacated the Nottingham benefice in 1498 and went on to become rector of St. Margaret's Friday Street, London, between 1505 and 1510. He was probably also the Master Thomas Turnour who was presented to the church of Stratford St. Andrew, Suffolk, in April 1507.[239]

Vyntener, Charles, of London.
A London vintner, Worsley's accounts often refer to him merely as Charles. He supplied wine to the Dean's household from at least 1481–82 until 1489–90.[240]

Walden, Essex, **John, abbot of**
John Sabrisford (d. 8 June 1509) was elected abbot in January 1485 following the death of his predecessor John Halstede. He occurs in Worsley's accounts in 1487–88.[241]

Watson *alias* **Weston, Thomas**, of Belchamp St. Paul, Essex.
Probably the man of northern origins studying at Cambridge by 1474–5 and ordained deacon in April 1476. He was instituted as vicar of Long Bennington, Lincolnshire in July 1479, but had vacated the benefice a year later. He served as a chaplain in Worsley's household between 1487 and 1490. Between 1487 and 1495 Watson also acted as the Dean's rent collector at Belchamp St. Paul, and also for the same period held the rectory there to farm. He died soon after, for prayers for his soul were provided for in the will of the former farmer of Belchamp St. Paul manor, Geoffrey Downing (q.v.), in August 1503.[242]

---

[237] Document 8, above.
[238] Document 12, above.
[239] Emden, *Cambridge*, p. 599; *CPR*, 1494–1509, pp. 427, 533; documents 2–5, above.
[240] Documents 2–8, above.
[241] *Monasticon Anglicanum*, iv. 135; *VCH Essex*, ii. 115; *CPR*, 1476–85, p. 535; document 6, above.
[242] Emden, *Cambridge*, p. 623; documents 6–9, above; PRO, PROB11/13, fols. 210v–211 (PCC 25 Blamyr).

Westby, Edward, of London.

Together with John Fox (q.v.) Westby was Worsley's farmer of Bowes and Polehouse between at least 1481 and 1490. Westby was a London gentleman with landholdings in various parts of Middlesex, including one called 'Aleynsbury' and tenements at Hampstead. He was predeceased by his wife Margaret who was buried in St. Bartholomew's hospital, West Smithfield. He made his will in early April 1501, asking to be interred alongside her, and died shortly after.[243]

Westminster, Mdx., John abbot of

John Esteney (d. 1498) was appointed abbot in 1474 when his predecessor Thomas Milling was elevated to the see of Hereford. Like many heads of religious houses he was on occasion appointed to collect clerical taxation and it was in this capacity that he came into contact with the Worsley household in 1488-89.[244]

Wilby, Master [Robert], of Woollaton, Notts.

In 1496-97 Wilby was an official of the archdeaconry of Nottingham. He was responsible for receiving some of Worsley's fees from inductions on behalf of the collector, Richard Samesbury (q.v.). He did this through a deputy, Simon Yates (q.v.). He may have been M. Robert Wilby, a son of Richard Wilby of Moulton. After study at Cambridge, this man assembled several Lincolnshire benefices, before becoming rector of Woollaton, Notts., in August 1491. He surrendered the rectory in October 1496, but lived on until 1500-01, becoming rector of Dartington, Devon, shortly before his death.[245]

Witheney, William, of London.

Witheney was a London brewer, who is only known to have supplied ale to the Dean's household on one occasion in 1484-85.[246]

Wode, John, of Molesey, Surrey.

Wode was an Exchequer official, who in 1481 was appointed to receive a clerical tenth alongside John Fitzherbert (q.v.), and appears in Worsley's accounts in this capacity. By this date he was the King's deputy treasurer. As such he was that year deputed to address convocation, where Worsley was present, and outline the need for a subsidy, which he notably did in English, rather than the customary Latin. He represented the borough of Midhurst, and the counties of Surrey and Sussex, respectively in eight Parliaments

243 Documents 3, 4, 6-8, above; PRO, PROB11/12, fols. 125v–126v (PCC 16 Moone).
244 *Monasticon Anglicanum*, i. 276-77; *VCH London*, 455; *CPR*, 1467-77, p. 472, 474; document 7, above.
245 Document 12, above; PRO, C1/329/4, 5, 7, 8; Emden, *Cambridge*, 624-25.
246 Document 5, above.

between 1435 and 1483, and became Speaker of the parliamentary Commons in 1483. He died the following autumn and was survived by his second wife, Margery, daughter of Sir Roger Lewknor.[247]

Worsley, Edmund, of London.

Resident in the London parish of All Saints Honey Lane, Edmund Worsley may have been a kinsman of Robert Worsley, a well-connected mercer active both in England and on the continent from the early 1420s until at least the late 1450s. He himself entered the same trade by the early 1490s.[248] In the 1490s he invested some of his wealth in the acquisition of an estate in Havering. Edmund may also have been related to the Dean, although their exact relationship is obscure, and was a member of his household by 1496. After the Warbeck conspiracy, Edmund Worsley, along with Philip Booth (q.v.), took on some of the responsibilities previously discharged by Roger Radcliff (q.v.), probably at least in part to keep control of the financial affairs of the Dean, for whom he mainperned in 1495. Alongside his position in the Dean's household, Edmund remained very much part of London's mercantile society, acting as feoffee for fellow mercers, such as Thomas Shelley (d. 20 January 1500). Worsley died unexpectedly and intestate by early 1502, survived by his wife, Agnes. For some years after his death the administrators of his estate were in litigation over his unfinished affairs, some cases dating back to the 1470s. One such case was a suit for debt brought by Edmund's former apprentice George Urswick. [249]

Worsley, Isabella, of Stockwell, Surrey.

Isabella was the daughter of the Dean's kinsman Otwell Worsley (d. 24 March 1470), who bequeathed 300 marks to her for her marriage and charged William Worsley with paying the money to her. Part of the payment, which was made on 1 May 1480 on her marriage to the Kentish landowner Richard Culpeper (d. 4 October 1484) is recorded in the receiver's account. Dean

247 Document 2, above; *CFR*, xxi, no. 657; *Reg. Bourgchier*, ed. Du Boulay, pp. 129, 134, 139–41; Roskell, *Commons and their Speakers*, pp. 291–93; *idem*, 'Sir John Wood of Molesey', *Surrey Archaeological Collections*, lvi (1959), 15–28; *The Commons 1439–1509*, ed. Wedgwood, pp. 965–66; Sainty, 198–99.

248 For biographical details of Robert Worsley see *The Bedford Inventories*, ed. J. Stratford (London, 1993), pp. 429–30; and also cf. SC6/1291/1/8/33, 9/55; A. F. Sutton, 'Caxton was a Mercer', in *England in the Fifteenth Century, Proceedings of the 1992 Harlaxton Symposium*, ed. N. Rogers (Stamford, 1994), 118–48, p. 128; *CCR*, 1435–41, pp. 101, 346, 399; *Acts of Court of the Mercers' Company*, ed. Lyell and Watney, pp. 225, 226, 306, 573, 577.

249 *CAD*, vi. C.6991; *CIPM Hen. VII*, no. 370; *CCR*, 1485–1500, no. 863; *CFR*, xxii. 716; PRO, SC2/172/36, rot. 13; SC2/172/40, rots. 4, 4d; C1/186/74, 233/70, 342/74, 371/79, 453/2–3; McIntosh, *A Community Transformed*, p. 339; F. W. Steer, 'A Medieval Household', *The Essex Review*, 63 (1954), p. 17; GL, MS 9168/3, fol. 93v; *VCH Essex*, vii. 69.

Worsley was later to act as one of Culpeper's feoffees. Isabella survived her first husband, by whom she had two daughters and, a few months before his death, a son. By early 1494 she had married Sir John Legh (d. 12 June 1523) of Stockwell. She also survived her second husband and acted as his executrix. She died in the spring of 1527, asking to be buried next to Sir John Legh in the chapel that he had built in the parish church of Lambeth.[250]

Wryght, Master John, of Ardleigh, Herts.
In 1495–96, as a bachelor of decrees, Wryght alongside William Stephens (q.v.) received a payment from the Dean for two procurements at Ardleigh. Three years later, when rector of Clothall, Herts., Wryght was appointed one of the executors of Edward Shuldham (q.v.).[251]

Wyle, William, of London.
Wyle was a London hosier who sold a range of items of apparel to the Dean in 1489–90. He may be the same man called 'Wylle' who supplied a pair of shoes for Worsley in 1481–82.[252]

Wylly, Edmund, of Westminster, Mdx.
Described in Worsley's accounts as the King's deputy Receiver, Wylly (d. by 20 January 1515) served as Foreign Apposer of the Exchequer under Henry VII and Henry VIII from 1495 until his death. In 1496–97 he served as undersheriff of Middlesex for Sir John Shaa (q.v.) and Sir Richard Haddon, sheriffs of London and Middlesex. He married Agnes, widow of Robert, brother of Thomas Langton, bishop of St. David's (1483–85), Salisbury (1485–93) and Winchester (1493–1501).[253]

Wynche, Richard, of Caddington, Beds.
During Worsley's final years, between at least 1493 and 1497, Wynche held the Dean's manor of Kensworth to farm. He was probably the Richard Wynche of Caddington 'the younger', who was active in Bedfordshire in 1502–3 and held lands in Caddington, Kensworth and Flamstead. He died childless by 1515 and was survived by his wife, Alice.[254]

---

[250] Document 1, above; PRO, C1/84/2–7; C67/53, m. 4; C140/57/54; C141/6/28; C142/40/12(2), 69; PROB11/21, fols. 112–116 (PCC 15 Bodfelde); PROB11/22, fols. 143–44 (PCC 18 Porche); M. Stephenson, 'A List of Monumental Brasses in Surrey', *Surrey Archaeological Collections*, xxix. 70–138, pp. 122–24.

[251] Document 9, above; PRO, PROB11/13, fol. 202 (PCC 24 Blamyr; C1/370/69–70).

[252] Documents 3, 8, above.

[253] Document 2, above; Sainty, p. 83; PRO, C1/145/21, 252/26; KB9/412/4; *CFR*, xxii. 58, 812.

[254] Documents 9, 11, 12, above; PRO, C1/54/206, 271/24, 302/8–9.

Yates, Simon, of Notts.

In 1497-98 Yates, as deputy of Master Wilby (q.v.), received some of Worsley's income from inductions in the archdeaconry of Nottingham on behalf of the collector there, Richard Samesbury (q.v.). In December 1504 he was presented to the parish church of Beckingham, Lincs., by the King.[255]

[-], William, of Tottenham, Mdx.

Otherwise obscure, this man occurs as one of the royal tax collectors at Tottenham in 1496-97.[256]

---

[255] Document 12, above; *CPR*, 1494-1509, p. 390.
[256] Document 12, above.

GLOSSARY

Glossary of Unusual English Words.
Sources: MED, OED. Latham, *Dictionary of Latin from British Sources,*
Assistance for cloth from John Oldland. W. S. Beck, *Drapers Dictionary,*
London, 1881 and Guy de Poerck, *La draperie medievale en Flandre et en
Artois: technique et terminologie* (Bruges, 1951). L. J. Wilhelmsen, *English
Textile Nomenclature* (Bergen, 1943).

Appruator	an official looking after the profit or interest of an employer, a steward or bailiff.
Bakens	?bricks baked in a kiln, dried or hardened.
Barehedde, barret	a covered wagon, a cart-cover made of rawhide, and also possibly a rawhide bag or trunk.
Blakechalk	pale and bleached cloth.
Blanket	undyed cloth or a thick, white cloth of average quality.
Bockeram	at this date, a fine linen or cotton fabric.
Brigander	body armour, originally for foot soldiers made of iron rings or plates sewn to canvas, linen or leather.
Chamelet	a costly velvet, often a gold one.
Chevage, chivagium	headpenny or chevage, a due paid by suitors at view of frankpledge or law-hundred.
Conysaunce	badges, pennons.
Correctors	auditors.
Corsse	a tunic.
Decrees	bachelor of, licentiate of, degrees in canon law.
Dolwood	see *Tallwodde.*
Doss	a dooser, dorser, an ornamental cloth or hanging, sometimes part of a vestment.
Dyaper worke	a linen cloth, a linen fabric, often quite expensive, with a characteristic design of lines crossing diamond wise with the intervals filled up.
Fustian	a coarse cloth made of cotton and flax, usually dyed a dark colour.
'Fustyances'	a coverlet of fustian, at this date not necessarily a cloth of coarse or poor quality.

179

Feeding Days	days on which it was the traditional responsibility of the Dean to provide food and drink for the minor clergy of the cathedral.
Grain, crimson in	cloth dyed with kermes dye, which produced a bright crimson or scarlet colour.
Grain, violet in	cloth dyed (probably in-the-wool or in-the-yarn) with woad and then redyed in the piece with kermes.
Grey	an expensive grey squirrel fur forbidden to cloistered clergy.
Grypege	an ostrich egg
Hayle, hale	a tent.
Hogshead	a cask containing sixty-three gallons.
Jack	a sleeveless tunic.
Kylderkyn	a cask holding ½ barrel = 16 gallons ale or 18 gallons of beer.
Liripipe	a peak, similar to that found on modern academic hoods.
Malmsey	a strong, sweet wine.
Mayle	mail, iron-clad.
Medley	pied cloth, made of wools dyed and mingled before being spun, and either of one colour or of different shades or colours.
Musterdevelis	a mixed grey woollen cloth.
Noble	a gold coin worth 6s. 8d.
Pipe	a large cask of more or less definite capacity, equivalent to half a tun, or two hogsheads, or four barrels.
Pollewodde	pollarded or cut wood.
Potell	half a gallon.
Procurator	deputy or agent.
Pyle	a pillow or cushion.
Quarter [qr.]	(as measurement of volume), 8 bushels.
Replevin, writ of	the legal process for the temporary restoration of confiscated property pending a court hearing.
Roundlet, runlet	a small cask of varying capacity. Large runlets appear to have varied between twelve and eighteen and a half gallons; small ones between a quart and three or four gallons.
Salette	*scaletta*, a cart-ladder; elsewhere, a helmet.
Staddles	staddle-stones, or stathels, supports for a sack of grain or stones placed beneath ricks and granaries to raise them and keep rats out.
Standard	a large packing case or chest.
Tallwodde, talwood	wood cut to size.

Tercion	a container holding 1/3 of a tun.
Virgate	an osier bed.
Virge	(in cloth) a yard; also 16 ½ ft.
Wodded black	woaded black, the best way to produce black, dyeing with woad in-the-wool and then re-dyeing in-the-piece with woad and other dyes to eventually produce black.

Feast Days and Term Dates used in the Accounts

St. Anne, 26 July
St. Peter *ad Vincula*, 1 August.
St. Matthew, 21 September.
Michaelmas, 29 September.
St. Martin in Winter, 11 November.
St. Thomas the Apostle, 21 December.
Christmas, 25 December.
Purification (of the Blessed Virgin Mary), 2 February.
Annunciation (to the Blessed Virgin Mary), 25 March.
The Nativity of St. John the Baptist, 24 June.

BIBLIOGRAPHY

I. Original Sources
1. Manuscripts
Borthwick Institute, York
Bishops' Registers
Register xx (William Booth)
Register xxii (Laurence Booth)
Register xxiii (Thomas Rotherham)

British Library
Additional Manuscripts
Harleian Manuscripts

Guildhall Library, London
MS 25125/92–99
MS 25281/1
MS 25287
MS 25301/1
MS 25311
MS 25342
MS 25375/2
MS 9168/1, 3
MS 9171/8
MS 9531/7
MS 9531/8 .

Lichfield Joint Record Office
Register B/A/1/10.

Public Record Office, Kew
C1   (Early Chancery Proceedings)
C47   (Chancery, Miscellanea)
C54   (Chancery, Close Rolls)
C65   (Chancery, Parliament Rolls)
C67   (Chancery, Supplementary Patent Rolls)
C82   (Chancery, Warrants for the Great Seal, Series II)
C106 (Exchequer and Chancery, Master Richards' Exhibits)

C139   (Chancery, Inquisitions post mortem, Henry VI)
C140   (Chancery, Inquisitions post mortem, Edward IV)
C141   (Chancery, Inquisitions post mortem, Richard III)
C142   (Chancery, Inquisitions post mortem, Henry VII–Charles I)
C146   (Chancery, Ancient Deeds, Series C)
C253   (Chancery, Sub Poena Files)
CP25(1) (Court of Common Pleas, Feet of Fines)
CP40   (Court of Common Pleas, Plea rolls)
E13   (Exchequer of Pleas, Plea Rolls)
E36   (Exchequer, Miscellaneous Books)
E101   (Exchequer, Miscellaneous Accounts)
E150   (Exchequer, Inquisitions post mortem)
E179   (Exchequer, Taxation records)
E210   (Exchequer, Ancient Deeds, Series D)
E314   (Exchequer, Court of Augmentations, Miscellanea)
E326   (Exchequer, Augmentation Office, Ancient Deeds, Series B)
E359   (Exchequer, Pipe Office, Account Rolls of Subsidies and Aids)
KB9   (Court of King's Bench, Ancient Indictments)
KB27   (Court of King's Bench, Plea rolls)
PROB11 (Prerogative Court of Canterbury, Registers of wills)
SC2   (Special Collections, Court Rolls)
SC6   (Special Collections, Ministers' Accounts)
SC7   (Special Collections)
SP46   (State Papers Domestic, Supplementary)
STAC1   (Court of Star Chamber, Proceedings, Henry VII)

University Library Cambridge
EDR G/1/5.

Westminster Abbey
WAM 5474
WAM 31795

2. Printed Sources
A Biographical Register of the University of Cambridge to 1500, ed. A. B. Emden
    (Cambridge, 1963).
A Biographical register of the University of Oxford to AD 1500, ed. A. B. Emden
    (3 vols., Oxford, 1957–59).
A Descriptive Catalogue of Ancient Deeds (6 vols., London, 1890–1915).
*A Roll of the Household Expenses of Richard de Swinfield, Bishop of Hereford,
    during part of the years 1289 and 1290*, ed. John Webb (2 vols., London,
    Cam. Soc. O. S. 59–60, 1854–55).
Abstracts of Inquisitions post mortem relating to the City of London, ed. G. S.
    Fry (3 pts., London, 1896–1908).

Acts of court of the Mercers' Company 1453–1527, ed. L. Lyell and F. D. Watney (Cambridge, 1936).

Calendar of Entries in the Papal Registers Relating to Great Britain and Ireland: Papal Letters (14 vols., London, 1893–1960).

Calendar of Letterbooks: Letterbook L, ed. R. R. Sharpe (London, 1912).

Calendar of the Patent Rolls (53 vols., London, 1891–1916).

Calendar of Plea and Memoranda Rolls, 1458–1482

Calendar of the Close Rolls (61 vols., London, 1892–1963).

Calendar of the Fine Rolls (22 vols., London, 1911–62).

Calendar of Inquisitions post Mortem, Henry VII (3 vols., London 1898–1955).

Complete Peerage.

Fasti Ecclesiae Anglicanae 1300–1541, ed. J. M. Horn and B. Jones (12 vols., London, 1962–67).

Grace Book A, ed. S. M. Leathes (Cambridge, 1897).

Household Accounts From Medieval England, ed. C. M. Woolgar (2 pts., Oxford 1992–93).

'Household Roll of Bishop Ralph of Shrewsbury', ed. J. A. Robinson in *Collectanea* (Som. Rec. Soc. xxxix, 1924), 72–165.

Letters and Papers, Foreign and Domestic, of the Reign of Henry VIII (22 vols. in 38, London, 1862–1932).

Memorials of King Henry VII: Historia Regis Henrici Septimi a Bernardo Andrea Tholosate Conscripta, ed. James Gairdner (London, R.S. 10, 1858).

Ninth Report of the Royal Commission on Historical Manuscripts (3 pts., London, 1883).

Novum Repertorium Ecclesiasticum Parochiale Londinense, ed. G. L. Hennessy (London, 1898).

Officers of the Exchequer, comp. J. C. Sainty (London, List and Index Soc. spec. ser. 18, 1983).

Radulphi de Diceto Opera Historica, ed. W. Stubbs (2 vols., London, R.S., 1876).

Records of the Honorable Society of Lincoln's Inn, vol. I: Admissions, A.D. 1420 to A.D. 1799, ed. W. P. Baildon (London, 1896).

Registrum Statutorum et Consuetudinum Ecclesiae Cathedralis Sancti Pauli Londinensis, ed. W. Sparrow Simpson (London, 1873).

Registrum Thome Bourgchier, ed. F. R. H. Du Boulay (Oxford, 1957).

Reisebeschreibung Niclas von Popplau Ritters, bürtig von Breslau, ed. Piotr Radzikowski (Kraków, 1998).

Rotuli Parliamentorum (7 vols., 1832)

Statutes of the Realm (11 vols., 1810–28).

Taxatio Ecclesiastica Angliae et Walliae auctoritate P. Nicholai IV. circa A.D. 1291, ed. T. Astle, S. Ayscough and J. Caley (London, 1802).

Testamenta Eboracensia, iv (Durham *et al.*, Surtees Soc. 53, 1869).

The Anglica Historia of Polydore Vergil A.D. 1485–1537, ed. D. Hay (London, Camden Soc. lxxiv, 1950).

The Ballard of Bosworth Feilde, Bishop Percy's Folio Manuscript (3 vol., London, 1868).

The Bedford Inventories, ed. J. Stratford (London, 1993).

The Collected Works of Erasmus, vol. 8: The Correspondence of Erasmus, ed. R. A. B. Mynors and P.G. Bietenholz (Toronto etc., 1988).

The Coronation of Richard III. The Extant Documents, ed. A. F. Sutton and P. W. Hammond (Gloucester, New York, 1983).

The Domesday of St. Paul's, ed. W. H. Hale (London, Camden Soc. o.s. 69, 1858).

The Durham household book: or The accounts of the bursar of the monastery of Durham. From Pentecost 1530 to Pentecost 1534, ed. James Raine (London, Surtees Soc. 18, 1844).

The First Book of the Churchwardens' Accounts of Heybridge, Essex, c. 1509–1532, ed. W. J. Pressey (Heybridge, 1938).

The Great Chronicle of London, ed. A. H. Thomas and I. D. Thornley (London, 1938).

The History of King Richard the Third (1619) by Sir George Buck, ed. A. N. Kincaid (Gloucester, 1979).

The Merchant Taylors' Company of London: Court Minutes 1486–1493, ed. M. P. Davies (Stamford, 2000).

The Notebook of Sir John Port, ed. J. H. Baker (London, Selden Soc. 102, 1986).

The Register of John Morton, Archbishop of Canterbury, 1486–1500, ed. C. Harper-Bill (2 vols. [Canterbury and York Soc. 75, 78], Leeds, Woodbridge, 1987–91).

The Register of Richard Fox while Bishop of Bath and Wells, A.D. MCCCCXCII–MCCCCXCIV, ed. E. C. Batten (n.l., 1889).

The Registers of Oliver King, Bishop of Bath and Wells 1496–1503, and Hadrian de Castello, Bishop of Bath and Wells 1503–1518, ed. H. Maxwell-Lyte (Som. Rec. Soc. liv, 1939).

The Registers of Robert Stillington, Bishop of Bath and Wells, 1466–1491, and Richard Fox, Bishop of Bath and Wells, 1492–94, ed. H. C. Maxwell-Lyte (Som. Rec. Soc., lii, 1937).

The Visitation of Suffolk, 1561, made by William Hervy, ed. Joan Corder (3 vols., London, Harl. Soc., n.s., 1981–84).

Visitations and Memorials of Southwell Minster, ed. A. F. Leach (London, Camden Soc. n.s. 48, 1891).

Visitations of Churches belonging to St. Paul's Cathedral in 1297 and 1458, ed. W. Sparrow Simpson (London, Camden Soc., n.s. 55, 1895).

185

II. Secondary Material

ARTHURSON, IAN, *The Perkin Warbeck Conspiracy* (Stroud, 1994).

AXON, E., 'The Family of Bothe (Booth) and the Church in the 15th and 16th Centuries', *Transactions of the Lancashire and Cheshire Antiquarian Society*, 53 (1938), 32–82.

BAKER, J. H., *The Legal Profession and the Common Law: Historical Essays* (London, 1986).

BROOKE, C. N. L., 'The Composition of the Chapter of St. Paul's, 1086–1163', *Cambridge Historical Journal*, x (1950–52), 111–32.

BROOKE, C. N. L., 'The Deans of St. Paul's, c. 1090–1499', *BIHR*, xxix (1965), 231–44.

BROOKE, C. N. L., 'The Earliest Times', in *A History of St Paul's Cathedral and the Men Associated with it* ed. W. R. Matthews and W. M. Atkins (London, 1957), 54–55.

CLARK, L. S., 'The Benefits and Burdens of Office: Henry Bourgchier (1408–83), Viscount Bourgchier and Earl of Essex, and the Treasurership of the Exchequer', in *Profit, Piety and the Profession*, ed. M. A. Hicks (Gloucester, 1990), 119–36.

REEVES, A. C., 'Bishop John Booth of Exeter, 1465–78', in *Traditions and Transformations in Late Medieval England*, ed. D. Biggs, S. D. Michalove and A. C. Reeves (Leiden *et al.*, 2002), 125–44.

REEVES, A. C., 'Lawrence Booth: Bishop of Durham (1457–76), Archbishop of York (1476–80)', in *Estrangement, Enterprise and Education in Fifteenth Century England*, ed. S. D. Michalove and A. Compton Reeves (Stroud, 1998), 63–88.

REEVES, A. C., 'William Booth, Bishop of Coventry and Lichfield (1447–52)', *Midland History*, iii (1975–76), 11–29.

REEVES, A. C., 'William Booth, Bishop of Coventry and Lichfield, Archbishop of York', in *Lancastrian Englishmen* (Washington D.C., 1981), 265–362.

CONDON, M. M., 'From Caitiff and Villain to Pater Patriae: Reynold Bray and the Profits of Office', in *Profit, Piety and the Professions in Later Medieval England*, ed. M. A. Hicks (Gloucester, 1990), 137–68.

CONDON, M. M., 'Ruling Elites in the Reign of Henry VII', in *Patronage, Pedigree and Power*, ed. C. Ross (Gloucester, 1979), 109–42.

DAVIES, R. R., 'Baronial Accounts, Incomes and Arrears in the Later Middle Ages', *Ec.H.R.*, 2nd ser., xxi (1968), 211–29.

DU BOULAY, F. R. H., 'Who Were Farming the English Demesnes at the End of the Middle Ages?', *Ec.H.R.*, 2nd Ser., xvii (1964–65), 443–55.

DUGDALE, W., *Monasticon Anglicanum*, ed. J. Caley, H. Ellis, and B. Bandinel (6 vols. in 8, London, 1817–30).

DUGDALE, W., *The History of St. Pauls Cathedral in London from its Foundation untill these Times* (London, 1658).

BIBLIOGRAPHY

DYER, C. C., *Lords and Peasants in a Changing Society: The Estates of the Bishopric of Worcester 680-1540* (Cambridge, 1980).

DYER, C. C., *Standards of Living in the Later Middle Ages* (Cambridge, 1989).

EDWARDS, K., *The English Secular Cathedral in the Middle Ages* (Manchester, 1967).

GRUMMITT, D., "For the Surety of the Town and Marches': Early Tudor Policy towards Calais 1485-1509', *Nottingham Medieval Studies*, xliv (2000), 184-203.

GUNN, STEVEN, 'Sir Thomas Lovell (*c.* 1449-1524): a New Man in a New Monarchy?', in *The End of the Middle Ages*, ed. J. L. Watts (Stroud, 1998), 117-54.

GUTH, D. J., 'Climbing the Civil-Service Pole during Civil War: Sir Reynold Bray (c.1440-1503)', in *Estrangement, Enterprise and Education*, ed. Michalove and Reeves, 47-62.

HAMPTON, W. E., 'Bishop Stillington's Chapel at Wells and his Family in Somerset', *The Ricardian*, iv (1977), 10-16, repr. in *Richard III*, ed. Petre, 166-72.

HAMPTON, W. E., 'Sir Thomas Montgomery, K.G.', *The Ricardian*, iii (1975), 9-14, repr. in *Richard III*, ed. Petre, 149-55.

HAMPTON, W. E., 'The Later Career of Robert Stillington', *The Ricardian*, iv (1976), 24-7, repr. in *Richard III*, ed. J. Petre (Gloucester, 1985), 162-65.

HARPER-BILL, C., 'Bishop Richard Hill and the Court of Canterbury, 1494-96', *Guildhall Studies in London History*, iii (1977-79), 1-12.

HARVEY, BARBARA, 'The Leasing of the Abbot of Westminster's Demesnes in the Later Middle Ages', *ibid.* xxii (1969), 17-27.

HARVEY, BARBARA, *Westminster Abbey and its Estates in the Middle Ages* (Oxford, 1977).

HOLT, RICHARD, *The Mills of Medieval England* (Oxford, 1988).

JAMES, M. R., *A Descriptive Catalogue of the Manuscripts in the Library of Corpus Christi College Cambridge* (2 vols., Cambridge, 1912), i. 381-90.

JENSEN, O., 'The 'Denarius Sancti Petri' in England', *Transactions of the Royal Historical Society*, n.s., xv (1901), 171-247.

JURKOWSKI, M., 'Parliamentary and Prerogative Taxation in the Reign of Edward IV', *Parliamentary History* 18 (1999), 271-90.

JURKOWSKI, M., SMITH, C. L., CROOK, D., *Lay Taxes in England and Wales 1188-1688* (Kew, 1998).

KLEINEKE, H., 'The Reburial Expenses of Sir Thomas Arundell', *The Ricardian*, xi (1998), 288-96.

LANDER, J. R., 'Council, Administration and Councillors, 1461-1485', *BIHR*, xxxii (1959), 138-80.

LUNT, W. E., *Financial Relations of the Papacy with England 1327-1534* (Cambridge, Mass., 1962).

LUNT, W. E., *Papal Revenues in the Middle Ages* (2 vols., New York, 1934).

LUPTON, J. H., *A Life of John Colet, D.D., Dean of St. Paul's and Founder of St. Paul's School* (London, 1909).

MACLEOD, R., 'The Topography of St. Paul's Precinct, 1200–1500', *London Topographical Soc.*, xxvi (1990), 1–14.

MCHARDY, A. K., 'Clerical Taxation in Fifteenth Century England: The Clergy as Agents of the Crown', in *The Church, Politics and Patronage in the Fifteenth Century*, ed. R. B. Dobson, 168–92.

MCINTOSH, M. K., *A Community Transformed, The Manor and Liberty of Havering 1500–1620* (Cambridge, 1991).

NICHOLSON, RANALD, *The Edinburgh History of Scotland*, ii: *Scotland: the Later Middle Ages* (Edinburgh, 1974).

OSCHINSKY, D., 'Medieval Treatises on Estate Accounting', *Ec.H.R.*, xvii (1947), 52–61.

PETRE, J. (ed.), *Richard III, Crown and People* (Gloucester, 1985).

PEVSNER, N., *Buildings of England, Essex* (2nd ed., Harmondsworth, 1965).

RASTALL, R., 'The Minstrels of the English Royal Households', *Royal Musical Association Research Chronicle*, iv (1967), 1–41.

REDDAWAY, T. F., *The Early History of the Goldsmiths' Company, 1327–1509* (London, 1975).

ROSKELL, J. S., CLARK, L. and RAWCLIFFE, C. (eds), *The History of Parliament, The Commons 1386–1421* (4 vols., Stroud, 1992).

ROSKELL, J. S., 'Sir John Wood of Molesey', *Surrey Archaeological Collections*, lvi (1959), 15–28.

ROSKELL, J. S., *The Commons and their Speakers in English Parliaments 1376–1523* (Manchester, 1965).

ROSS, C., *Edward IV* (London, 1974).

ROSS, C., *Richard III* (London, 1981).

SCARISBRICK, J. J., 'Clerical Taxation in England, 1485 to 1547', *Journal of Ecclesiastical History*, xi (1960), 41–54.

SHAW, W. A., *The Knights of England* (2 vols., London, 1906).

SHEPPARD, F. H. W. and GREENACOMBE, J. (eds), *A Survey of London*, 45 vols., London 1900–).

SOUTHWORTH, J., *Fools and Jesters at the English Court* (Stroud, 1998).

SOUTHWORTH, J., *The English Medieval Minstrel* (Woodbridge, 1989).

STEER, F. W., 'A Medieval Household', *The Essex Review*, 63 (1954).

STEPHENSON, M., 'A List of Monumental Brasses in Surrey', *Surrey Archaeological Collections*, xxix. 70–138.

SUTTON, A. F., 'Alice Claver, Silkwoman', in *Medieval London Widows*, ed. C. Barron and A. F. Sutton (London and Rio Grande, 1994), 129–42.

SUTTON, A. F., 'Caxton was a Mercer', in *England in the Fifteenth Century, Proceedings of the 1992 Harlaxton Symposium*, ed. N. Rogers (Stamford, 1994), 118–48.

SUTTON, A. F., 'John Kendale: A Search for Richard III's Secretary', *Richard III*, ed. Petre, 224–38.

SUTTON, A. F., *A Merchant Family of Coventry, London and Calais: The Tates, c.1450–1515* (London, 1998).

SUTTON, A. F., and VISSER-FUCHS, L., 'The Royal Burials of the House of York at Windsor', *The Ricardian*, xi (1998), 366–407.

SUTTON, A. F., and VISSER-FUCHS, L., 'The Royal Burials of the House of York at Windsor: II. Princess Mary, May 1482, and Queen Elizabeth Woodville, June 1492', *The Ricardian*, xi (1999), 446–62.

SUTTON, A. F., and VISSER-FUCHS, L., with HAMMOND, P. W., *The Reburial of Richard Duke of York, 21–30 July 1476* (London, 1996).

SWANSON, R. N., 'Episcopal Income from Spiritualities in Later Medieval England: The Evidence for the Diocese of Coventry and Lichfield', *Midland History*, xiv (1988), 1–20.

SWANSON, R. N., 'Episcopal Income from Spiritualities in the Diocese of Exeter in the Early Sixteenth Century', *Journal of Ecclesiastical History*, 39 (1988), 520–30.

SWANSON, R. N., *Church and Society in Late Medieval England* (Oxford, 1989).

THOMPSON, A. H., *The English Clergy and their Organization in the Later Middle Ages* (Oxford, 1947).

THRUPP, S., *The Merchant Class of Medieval London* (Chicago, 1948).

VCH Berkshire (4 vols., London 1906–24)

VCH Essex (9 vols., London, 1903–94).

VCH London (London, 1909).

VCH Middlesex (10 vols., London, 1909–95).

VCH Warwickshire (8 vols., London, 1904–69).

VIRGOE, R., 'The Composition of the King's Council, 1437–61', *BIHR*, xliii (1970), 134–60.

WEDGWOOD, J. C. (ed.), *The History of Parliament: Biographies of the Members of the Commons House 1439–1509* (London, 1936).

WEEVER, JOHN, *Ancient Funeral Monuments* (London, 1767).

WOOLGAR, C. M., *The Great Household in Late Medieval England* (New Haven, London, 1999).

III. Unpublished Theses

BUTLER, L. H., 'Robert Braybrooke, Bishop of London (1381–1404) and His Kinsmen' (University of Oxford, D.Phil. thesis, 1951).

JENSEN, O., 'Der englische Peterspfennig und die Lehensteuer aus England und Irland an den Papststuhl in Mittelalter' (Doctoral thesis, Heidelberg, 1903).

NEW, E. A., 'The Cult of the Holy Name of Jesus in Late Medieval England, with Special Reference to the Fraternity in St. Paul's Cathedral, London c.1450–1558' (Univ. of London Ph.D. thesis, 1999).

TAYLOR, P. J., 'The Estates of the Bishopric of London from the Seventh Century to the early Sixteenth Century' (2 vols., Univ. of London Ph.D. thesis, 1976).

INDEX

This index aims to be comprehensive for all personal and place names. Subjects have been included selectively, mostly grouped under the headings of 'textiles and clothing', 'food and drink', 'manorial produce and management', and 'plate and jewels'. References to notes where both the main text and a footnote are relevant appear in the form '19 + n. 93', and in the form '19: n. 93' where only the note is relevant. Where other references follow a note reference, a semi-colon is used to divide them.

Abingdon (Berks.) 129
Abingdon, abbot of, *see* Asshenden, Sant
   plot of 129
Acaster (Yorks.) 132
Acton (Mdx.) 18, 20, 21, 25, 49, 69, 75, 80, 97, 104, 148
   'Deane Wodde' in 25, 119
Aleyn families
   Anne 129
   Barbara 129
   Hugh, ironmonger of London 129, 135
   William, of Raylegh 129
   William, baker of London 129
   William, clerk 129
   William, farmer of Runwell 23, 99, 106, 120, 129, 133
   William, mercer of London 129, 150
Alyff, John 28, 101, 106, 130, 163
Angus, earl of, *see* Douglas
Appelby, John de, dean of St. Paul's 12: n. 54
Arches, court of 151
Ardern (Essex) 168

Ardleigh (Herts.) 19 + n. 93; 21, 26, 28, 38, 43, 47, 57, 65, 66, 67, 72, 73 + n. 55; 79, 85, 91, 98, 102, 104, 106, 113, 121, 132, 138, 148, 165, 169, 171, 176
   'le Parke' at 25, 121
   Wadende in 67, 73: n. 55; 79, 85, 91, 98, 148
      'Cootes' tenement in 19, 20, 121
Armar, John, armourer of London 54, 130
Arnoldson, Arnold 84, 130
Arthur Tudor, prince of Wales 135
Ashbury (Berks), rectory of 161
Asshendon, William, abbot of Abingdon 129
At Hey (Athey, Hey), John 58, 67, 73, 83, 151, 152
Audley, Edmund
   archdeacon of Essex 130
   bishop of Hereford 18, 24, 130
   bishop of Rochester 130
   bishop of Salisbury 130
   canon of St. Paul's 8, 98, 127, 130

canon of Windsor 130
chancellor of the Order of the
Garter 130
Audley, Lord, *see* Tuchet
Ayloff family
Thomas 130
William jun. 16: n. 84
William sen. 16 + n. 84; 20,
130
Ayskows family
Anne, *see* Vaughan
Elizabeth, *see* Page
Margaret jun., *see* Jones
Margaret sen. 131
Nicholas 131
Thomas 120, 131
widow of, *see* Wales
William 131

Babington family
Joan, *see* Fitzherbert
Robert 146
Baker family
Agnes 172
John 172
Baldewyn, John 126, 131
Ballard family 131
Richard 81, 131
Richard of Romford 131
Robert, treasurer of St. Paul's
131
Bangore, William, draper of
London 150
Bardolf family
Edmund jun. 131
Edmund sen. 131
Edmund, farmer of Ardleigh
98, 121, 131, 132
Elizabeth jun. 131
Elizabeth sen. 131
Henry 131
Margaret 132
William 121, 132
Barling (Essex) 18, 81, 87, 93, 136

Barlowe family
John, skinner of London 132
Robert 111, 132
Roger, tailor of London 132
Barthorn, John 69, 132
Barton (Lancs.) 3, 134
Barville, John, canon of St.
Paul's 128
Bate, Walter, canon of St. Paul's
128
Bath and Wells, bishopric of 157
bishops of, *see* Bekynton,
Stafford, Stillington
Beaufort, Margaret, countess of
Richmond 136
Beckingham (Lincs.) 177
Bedmaker, Thomas 54, 133
Bek, John 23, 80, 86, 92, 99, 111,
129, 133, 151, 152
Bekynton, Thomas, bishop of
Bath and Wells 132
Belchamp Otton (Essex) 144
Belchamp St. Paul (Essex) 18, 21,
24, 26, 28, 36, 43, 47, 52,
58, 62, 68, 70, 71, 72, 74,
76, 77, 80, 83, 84, 86, 89,
90, 92, 95, 97, 101, 104, 105,
144, 158, 173
'Hamondes' garden in 144
'Mellegrene' in 144
rectory of 58, 77, 80, 86, 92,
96, 97
Belchamp William (Essex) 144
Bell, Richard, bishop of Carlisle
2: n. 3
Berebrewer, Alexander, brewer
of London 45, 51, 62, 70,
76, 82, 133
Bergham (Suffolk) 3, 134
Bernard family
John jun. 49, 60, 69, 75, 133,
149
John sen. 133

Bernyngham, John canon of St.
Paul's 18: n. 93; 19 + n. 97
Berwick upon Tweed
(Northumb.) 11
Bette, Robert 117
Beverley (Yorks.), prebend of St.
Mary's altar at 4
Bexley (Kent) 153
Bignell (Oxon.) 171
Bilton (Warws.) 4
Bishop's Wickham (Essex) 142
Blakwalle, Robert 141
Bogas (Bocas), Thomas 25, 68,
74, 80, 86, 92, 98, 109, 110,
114, 116, 134
Bolton le Moors (Lancs.) 4
Bonville family
Cicely, see Grey
William, Lord 144
Booth family 3, 4, 39
Adriana, see Litton
Charles 4
John, bishop of Exeter 134
John, canon of York 4
John, of Barton 3, 134
Katharine, née atte Oke 134
Laurence
archbishop of York 3 + n.
8; 4, 5, 7, 64, 134
bishop of Durham 7, 134
burial of 5
chancellor of Cambridge
university 4, 5
chancellor of England 14
chantry of, see Southwell
dean of St. Paul's 5, 9, 10,
13, 20, 32, 134
Margaret, see Langford,
Worsley
Margaret, née Hopton 134
Philip 15, 16, 24, 33, 113, 114,
115, 117, 118, 120, 121, 134,
135, 158, 175

Ralph, archdeacon of York 4
Richard 3 + n. 8; 134
Robert, dean of York 3, 134
Thomas 3
Thomas, canon of York 3
William
archbishop of York 3, 4, 5,
7, 15, 31, 134
bishop of Coventry and
Lichfield 134
burial of 5
will of 4, 5, 18
Booth in Eccles (Lancs.) 3
Bordeman family
Agnes, see Cheell
John 135
Margery 135
Robert 54, 135
Bosworth, battle of (1485) 12: n.
57; 30, 140, 144, 160
Botery, William 50, 135, 143,
148
Botiller family
Elizabeth, see Montgomery
Ralph, Lord Sudeley 160
Bourgchier family 30
Agnes, née Charlton 30, 145
Henry, 1st earl of Essex 52,
60, 69, 145; Lord Treasurer
of England 145
Henry, 2nd earl of Essex 75,
145, 168
Isabel, née Plantagenet,
countess of Essex 145
John, archdeacon of
Canterbury 10; canon of St.
Paul's 8, 128
Mary, née Say, countess of
Essex 145, 168
Sir Thomas 30, 145
Sir William 145
Bovour (Bover), Thomas 109,
115, 136

Bowar, Joan 136
Bowecer, Roger, mercer of
London 140
Bower, Richard 81, 87, 93, 136
Bowes, see Edmonton
Braddows, Robert, commissary
general of the Dean and
chapter of St. Paul's 28, 49,
136, 141
Bray families
John 24, 68, 72, 74, 80, 86, 92,
99, 112, 117, 136, 143, 164
Sir Reginald 15 + n. 77; 16,
100, 103, 107, 136, 144, 168,
169
chancellor of the duchy of
Lancaster, Lord Treasurer
of England 136
undertreasurer of England
136, 158
Thomas 118, 137
Braybroke, Robert, bishop of
London 1, 2: n. 3
Brewer, Gilbert de 137
Breych, Richard 29, 44, 137
Broke, John 110, 137
Bromley, Thomas 33, 53, 137
Broughton (Bucks.) 171
Brown family
Agnes 163
John 163
Stephen, grocer of London
163
Broxbourne (Herts.) 145, 168
Buckworth (Hunts.) 169
Bukke, William, draper of
London 45, 51, 62, 70, 82,
88, 94; tailor of London 137
+ n. 60
Bulman, John 67, 138
Bunewell, Thomas 28, 34, 46, 53,
55, 65, 72 + n. 53; 73 + n.

55; 79, 85, 91, 97, 98, 103,
106, 121, 123, 138
Burchester (Oxon.) 171
Burgh family
Benedict, archdeacon of
Colchester 128
John 109, 110, 115, 138
Burton family
John, mercer of London 155
Margaret, see Kemp
William 155
Butler, Laurence
chamberlain of St. Paul's 94,
138, 145
clerk of the bakehouse of St.
Paul's 94, 100, 138, 145
Bygland, John, tailor of London
20
Byngham, Thomas 162
Byrd, Ralph, canon of St. Paul's
8, 127

Caddington (Beds.) 18, 24 + n.
118; 38, 43 + n. 1; 47, 58,
68, 72, 74, 80, 86, 90, 92,
99, 101, 106, 108, 112, 113,
117, 136, 137, 143, 176
Calais 12: n. 57; 14
lordship of Ballingham in 12:
n. 57
Cambridge university 4, 5, 33,
134, 142, 156, 160, 162, 165,
170, 171, 173, 174
chancellor of, see Booth
Corpus Christi College in 141,
156
King's College in 165
dean of, see Reynold
Pembroke College in 5, 134
Trinity Hall in 169
Cambridge, earl of, see
Plantagenet

Candish, John 44, 48, 68, 138, 164

Canterbury (Kent) 35, 45
  archbishop of, *see* Morton
  court of 141
  archbishopric of 20, 21: n. 111
  archdeacon of, *see* Bourgchier
  province of,
    convocation of 10, 21, 53, 89, 95, 174
      committees of 10
      speaker of 10, and *see* Pykenham

Carder, Mary 144

Carlisle, bishop of, *see* Bell

Carter family
  John 25, 43, 47, 58, 68, 74, 80, 86, 92, 139
  William 23, 25, 98, 108, 113, 139

Cartwryght, Thomas 52, 63, 71, 139
  vicar choral of Southwell 33, 139

Chace family
  Elizabeth, *see* Merston
  John 102, 139
  Maud, *née* Godelake 139

Chaddekyrke, Henry 54, 140

Chadsworth, manor of 30, 50, 60, 69, 75, 87, 93, 99

Chalk, John 46, 140

Chancery 141, 163
  court of 6, 16, 170

Chapel Royal, deans of, *see* Jane, Nykke

Charlton family 77: n. 62
  Agnes 140
  Agnes, *see* Bourgchier
  Sir Richard 30, 52, 60, 69, 75, 99, 140, 145
  Sir Richard, heirs of 81, 87, 93, 99

Sir Thomas, speaker of Parliament 140

Charlwood (Surrey) 155, 167
  Gatwick in 155

Chaterton family
  Katharine 140
  Thomas 59, 140

Chauncy, George 37: n. 176

Chaundeler, Thomas, canon of St. Paul's 8, 127

Cheell family
  Agnes, *née* Bordeman 135
  William 135

Chepyng Lambourn (Berks.) 102, 133, 149
  rectory of 18, 20, 30 + n. 139; 31, 49, 53, 60, 69, 75, 80, 95, 97, 102, 133, 149

Chichester, bishops of, *see* Moleyns

Chichester, dean of 10: n. 47

Chipping Ongar (Essex) 152, 167

Chiswick 172

Clarkson, William, steward of the soke of St. Paul's in Essex 28, 35, 83, 84, 89, 90, 95, 141

Clerk, John 38, 49, 55, 56, 57, 60, 67, 79, 85, 91, 141, 172

Clerkenwell priory 172

Cleveland, archdeacon of, *see* Reynold

Cleydon, John 110, 141

Clifton family 162

Clothall (Herts.) 176

Cobham family 155

Colchester (Essex) 159, 170
  Hospital of St. Mary Magdalen in 170
    master of, *see* Skypwith

Colchester, archdeacon of 22, and *see* Burgh, Milford, Plesseys

Coleshill (Warws.) 144

Colet, John, dean of St. Paul's
10, 20, 34

Colles (Scholes), Nicholas 28, 80,
86, 92, 141

Colman family
Joan 143
William 143

Colyngham, Robert 29, 122, 142

Combes (Comber), Robert 76,
83, 89, 94, 142

Coningsby family
Alice 171
Sir Humphrey 171

Convocation, see Canterbury

Cook families
Clement 48, 59, 69, 74, 81, 87,
93, 142
John 125, 142
Matthew 43, 48, 142

Cornish Rising (1497) 169

Cotez, John 54, 142

Counteys, Edmund 24 + n. 118;
47, 58, 68, 72, 74, 80, 86,
92, 143

Coventry and Lichfield, bishops
of, see Booth, Hales

Crall alias Sudbury, John,
archdeacon of Essex 128

Cranfield (Beds.) 169

Cressal, Richard, prior of St.
Mary without Bishopsgate,
London 167

Cressy, Marmaduke 46, 143

Culpeper family
Isabella, née Worsley 14, 157,
175-6
Richard 12n, 14, 157, 175, 176

Dallyng, Geoffrey 19, 23, 28, 81,
87, 93, 98, 111, 117, 143

Damlet, Laurence 129
minor canon of St. Paul's 143
subdean of St. Paul's 135, 143

executors of 65, 129

Dartington (Devon) 174

Daubeney family
Giles, Lord 15 + n. 77
William 13

Davyson, John, canon of St.
Paul's 8, 128

De Vere family
Elizabeth, née Howard,
countess of Oxford 163
John, 12th earl of Oxford 163
John, 13th earl of Oxford 28,
101, 130, 163

Dene (Deyne) family
Richard, brewer of Hackney
100, 107, 143
Joan 143
Richard, skinner of London
143

Dey, Thomas 120, 121, 143

Diceto, Ralph, dean of St. Paul's
17

Digby family
Alice 144
Everard 144
John 144
Reynold 144
Simon 14, 16, 101, 103, 136,
144

Dinham, John Lord 151; Lord
Treasurer of England 136

Doreward, John 170

Dorset, Marquess of, see Grey

Douglas, Archibald, earl of
Angus 11

Downing family
Alice 144
Geoffrey 80, 86, 92, 97, 144,
173
John 144
Margery 144
Mary 144

Drayton (Mdx.) 18, 19: n. 93; 24, 25, 48, 59, 69, 74, 77, 81, 84, 87, 90, 93, 96, 98, 130, 142, 164
  mill 19, 48, 59, 69, 81, 87, 93, 142
Dukinfield (Ches.) 168
Durham priory 37: n. 176
Durham, bishops of, *see* Booth
Dyer, Christopher 31
Dymmok, Andrew 15 + n. 74

Eakring (Notts.), rectory of 5, 12, 79, 85, 91
East Greenwich (Kent) 172
East Stoke (Notts.) 142
Edmonton (Mdx.) 22, 30, 35, 89, 95, 120, 131, 140, 145, 147, 173
  Bowes in 18, 21, 22, 23, 24, 25, 30, 38, 43, 47, 52, 57, 60, 67, 69, 73, 75, 79, 81, 85, 87, 89, 91, 93, 98, 99, 102, 106, 113, 119, 148, 174
  lord of 89, 95
  Polehouse in 18, 21, 22, 23, 24, 25, 30, 38, 43, 47, 52, 57, 60, 67, 69, 73, 75, 79, 81, 85, 87, 89, 91, 93, 98, 99, 106, 113, 119, 148, 174
  marsh in 65
Edward IV, King of England 10, 11, 12, 13, 14, 30, 53, 133, 134, 140, 144, 158, 160, 168
  death of 12
  executors of 14
  funeral of 36 + n. 173; 70
  Scottish expedition of (1481) 11, 12, 25, 36, 53, 130, 133, 135, 137, 140, 142, 147, 149, 166, 167, 171
Edward of York, Prince of Wales 140

Elizabeth Wydeville, Queen of England 144
Elsing (Mdx.) 159
Eltham (Kent) 77
Elys, Thomas, minor canon and subdean of St. Paul's 135, 143
Empson, Richard 15
Enfield (Mdx.) 90, 159
England
  Chancellor of 163, and *see* Booth, Morton, Stillington
  Lord Treasurer of, *see* Bray, Dinham
  undertreasurer of, *see* Bray, Litton
Erasmus, Desiderius, al. of Rotterdam 34
Essenden (Herts.) 145
Essenwolde family
  John, brewer of London 45, 50, 145
  Robert, brewer of London 145
Essex, archdeacons of 22, and *see* Audley, Crall *alias* Sudbury, Jane
Essex, county of 72
  Rochford hundred in 30, 52, 157
  soke of St. Paul's in 20, 25 + n. 122; 26, 27, 28, 35, 38, 106, 108, 109, 114, 130, 134, 137, 141, 147, 154, 161, 166
  Frevelland in 109, 115
  steward of, *see* Clarkson, Forster
  Worsley's estates in 101
Essex, earls of, *see* Bourgchier
Esteney, John, abbot of Westminster 89, 174
Ewell (Surrey) 167

Exchequer 33, 52: n. 19; 55, 146,
147, 151, 158, 161
chancellor of, see Lovell
officials of 146, 151, 155, 158,
176
Exeter, archdeacons of, see
Nykke
bishops of, see King
canons of, see Odeby
Exeter, duke of, see Holand

Farman, John, chaplain 28, 83,
89, 94, 100
chamberlain of St. Paul's 94,
100, 138, 145
clerk of the bakehouse of St.
Paul's 94, 138, 145
rent collector of the Dean and
chapter of St. Paul's 145, 173
Faulkbourn (Essex) 160
Felix, John, butcher of
Kirby-le-Soken 114, 146
Felkirk (Yorks.), 4
Felyx family
Robert, church warden of
Kirby-le-Soken 146
William, church warden of
Kirby-le-Soken 146
Ferrers of Groby, Lord, see Grey
Fitton, George, vicar of
Kirby-le-Soken 113, 146
Fitzherbert family
Eustace 146
Henry 146
Joan, née Babington 146
John 53, 143, 146, 162, 174
Sir Nicholas 146
Fitzwalter, Lord, see Radcliff
Fitzwarren, Thomas
goldsmith of London 45, 146
leatherseller of London 146
verger of St. Paul's 146

Flamstead (Herts.) 176
Flynte, Nicholas, goldsmith of
London 45, 147
Food and drink
victuals (general) 14, 34, 44,
50, 70, 75, 87, 93, 99, 102
ale 32, 34, 35, 45, 50, 61, 70,
75, 82, 88, 94, 100, 102, 107,
133, 164, 174
beer 32, 34, 45, 51, 62, 70, 76,
82, 133
bread 34, 44, 50, 61, 70, 75, 88,
94, 100
fish 14, 34, 35, 99, 102; salted
45
flour 21
meat 44, 50, 61, 70, 75, 81, 87,
93, 99, 102
oatmeal 21
spices 34, 37, 51, 52, 62, 71,
77, 84, 94, 101; saffron 77
sweetmeats 102
wine 32, 51, 62, 71, 76, 82, 88,
94, 100, 109: n. 97; 173
claret 34, 62, 71, 76, 82, 88,
94
Malmsey 34, 51, 71, 94;
old 69
Rhenish 34, 51
Ford (Forth), Roger, taverner of
London 124, 125, 147
Ford, William 33, 55, 147
Forster family
John, canon of St. Paul's and
archdeacon of London 28,
32, 130, 147
Robert, steward of the soke of
St. Paul's in Essex 28, 32, 35,
52, 63, 66, 71, 72, 76, 77,
130, 141, 147
Fourth, [-], of Oakley 114, 147

Fox family
  John 23, 25, 53, 57, 79, 85, 91,
    98, 102, 103: n. 91; 119, 147,
    174
  William 148
Fray family
  Elizabeth, see Say, Waldegrave
  Sir John 168
Freman, Robert 102, 148
Frende family
  Joan 25, 80, 148
  Robert 25, 84, 97, 148
  Roger 20, 21, 25, 46, 49 + n.
    10; 69, 75, 148
Friday, Adam, clerk of the
  bakehouse of St. Paul's 44,
    50, 135, 148, 170
Frost, William 20, 67, 73 + n.
    55; 79, 85, 91, 98, 121, 148
Fuldon (Fulledene), John 28, 46,
    55, 67, 68, 73 + n. 55; 148

Garrard, Thomas 20, 80, 97, 133,
    149
Garter, order of the, chancellor
  of, see Audley
Gawge, Thomas 164
Gerardson, Simon 170
German, John 43, 48, 58, 68, 74,
    149
Gestingthorpe (Essex) 139, 150
Giffard family
  Mary, née Staveley 171
  Thomas 171
Gloucester, duke of, see
  Plantagenet
Godde family
  Robert, 29, 97, 149
  William, canon of Wells 149
Godelake family
  Geoffrey 139
  Maud, see Chace
Gosberkirk (Lincs.) 135

Great Stambridge (Essex) 157
Great Wardrobe 158
Greenford (Mdx.) 152
Grege, John 54, 149
Grene families
  Anne, see Reynew
  Barbara 129
  John 48, 59, 68, 77, 81, 84, 86,
    92, 98, 149, 150
  John, mercer of London 150
  Robert 129
Grey family
  Anne, née Holand 144
  Cicely née Bonville, countess
    of Huntingdon and
    marchioness of Dorset 144
  Henry, Lord Grey of Codnor
    7
  John, Lord Ferrers of Groby
    144
  Thomas, Lord Ferrers of
    Groby, earl of Huntingdon
    and Marquess of Dorset 11,
    14, 36, 64, 144
Grymston, John 64, 166; chantry
  chaplain at St. Paul's 150
Gurnell, Thomas, vicar choral at
  Southwell 6, 7

Hackney (Mdx.) 5, 15, 18, 27, 28,
    29, 31, 34, 43, 47, 55, 58,
    68, 74, 78, 79, 82, 84, 85,
    88, 90, 91, 96, 97, 99, 100,
    103, 104, 106, 107, 118, 121,
    122, 133, 136, 138, 143, 146,
    148, 149, 151, 164, 166, 168
  'Brooke House' in 31
  Worsley's house in 31, 120,
    143
Haddon, Sir Richard 176
Hale family
  William 60, 124: n. 147; 150
  William jun. 150

Hales, John, bishop of Coventry
and Lichfield 2: n. 3
Halfched family 132
Margaret 132
Haliwell, *see* Shorditch
Hall, Thomas, canon of St.
Paul's 8, 127
Halstede, John, abbot of Walden
173
Hampstead (Mdx.) 174
Hampton, John, prior of Hurley
154
Harlesley, John 124, 150
Harnes (Herneys), John 23, 98,
109, 114, 151, 168
Haryngton family
John, advocate 151
John, chaplain 32, 100, 151
William, canon of St. Paul's
32, 151
Havering (Essex) 175
Hendon (Mdx.) 147
Henry VI, King of England 134,
160
council of 9
Readeption of 133, 134, 163
Henry VII, King of England 12,
13, 14, 15, 36, 103, 107, 129,
135, 136, 144, 147, 151, 154,
159, 160, 163, 166, 173
coronation of 136
council of 101, 153
Henry VIII, King of England
129, 135, 145, 151, 159, 163
Herde, John 73, 83, 151, 152
Herdyng, William 117, 151
Hereford, bishops of, *see* Audley,
Milling, Odeby
Heron family
John 103, 107, 151
Margaret 151
Hert, Walter, canon of St. Paul's
128

Hertwell family
Mary, *née* Hulme 154
Thomas 154
Hethe, Robert, collector of Dean
and chapter of St. Paul's 49,
151
Hewet family 25
John 49, 60, 69, 75, 152
William 80, 152
Hewyk family
Isabel 152
John 27, 35, 48, 52, 63, 66, 71,
72, 76, 77, 152, 167
Heybridge (Essex) 18, 23, 25, 27
+ n. 129; 28, 29, 38, 44, 48,
50, 59, 61, 68, 70, 74, 75,
77, 78, 81, 82, 87, 93, 94,
98, 100, 105, 108, 111, 113,
117, 132, 138, 140, 143, 151,
157, 159, 164
bridge at 143
'Cowebryge' at 111
fulling mill 111
mills 19, 20, 23, 25, 44, 48, 59,
68, 74, 81, 93, 98, 111, 117,
138, 151, 164
'Mynhouez' in 157
water mill 111
High Ongar (Essex) 152
Hill families
Edmund 25, 86, 92, 152
Genevieve, *see* Say
John of Spaxton 168
Richard, bishop of London
93, 99, 132, 153, 158, 159
William, farmer of Norton
Folgate 25, 49, 59, 69, 75
rent collector of the Dean
and chapter of St. Paul's
33, 49, 151, 152
minor canon and subdean
of St. Paul's 24, 28, 33,
152

master of the hospital of
St. Thomas of Acon 152
Hillingdon (Mdx.) 140
Hilston, John, prior of Hurley
84, 154
Hobart, James 15
Hodges, Joan, embroidress of
Holy Trinity Aldgate,
London 153
Holand family
Anne, *see* Grey
Thomas, duke of Exeter 144
Holes, Andrew
archdeacon of Taunton 12: n.
59
archdeacon of Wells 12: n. 59
Holt, Stephen 46, 152
Honyborne, John 125, 153
Hopton, Sir William 134
Hornchurch (Essex) 28, 131
'Breteyns' manor in 16: n. 84
Horward, John 23, 113, 153
Hudson, [-], farmer of Ratcliff
mill 97, 153
Hugh, John 110, 154
Hulme family
Joan 154
Margaret 154
Mary, *see* Hertwell
William, draper of London 76,
154
Huntingdon,
archdeaconry of 66, 169
official of, *see* Shuldham
Hurley priory (Berks.) 154
priors of, *see* Hampton,
Hilston, Preston
Hykman, John 109, 115, 154

Isaak, John, canon of St. Paul's
128
Isleworth (Mdx.) 139
Islington (Mdx.) 147

James I, King of Scots 14
James III, King of Scots 11
Jane, Thomas, canon of St.
Paul's 8, 77, 125, 127, 130,
154
archdeacon of Essex 24, 154
bishop of Norwich 154, 161
dean of the chapel royal 154
Jenyns, Stephen 137
Jolyff family
Martin, chamberlain of St.
Paul's 81, 88, 94, 155
clerk of the bakehouse of
St. Paul's 70, 75, 81, 88,
94, 154, 170
keeper of the guild of Jesus
at St. Paul's 155
Richard 155
Jones family
David 131
Margaret, *née* Ayskows 131
Jordan family
Alice 155
John 155, 167

Kemp families
John 155
Margaret, *née* Burton 155
Ralph, mercer of London 125,
155, 164
Thomas, bishop of London 7,
36, 44, 45, 50, 53, 60, 69, 75,
81, 87, 154, 155, 158, 160
Kempe, William, canon of St.
Paul's 8, 128
Kendale family
John, registrar of the
archdeaconry of
Nottingham 29, 122, 155
John, secretary of Richard III
155
Kensworth (Beds.) 18, 24 + n.
118; 38, 43 + n. 1; 47, 58,

68, 72, 74, 80, 86, 90, 92,
99, 101, 106, 108, 111, 113,
118, 143, 176
Kent family
John 19: n. 95; 48, 59, 68, 74,
80, 151, 156, 167
Thomas 131
William 124, 156
Kilburn priory (Mdx.) 156
Katharine prioress of 46, 156
King, Oliver, archdeacon of
Taunton 12: n. 59; bishop
of Exeter 12: n. 59
Kingston (Som.) 28, 29, 149
Kirby-le-Soken (Essex) 18, 38,
39: n. 178; 43, 47, 48, 52,
58, 63, 68, 71, 74, 76, 80,
83, 84, 86, 89, 90, 92, 95,
98, 105, 108, 109 + n. 96;
110, 113, 115, 116, 134, 139,
146, 147, 149, 154, 160, 166
churchwardens of, see Felyx
rectory of 25, 48, 58, 68, 74,
80, 86, 92, 115, 116, 134, 149
vicar of, see Fitton
Knightley, Walter, treasurer of
St. Paul's 128

Lacy, Richard 13
Lambe, John, embroiderer of
London 131
Lambeth (Surrey) 172, 176
Lancaster, duchy of, chancellor
of, see Bray
Landymer Hall (Essex) 160
Langford family
Dorothy 146
Margaret, née Booth 3
Nicholas 156
Ralph, half-brother of Dean
Worsley 3: n. 6; 33, 122, 156
Ralph (another) 146
Sir Ralph 3 + n. 6; 156

Langport, Richard, archdeacon
of Taunton 12: n. 59
Langton family
Agnes 176
Robert 176
Thomas, bishop of St.
David's, Salisbury,
Winchester 176
Lawshull family
John 157
William 30, 52, 157
Layn, Robert, vicar choral of
Southwell 139
Lee family
Joyce 157
Richard jun. 157
Richard sen. 20, 157
Richard, grocer of London 14,
45, 157
Legh families
Alexander 11 + n. 53
Isabella, née Worsley 176
Sir John 176
Leicester
Newarke College in 169
canons of, see Shuldham
Lewknor family
Margery, see Wode
Sir Roger 175
Leyke, Thomas 44, 157
Lichfield cathedral,
canons of, see Reynold,
Worsley
prebend of Tachbrook at 4, 5
Lichfield, Richard, canon of St.
Paul's and archdeacon of
Middlesex 8, 127
Lihert, Walter, bishop of
Norwich 138
Lincoln, canons of, see Shuldham
Lindsey family
Alice 157
Joan 157

John 25, 28, 44, 48, 59, 68, 74, 78, 157
John jun. 157
John sen. 157
Lisieux, Thomas, dean of St. Paul's 8, 9, 10, 32: n. 147; keeper of the Privy Seal 9; will of 32: n. 147
Litton family
  Adriana, *née* Booth 134, 158
  Elizabeth 158
  Robert jun. 135
  Sir Robert 121, 134, 158; undertreasurer of England 158
Lokear, John 24, 28, 36, 43, 47, 52, 58, 68, 71, 74, 76, 77, 158
Lokkey, William 46, 158
London 11, 24, 27, 28, 29, 31, 43, 46, 47 + n. 7; 77, 101, 102, 103, 104, 106, 121, 131, 133, 135, 141, 142, 146, 148, 152, 153, 160, 162, 163
archdeaconry of 83
archdeacons of, *see* Forster, Martyn
bishop of 30, and *see* Braybroke, Hill, Kemp, Savage
  receiver general of 27, 37: n. 176
bishopric of, estates of 19: n. 96; 20
companies:
  Goldsmiths' company 168
  Mercers' company 14, 135, 155, 163
  Merchant Tailors' company 137
deanery property in 17, 20, 38, 49, 53, 56, 57, 60, 67, 73, 77, 79, 85, 86, 91, 98, 124, 164, 166, 167
diocese of 22
Great Chronicle of 16
mayor of 138
mayor's court of 129, 135, 163
parishes and parish churches:
  All Saints Honey Lane 175
  Allhallows in the Wall 136
  St. Bartholomew the less 155
  St. Benet 146
  St. Bride Fleet Street 171, 172
    fraternity of Our Lady in 172
  St. Christopher le Stocks 154
  St. Clement Danes 139
  St. Dunstan in the East 136
  St. Faith 166
  St. Giles Cripplegate 172
  St. Gregory by St. Paul's 152
  St. Katharine by the Tower 131
  St. Laurence Jewry 137
  St. Margaret Friday Street 173
  St. Margaret Moses 162
  St. Martin le Grand 132
  St. Mary Aldermanbury 137
  St. Mary Colechurch 132
  St. Mary Magdalen in the Fishmarket 160
  St. Mary Woolnoth 28, 136
  St. Michael Bassishaw 163
  St. Nicholas Acon 154
  St. Pancras Soper Lane 159: n. 173

London / parishes, continued
  St. Stephen Walbrook 13,
    20, 157
places in:
  bishop of Norwich's
    palace 150
  Bridgestreet 166
  Fleetstreet 172
  Gray's Inn 149
    steward of 55, 149
  'le Hermitage' 51, 70, 133
  'le Herteshorne' 82, 88, 94,
    100
  Ivy Lane 17, 95, 124, 161,
    165
  Knightrider Street 17, 49,
    124, 156, 168
  Lincoln's Inn 16: n. 84; 28,
    141
  Moreland 125
  Newgate prison 163
  'Paules Cheyn' 124, 150,
    166
    'Powles Hede' in 124,
      125, 147
  Paul's Cross 64
  Pope's Alley 138
  Redcrossestreet 172
  Smithfield 49
  St. Bartholomew's close,
    West Smithfield 146
  'la Sonne' 171
  'le Spaldynghouse' 125,
    150
  Tower of London 14, 16,
    82: n. 64; 102, 103, 133,
    144, 148
    constable of, see Lovell
    mint at 147, 160, 168,
      169
  Turnmillstreet 172
  'the Rose' in 172
religious houses and hospitals:
  Holy Trinity Aldgate,
    priory of 95, 132, 153
    embroidress of, see
      Hodges
    prior of, see Percy
  St. Bartholomew, West
    Smithfield, hospital of 174
  St. Mary without
    Bishopsgate, hospital of
    .125, 167
    prior of 125, and see
      Cressal, Sutton
  St. Thomas of Acon,
    hospital of 152
    Master of, see Hill
  sheriffs of 130
  St. Paul's cathedral 31, 32,
    101, 118
    altar of the Holy Ghost in
      170
    bakehouse of 27, 29, 138
    brewery of 27
    canons of, see Audley,
      Barville, Bate,
      Bernyngham, Byrd,
      Chaundeler, Davyson,
      Forster, Hall, Haryngton,
      Hert, Isaak, Jane, Kempe,
      Lichfield, Luke, Martyn,
      Moreland, Morton,
      Odeby, Peese, Pevesey,
      Pykenham, Shaa, Smith,
      Stanley, Sutton, Tapton,
      Woodcock, Worsley,
      Wylde
    chamberlain of 27, 29, 44,
      50, 61, 70, 75, 81, 88, 94,
      100, 107, and see Jolyff,
      Steward
    chancellors of, see Saver,
      Smith
    chantries at 171
      Brewer chantry 137

London / St. Paul's / chantries
continued
Dungeon chantry 135
Foliot Chantry 166
perpetual chantry at the
altar of the Holy Ghost
170
Pultenay's chantry 138
Wendover chantry 150
chantry chaplains at, see
Grymston, Rogers, Roke
chapel of St. Laurence in
16, 17
chapter of 8, 9, 29, 127,
130, 141
chapter house of 10
choir of 16
clerk of the bakehouse of
34, 70, 75, 81, 88, 94, 100,
107, and see Friday, Jolyff,
Skypwith
dean and chapter of 18, 19:
n. 93; 20, 25, 28, 98, 138,
148, 157, 160, 166
commissary general of,
see Braddows
hospitality of 11, 34
rent collector of, see
Farman, Hethe, Hill,
Nutson, Pope
dean of 39, and see Booth,
Colet, Diceto, Lisieux,
Say, Sherborne,
Winterbourne, Worsley
London mansion of 17,
31, 35, 65, 72, 77, 83, 84,
89, 95, 140
office of 8, 9
deanery of 29, 56, 92, 105,
153
collector of 155
commissary of 26, 80

fraternity of the Holy
Name at 9
guild of Jesus at 155
keeper of, see Jolyff
Jesus chapel in 9
ministers of 102
minor canons of 16, and
see Damlet, Elys, Hill,
Roke, Steward
prebends at
Brownswood 154
Caddington Major 128
Caddington Minor 128
Chamberlainwood 128
Ealdland 128
Ealdstreet 128
Harleston 18, 128, 162
Holborn 128
Hoxton 7
Islington 151
Mora 130
Newington 8
Oxgate 128
Reculversland 154
Rugmere 7, 154
St. Pancras 128
Tottenham 8
Twiford 128
Willesden 5, 9, 17, 18, 29,
30 + n. 139; 31, 53, 77,
80, 83, 86, 89, 95, 102,
107, 118, 119, 161
statutes of 9, 10, 34
subdeans of, see Damlet,
Elys, Hill
treasurers of, see Ballard,
Knightley
verger of, see Fitzwarren
St. Paul's school 10
trades and occupations:
armourers, see Armar
bakers, see Aleyn
bowyers, see Symsone

London / trades continued
brewers, see Berebrewer,
Essenwolde, Prowell,
Witheney
butchers, see Stalon
drapers, see Bangore,
Bukke, Hulme
embroiderers, see Lambe
goldsmiths, see Fitzwarren,
Flynte, Rokes, Shaa
grocers, see Brown, Lee
ironmongers, see Aleyn
leathersellers, see
Fitzwarren
mercers, see Aleyn,
Bowecer, Burton, Grene,
Kemp, Shelley, Symsone,
Tate, Worsley
saddlers, see Milard, Milen
skinners, see Barlowe,
Dene
stationers, see Sylverton
tailors, see Barlowe,
Bukke, Bygland
taverners, see Ford
vintners, see Vyntener
Long Bennington (Lincs.) 173
Lovell, Master 90
Lovell, Sir Thomas 15, 16, 30,
99, 100, 103, 107, 166
chancellor of the Exchequer
159
constable of the Tower of
London 159
speaker of Parliament 159
Lucas, Thomas 15: n. 74
Luke, Richard, canon of St.
Paul's 8, 127, 130
Lynde, Joan, prioress of Haliwell
150

Maldon (Essex) 117, 151

Manorial produce and
management:
arrears 23-4, 108-24, 133
demesne leasing 19-21
fuel 35, 46, 87, 99
charcoal 35, 119
coal 99
grain 44, 45, 50, 55, 61, 70, 75,
78, 81, 84, 88, 94, 100
hay 55
livestock 45, 51, 54, 84, 90, 96,
104, 106, 115
timber and firewood, 20: n.
107; 25, 35, 59, 74, 80, 86,
91, 92, 111, 119, 120, 121,
140, 155
Mansfield (Notts.) 142
Margaret of Anjou, Queen of
England 134
Marke family
Master 27: n. 129; 78
Richard 159, 170
Thomas, archdeacon of
Norwich 159: n. 173
Thomas, rector of St. Pancras,
Soper Lane 159: n. 173
Thomas (another) 159: n. 173
Markshall (Essex) 28, 136
Martyn family
Richard, canon of St. Paul's
and archdeacon of London
7, 127
Richard, clerk of Chancery
141
Matyn, Thomas 33, 55, 160
Merston family
Elizabeth, née Chace 139
William 139
Michell, Thomas 109: n. 96; 160
Middlesex, archdeacon of 22, and
see Lichfield
archdeaconry of 53, 83
Midhurst (Sussex) 174

Milard, Richard, saddler of
London 160
Milen, Richard, saddler of
London 96, 160
Milford, William, archdeacon of
Colchester 138
Milling, Thomas, abbot of
Westminster 174; bishop of
Hereford 174
Minstrels 34, 55, 66, 77, 84, 89,
96
Molesey (Surrey) 174
Moleyns, Adam, archdeacon of
Taunton, bishop of
Chichester 12: n. 59
Montgomery family
Elizabeth, née Botiller, lady of
Say 160
Sir John 160
Sir Thomas 14, 33, 71, 76, 83,
89, 95, 160
More, John 43, 47, 58, 161
Moreland, William, canon of St.
Paul's 128
Morton family
John, archbishop of
Canterbury 132, 153, 158
Chancellor of England 132
John, attorney 33, 52: n. 19;
55, 147, 161
Robert, canon of St. Paul's 8,
127
Morys, Thomas 32, 90, 96, 161
Moulton (Lincs.) 174
Mountford, Sir Simon 13

Nayler family
Elizabeth 161
Richard, tailor of London 161
Nayller, John 25: n. 122; 48, 161
Neville family 134
Nevyll, Robert 48, 59, 69, 74, 79,
85, 161, 172

Nicholas IV, Pope 30
Northcote, William 68, 74, 80,
86, 92, 161, 172
Norton Folgate see Shorditch
Norton Mandeville (Essex) 172
Norwell Overall see Southwell
Norwich (Norfolk) 154, 161
Norwich, archdeacon of, see
Marke
Norwich, bishops of, see Jane,
Lihert, Nykke
Nottingham (Notts.) 11
archdeaconry of 26, 29, 33, 38,
43, 44, 47, 73, 79, 85, 91, 97,
113, 122, 137, 142, 155, 157,
162, 167, 174, 177
registrar of, see Kendale
archdeacons of, see Worsley
St. Mary's church in 173
St. Peter's church in 29, 142
Nowell (Notts.) 18
Nundy, Robert 20
Nutson, Thomas, collector of
Dean and chapter of St.
Paul's 146
Nykke, Richard
archdeacon of Exeter 161
archdeacon of Wells 161
bishop of Norwich 24, 150,
161
canon of Southwell 161
canon of Wells 95, 161
dean of the Chapel Royal 161

Oakley (Essex) 147
Odeby family
[-] 146
Walter, canon of Exeter 162
canon of Hereford 162
canon of St. Paul's 18, 91,
162
canon of St. Stephen's,
Westminster 162

Offington *see* Winkburn
Oke family
Katharine atte, *see* Booth
Philip atte 134
Orreys, Robert 80, 162
Orston, Thomas 15, 29, 33, 44,
67, 97, 105, 156, 157, 162
Oxford (Oxon.) 133
Oxford university 4, 5, 132, 160
All Souls College in 159: n.
173
Deep Hall in 132
Lincoln College in 130
Magdalen College in 141
New College in 141
Oxford, earls of, *see* De Vere

Page family
Elizabeth, *née* Ayskows 131
Robert 131
Palmer, Robert 23, 114, 115, 163
Panter, David 147
Parliament 21, 174; (1472) 168;
(1478) 170; (1483) 175;
(1485) 159; (1491) 168;
(1495) 15, 168; (1497) 120,
131, 173
speaker of, *see* Charlton,
Lovell, Wode
Peckham family
Agnes 163
Elizabeth 163
Peter 33, 101, 103, 163
Peese, John, canon of St. Paul's
128
Percy family
John 19: n. 95; 23, 80, 86, 92,
98, 108, 115, 162, 163
Thomas, prior of Holy
Trinity Aldgate, London 95,
132, 153, 159
Pere family 25
John jun. 74, 81, 164

John sen. 164
Robert 59, 138, 164
Pevesey, Robert, canon of St.
Paul's 8, 127
Plantagenet family
Edward, earl of Warwick 129
Richard, duke of Gloucester
11
Richard, duke of York 13
Richard, earl of Cambridge
145
Thomas, duke of Gloucester
145
Plate and jewels:
crosses 64
cruets 65
cups 45; with an ostrich egg 44
salt-cellars 45, 65
Plesseys, John, archdeacon of
Colchester 138
Plumstead (Kent) 172
Plympton Erle (Devon) 168
Polehouse, *see* Edmonton
Pomfret, Alice, widow of
London 125, 164
Pope, William 152
Poppes, Alice 149
Powys, Thomas 13
Prentesse, Edmund 25, 48, 59,
69, 74, 77, 81, 84, 87, 93,
164
Preston, Thomas, prior of
Hurley 154
Privy Seal, keeper of, *see* Booth
Prowell, Richard, brewer of
London 61, 70, 164
Prudde, Elizabeth, prioress of
Haliwell 150
Pykenham, William, archdeacon
of Suffolk 10
canon of St. Paul's 8, 127
speaker of convocation 10

Radcliff family
  arms of 39
  Alice 165
  John 165
  John, Lord FitzWalter 13
  Robert 164, 165
  Roger, dean of St. Paul's 9, 32,
    164, 165, 168
  Roger, receiver general of
    Dean Worsley 1, 14, 15, 16,
    17, 21, 23, 24, 26, 29, 32, 33,
    36, 37, 38, 50, 53, 55 + n.
    21; 57, 61, 62, 66, 72, 77, 84,
    85, 90, 94, 95, 96, 101, 102,
    104, 105 + n. 92, 108, 111,
    112, 115, 118, 119, 121, 125,
    132, 138, 141, 157, 164-5,
    172, 175
Raderford (Ratherford, Retford)
  family
  George 67, 79, 85, 91, 165
  James 43, 47, 58, 68, 134, 165
Ratcliff mill see Stepney
Ratcliffe, Robert 13
Rayleigh (Essex) 52, 129
Reading, abbot of, see Thorne
Rede, Bartholomew 15
Retford see Raderford
Reynew family
  Anne, née Grene 150
  George 150
  Joan 150
Reynold family
  John, archdeacon of Cleveland
    165
    canon of Southwell 165
    canon of York 165
    dean of King's College,
      Cambridge 165
  Master 124, 165
  Thomas, canon of Lichfield
    165
Ricas, Thomas 165

Richard III, King of England 10,
    12, 30, 133, 140, 146, 152,
    160, 162
  secretary of, see Kendale
Richford, William 13
Richmond, countess of, see
    Beaufort
Rivers, earl, see Wydeville
Robson family
  Katharine 166
  Robert 53, 64, 166
Rochester, bishop of, see Audley
Rochford (Essex) 168
Rogers, John, chantry chaplain
    at St. Paul's 150
Roke family
  William sen. 166
  William, chantry chaplain and
    minor canon of St. Paul's 15,
    33, 52, 63, 71, 76, 83, 89, 94,
    100, 166
Rokes family
  John 110, 166
  Thomas, goldsmith of
    London 166
Rome 55, 160
  English hospital at 33
  Hospital of St. Thomas the
    Martyr in 160
  Papal curia at 33, 55, 160
Rome, John, priest 129
Romford (Essex) 131
Roos family
  Edmund, Lord 30, 81, 87, 93,
    166
  Thomas, Lord 166
Ross herald 11
Runwell (Essex) 18, 20 + n. 108;
    23, 38, 43, 47, 58, 67, 80,
    83, 86, 92, 99, 106, 108, 111,
    113, 120, 129, 133, 151, 152

Sabrisford, John, abbot of
    Walden 83, 84, 173
Saddler, Richard 49, 166
Salisbury, bishops of, *see* Audley,
    Langton
    diocese of 53
Salmans (Surrey), manor of 155
Samesbury family
    Richard 29, 54, 122, 142, 167,
        174, 177
    Thomas 167
Sanders (Saunder) family
    Henry of Charlwood 167
    Henry of Ewell 28, 98, 155,
        167
Sant, John, abbot of Abingdon
    95, 129
Saperton family
    Isabel 167
    John 17, 27, 35, 83, 84, 86, 89,
        90, 92, 95, 101, 104, 106,
        116, 123, 152, 167
Savage, Thomas
    bishop of London 17, 159
    archbishop of York 159
Saver (Saber) family
    John 25, 80, 167
    Henry, chancellor of St. Paul's
        168
    William jun. 25, 86, 92, 167,
        168
Say family 140
    Elizabeth, *née* Fray 168
    Genevieve, *née* Hill 168
    Lady of, *see* Montgomery
    Mary, *see* Bourgchier
    Sir John 168
    William of Broxbourne 24, 49,
        67, 124, 145, 156, 168
    William, dean of St. Paul's 20,
        34, 148
Scotland, marches towards 11 +
    n. 54

Scots,
    Kings of, 12: n. 54, and *see*
        James I, James III
    'rough-footed' 147
Shaa (Shaw) family
    Sir Edmund, goldsmith of
        London 24, 25, 79, 168
    Hugh 25, 168
    John of Dukinfield 168
    John of Rochford 168
    Sir John, goldsmith of
        London 15, 18, 24, 25, 85,
        91, 98, 136, 168-9, 176
    Juliana 168
    Ralph, canon of St. Paul's 32,
        128, 168
    Thomas 16, 32, 77, 96, 113,
        114, 115, 116, 117, 120, 169
        wife of 32, 96, 169
Sheen (Surrey) 102
Shelley, Thomas, mercer of
    London 175
Sherborne, Robert
    dean of St. Paul's 149
    archdeacon of Taunton,
        bishop of St. David's 13: n.
        59
Shingleford (Essex) 30, 81, 93,
    99, 161
Shorditch (Mdx.),
    Haliwell in 159
    Haliwell priory 125, 126
        prioress of 125, 126 and *see*
            Lynde, Prudde
    Norton Folgate in 18, 19: n.
        93; 25, 26, 27, 36, 38, 49, 52,
        59, 63, 69, 75, 81, 83, 86, 92,
        98, 105, 113, 123, 124, 131,
        150, 152, 171
Shuldham, Edward
    canon of Lincoln 169, 176
    canon of Newarke College,
        Leicester 169

official of the archdeaconry of
Huntingdon 66
Skypwith, Thomas
clerk of the bakehouse of St.
Paul's 44, 50, 61, 70, 148,
155, 170
master of the Hospital of St.
Mary Magdalen, Colchester
170
Slade, John 33, 96, 170
Smith families
Thomas of Colchester 170
Thomas of Thorpe Hall 48,
58, 68, 74, 142, 162, 170
Thomas, canon and chancellor
of St. Paul's 128, 170;
executor of Adam Friday 50,
135, 148
Thomas, chaplain 33, 102,
118, 170-71
William, archdeacon of
Winchester, bishop of
Coventry and Lichfield 2: n.
3
Southoe (Hunts.) 169
Southwell (Notts.) 12, 36, 55,
122, 137, 139, 156, 162, 167
archbishop's park at 167
Southwell minster 4, 5, 6, 7, 8,
33, 162, 167
canons of, see Nykke,
Reynold, Talbot, Terold,
Worsley
Laurence Booth's chantry at 4
prebend of Norwell Overall at
5, 15, 18, 43, 73, 79, 85, 91,
97, 105
vicars choral of, see
Cartwryght, Gurnell, Layn
Spaxton (Som.) 168
St. David's, bishops of, see
Langton, Sherborne

Stafford, John, bishop of Bath
and Wells 139
Stalon, William, butcher of
London 153
Stanford Rivers (Essex) 152
Stanley, James, canon of St.
Paul's 8, 127
Stanwell (Mdx.) 158
Staveley family
Alice 171
George 171
Isabel 171
John 171
Mary, see Giffard
William 49, 171
William jun. 171
Stephens family
Joan 25, 123, 171
John 25, 92, 98, 105, 123, 171
William 102, 171, 176
Stepney (Mdx.) 49, 60, 162
marsh at 30, 45, 53
Ratcliff mill in 18, 21, 25, 49,
53, 65, 69, 72, 75, 77, 80, 95,
97, 101, 152, 153
Steward, William
chamberlain of St. Paul's 44,
50, 171
minor canon of St. Paul's 171
Stillington, Robert
archdeacon of Taunton 12: n.
59; 132
bishop of Bath and Wells 12:
n. 59; 24, 48, 132, 133
canon of Wells 132
chancellor of England 133
Stockwell (Surrey) 175, 176
Stratford St. Andrew (Suffolk)
173
Stykeswolde, Robert 53, 77,
171-2
Sudeley, Lord, see Botiller

Suffolk, archdeacon of, *see*
    Pykenham
Sutton (Essex) 18, 24, 44, 48, 59,
    69, 74, 79, 85, 91, 133, 161,
    162, 172
Sutton family
    John, canon of St. Paul's 7,
    127
    William, prior of St. Mary
        without Bishopsgate,
        London 167
    William, rector of St. Stephen
        Walbrook, London 13 + n.
        62; 14, 157
Swete, William 80, 84, 86, 89, 92,
    95, 97, 105, 118, 161, 172
Sylverton, Nicholas, stationer of
    London 143
Symsone family
    Agnes 172
    Agnes jun. 172
    Elizabeth 172
    John, bowyer of London 54,
    172
    John, mercer of London 172
    Maud 172

Talbot, William, canon of
    Southwell 156
Tapton, John, canon of St.
    Paul's 128
Tate, John, mercer of London
    163
Taunton (Som.) 101, 149
    archdeaconry of 13, 15, 26, 28,
        29, 97, 105, 149
    archdeacons of, *see* Holes,
        King, Langport, Moleyns,
        Sherborne, Stillington,
        Worsley
    prior of 149
Taxation
    papal 21, 30, 31

'Peter's Pence' 22, 26, 89,
    95, 99, 120, 122
royal 21, 22, 30, 31, 53, 77, 83,
    84, 89, 95, 102, 107, 118,
    120, 129, 131, 139, 146, 147,
    148, 150, 154, 165, 171, 173,
    174, 176
Terold, John, canon of
    Southwell 6
Textiles and clothing:
    cloth 37, 137, 144
    'blakechalk' 54
    blanket 65
    buckram 64, 65
    canvas 65
    chamelet 65
    cloth of gold 64
    fustian 53, 64
    linen 64, 65, 96
        'dyaper worke' 65
    russet 63
    silk 64
    velvet 46, 53
    woollen cloth 45, 51, 62,
        70, 76, 82, 88, 94, 96
    copes 64
    doublets 54, 65
    funerary livery 70
    fur 63
    gowns 51, 62, 63, 64, 65, 70,
        77, 84, 90, 104, 118
    hoods 46, 96
    hose 64, 65
    jackets 65
    napkins 64
    sheets 64
    shirts 65
    shoes 64 + n. 37; 65, 96
    towels 64, 65
Thames, river 95, 159
Therfield (Herts.) 169
Thomas, Thomas 48, 59, 172

Thorne, John, abbot of Reading
102, 165
Thorpe-le-Soken (Essex) 18, 19,
23, 38, 39: n. 178; 43, 47,
52, 58, 63, 68, 71, 74, 76,
80, 83, 84, 86, 89, 90, 92,
95, 98, 105, 108, 109, 110,
113, 114, 115, 116, 136, 139,
141, 142, 147, 151, 156, 162,
163, 165, 167, 170, 172
 Kent's tenement in 19 + n.
 95; 22, 23, 25, 80, 86, 92, 98,
 109, 110, 114, 116, 151, 156,
 167
 'Hobbesdale' in 109, 115, 116,
 172
 rectory of 19 + n. 95; 48, 59,
 68, 74: n. 58; 86, 92, 108,
 114, 156, 163
 Thorpe Hall in 19: n. 95; 43,
 48, 58, 68, 74, 80, 98, 142,
 148, 162, 163, 170
 watermill in 109, 136
Thurston, William 109, 115, 172
Thwaites, Sir Thomas 13
Tillingham (Essex) 18, 24, 25, 79,
85, 91, 98, 168, 169
Tilton-on-the-Hill (Leics.) 144
Toose (Toyse), John 23, 43, 48,
59, 68, 74, 80, 86, 92, 98,
108, 109, 113, 115, 153, 172
Tottenham (Mdx.) 5, 15, 18, 21,
120, 147, 168, 177
Towton, battle of (1461) 160
Trent, William 91, 141, 172
Tresham, Sir Thomas 171
Tuchet, James, Lord Audley 130
Turle, John 120, 173
Turnour, Thomas 33, 52, 63, 71,
76, 173

Uphavering (Essex) 14
Urswick family
 Anne 14
 George, mercer of London
 175
 Sir Thomas 14

Vaughan family
 Anne, *née* Ayskows 131
 Robert 131
Vyntener, Charles, vintner of
 London 51, 62, 69, 71, 76,
 82, 88; 94, 173

Waldegrave family
 Elizabeth, *née* Fray 168
 Sir Thomas 168
Walden (Essex) 140
 abbot of, *see* Halstede,
 Sabrisford
Wales family
 Margaret, widow of Thomas
 Ayskows 131
 Robert 131
Wales, princes of, *see* Arthur,
 Edward
Waltham (Lincs.), rectory of 4
Walton-le-Soken (Essex) 18, 23,
38, 39: n. 178; 43, 47, 48,
52, 58, 59, 63, 68, 71, 74,
76, 80, 83, 84, 86, 89, 90,
92, 95, 98, 105, 108, 109,
110, 113, 115, 116, 138, 146,
153, 165, 172
 bakehouse in 109, 110, 115,
 138
 Bancroft rectory in 23, 25, 43,
 47, 58, 68, 74, 80, 86, 92 +
 n. 78; 98, 108, 113, 139
 churchwardens of 139
 sea dyke in 110
Walton Hall in 80

Warbeck, Perkin 13
    conspiracy of 12, 13, 14, 24,
        28, 33, 37, 132, 135, 151,
        157, 159, 163, 165, 166, 175
Warwick, earl of, *see* Plantagenet
Watson (Weston), Thomas 28,
    33, 36, 80, 83, 86, 89, 95,
    97, 98, 101, 144, 173
Watton (Herts.) 131
Wells cathedral
    archdeacons of, *see* Holes,
        Nykke
    canons of, *see* Godde, Nykke,
        Stillington
    dean of 10: n. 47
    prebend of Milverton at 12,
        18, 132
    prebend of Warminster at 149
Westby family
    Edward 24, 57, 67, 79, 85, 91,
        148, 174
    Margaret 174
Westminster (Mdx.) 11, 147, 176
    royal courts at 147
    St. Stephen's, canons of, *see*
        Odeby
Westminster Abbey 2: n. 3; 39,
    154, 156
    abbots of, *see* Esteney, Milling
Weston *see* Watson
Whitton (Mdx.) 142
Wickham St. Paul (Essex) 18, 21,
    28, 36, 39: n. 178; 43, 48,
    59, 62, 68, 70, 71, 72, 74,
    76, 77, 81, 83, 84, 86, 89,
    90, 92, 95, 96, 98, 101, 104,
    141, 149, 158
    'Walshes' house in 150
    churchwarden of 149
    rectory of 43
Wilby family
    Richard 174
    Robert 29, 122, 174, 177

Willesden (Mdx.) 20, 21, 38, 43,
    47, 58, 68, 74, 80, 86, 87,
    90, 92, 93, 96, 97, 99, 101,
    104, 105, 139, 148, 161, 172
    rectory of 18, 30, 84
    wood at 25, 87, 93
William I, King of England 22
William, tax collector at
    Tottenham 120, 177
Willis family
    Joan 136
    Robert 136
Wimpole (Cambs.) 77 + n. 62;
    172
Winchester College 3: n. 4; 4
Winchester, bishops of, *see*
    Langton
Windsor castle
    St. George's chapel in 130
    canons of, *see* Audley
Winkburn and Offington
    (Notts.), rectory of 113, 122
Winterbourne, Thomas, dean of
    St. Paul's 7, 8, 9, 128
Witheney, William, brewer of
    London 75, 174
Wode family
    John, speaker of the House of
        Commons 53, 174-5
    Margery, *née* Lewknor 175
Woking (Surrey) 136
Wolverhampton (Staffs.) 4
Wolverhampton chapel, prebend
    of Kynwaston alias Stonhall
    at 4
Woodcock, William, canon of
    St. Paul's 128
Woollaton (Notts.) 29, 174
Woolwich (Kent) 154
Worcester
    bishop of 35
    bishopric of, estates of 19: n.
        94; 24: n. 119

Worsley family 3, 4, 14
Agnes 175
arms of 39
Benjamin 4
Edmund, mercer of London
14, 15, 16, 24, 33, 113, 114,
115, 117, 118, 119, 120, 121,
135, 137, 146, 175
Edward 12 + n. 57
Isabella 33, 45, and *see*
Culpeper, Legh
John, canon of York 4
Otwell 33, 175
Richard 4
Robert 3
Robert, mercer of London 175
Seth 12 + n. 57
Thomas, canon of Lichfield 4,
5, 16, 162
Worsley, William
archdeacon of Nottingham 7
archdeacon of Taunton 12
canon of Lichfield 4, 5
canon of Southwell 5, 6, 7; 8,
127, 130
council 101
dean of St. Paul's 1, 2, 7, 8, 11,
12, 13, 14, 37, 44, 53, 61, 63,
64, 65, 66, 70, 71, 72, 75, 77,
78, 81, 84, 85, 90, 95, 96, 97,
102, 103, 104, 106, 149
education 4, 5
election 127, 130, 154, 158
epitaph 17
estate administration 27
funeral 16
health 16
image 39
imprisonment 14, 16, 102,
103, 148
income 17, 29, 31
institution 37

Margaret, *née* Booth, mother
of 3
pardon 151
parents 150, 156, 166
Seth, father of 3, 4
signature 66: n. 41; 72, 101,
103
tomb 39
tomb brass 17
will 1, 16, 17: n. 85; 130
youth 3
Wrentham (Suffolk) 171
Wryght, John 102, 169, 176
Wydeville, Richard, 1st earl
Rivers 144
Wylde, William, canon of St.
Paul's 8, 127
Wyle (Wylle), William, hosier of
London 65, 96, 176
Wylly family
Agnes 176
Edmund 53, 176
Wynche family
Alice 176
Richard 24, 76, 99, 111, 118,
119, 143
Wyott, Henry 147

Yates, Simon 122, 174, 177
York
archbishops of, *see* Booth,
Savage
archdeacons of, *see* Booth
canons of, *see* Booth, Reynold,
Worsley
chapel of St. Mary and the
Holy Angels at 4
deans of, *see* Booth
duke of, *see* Plantagenet
minster 39
prebend of Ampleforth at 4
prebend of Rikhill at 4

York, continued
prebend of South Cave at 5,
18, 43, 47, 67, 79, 85, 91, 97,
105

Zouche, John Lord 136